THE SOCIOCULTURAL TURN IN PSYCHOLOGY

Charles Seale-Hayne Library

University of Plymouth

(01752) 588 588

LibraryandITenquiries@plymouth.ac.uk

THE SOCIOCULTURAL
TURN IN PSYCHOLOGY

The Contextual Emergence of Mind and Self

EDITED BY

Suzanne R. Kirschner
and Jack Martin

Columbia University Press   New York

Columbia University Press

Publishers Since 1893

New York   Chichester, West Sussex

Copyright © 2010 Columbia University Press

Library of Congress Cataloging-in-Publication Data

The sociocultural turn in psychology : the contextual emergence of mind and self /
edited by Suzanne R. Kirschner and Jack Martin.

p. cm.

Includes bibliographical references and index

ISBN 978-0-231-14838-2 (cloth : alk. paper) — ISBN 978-0-231-14839-9 (pbk. : alk. paper) —
ISBN 978-0-231-51990-8 (ebook)

1. Psychology—Social aspects. 2. Social cognition. 3. Social psychology. 4. Culture—
Psychological aspects.   I. Kirschner, Suzanne R.   II. Martin, Jack, 1950–   III. Title

BF57 S63   2010

150—dc22   2009043202

Columbia University Press books are printed on
permanent and durable acid-free paper.

This book is printed on paper with recycled content.

Printed in the United States of America

Contents

Acknowledgments

Rom Harré's chapter first appeared in *Theory & Psychology* 12.5 (2002). It is included here with the permission of Sage Publications. Portions of Mark Freeman's chapter appeared earlier in *Warum Menschen sich erinnern können*, ed. H. Welzer and H. J. Markowitsch (Stuttgart: Klett-Cotta, 2006), and *Interchange: A Quarterly Review of Education* 38.3 (2007). These writings are reprinted here with the permission of their respective publishers.

The editors wish to express their appreciation to Lauren Dockett, executive editor at Columbia University Press, for her enthusiasm about this project, and to the anonymous reviewers for their very helpful feedback.

Suzanne Kirschner would like to thank Timothy Austin, vice president for academic affairs and dean of the College of the Holy Cross, and Richard Schmidt, chair of the Psychology Department at the College of the Holy Cross, for granting her a research leave in order to ensure completion of this book. She owes her deepest gratitude and love to her family. She thanks Len for his unfailing, unselfish love and encouragement, and for the many forms of support he has provided. She thanks Alex for the pleasure of his company all the times he sat nearby and played or read while she worked on the manuscript, as well as for the privilege of being his mother and watching him grow.

Jack Martin wishes to acknowledge the support of Simon Fraser University's Burnaby Mountain Endowment Trust for supporting his work and for funding in aid of some of the preparation and indexing of this volume. He would also like to thank Wyn for her support, encouragement, and patience with yet another lengthy period of writing and editing over many hours and occasions.

THE SOCIOCULTURAL TURN IN PSYCHOLOGY

The Sociocultural Turn in Psychology

An Introduction and an Invitation

SUZANNE R. KIRSCHNER AND JACK MARTIN

In recent years constitutive sociocultural perspectives have become increasingly visible and influential within psychology. Such perspectives envision psychological processes, such as the mind and the self, as phenomena that are socioculturally constituted—that is, actually made up within, as opposed to merely facilitated by, culture and society. These constitutive approaches to psychology understand cognition, emotion, memory, identity, personality, and other psychological constructs as relational entities that emerge out of interactions with others within a sociocultural context. Moreover, the perspectives included under this rubric all have a cultural-historical aspect that moves consideration of the sociocultural beyond the immediate interpersonal and social situation.

Constitutive sociocultural approaches have been articulated over the past several decades by a diverse group of psychologists and social researchers whose work has emphasized, in various ways, the inseparability of the psychological and sociocultural realms. These researchers include Urie Bronfenbrenner (1979), Jerome Bruner (1990), Roy D'Andrade (1990), Pierre Dasen (1977), Yrjö Engeström (1990), Jacqueline Goodnow (Goodnow, Miller, and Kessel 1995), Patricia Greenfield (1984), Sara Harkness (Harkness and Super 1992), Edward Hutchins (1991), Vera John-Steiner (1985), Shinobu Kitayama (Markus and Kitayama 1991), Jean Lave (1988),

Hazel Markus (Markus and Kitayama 1991), Carl Ratner (2002), Barbara Rogoff (2003), Geoffrey Saxe (1991), Sylvia Scribner (Scribner and Cole 1981), Robert Serpell (1976), Richard Shweder (1990), James Stigler (Stigler, Lee, and Stevenson 1990), Charles Super (1981), Michael Tomasello (1999), Jaan Valsiner (1998), Dan Wagner (1993), James Wertsch (1998), Sheldon White (Cahan and White 1992), and many others (including the contributors to this current volume). At this writing, several major psychology journals (including *Mind, Culture, and Activity, Theory & Psychology, Culture & Psychology, Narrative Inquiry,* and *Subjectivity*) regularly publish work in sociocultural psychology that adopts constitutive, strongly relational perspectives. Moreover, many colleges and universities now offer courses in fields such as cultural psychology and narrative psychology; a growing number of graduate programs even afford students the opportunity to specialize in sociocultural theories and methods. Beyond psychology, these types of contemporary sociocultural approaches to psychological phenomena and issues are currently being applied widely in education, social work, psychotherapy, business, nursing, language instruction and learning, and many other areas (e.g., Hoshmand 2006; John-Steiner, Panofsky, and Smith 1994; Kozulin 1998).

However, sociocultural perspectives are by no means new. Even constitutive sociocultural approaches, such as those presented in this volume, have deep roots in several classical and early modern intellectual traditions. Richard Sorabji (2006) has recently pointed out that the ancient Greeks tended to a view of self and self-knowledge as relational not only by means of their connection to the cosmos, but also, more specifically, by means of the self's connection to social others. In contrast to the detached, inner "cogito" of Augustine and Descartes, Plato held that self-knowledge is hard to attain, and that seeing our selves reflected in others is often the best source of such understanding. Indeed, it was largely for this reason that Aristotle extolled the value of friendship, for it is through friendship that one comes to perceive and know both others and one's self, and is able to enter into the greater good.

Although many scholars (e.g., Guignon 2004; Taylor 1989) have correctly associated much Enlightenment and Romantic thought with a deeply interior, reflective, and ruminating conception of the psychological person (the infamous Cartesian self dwelling in splendid isolation from the world and others), it would be a mistake to think that relational and cultural-historical conceptions of psychological persons did not permeate much Western Enlightenment, Romantic, and modern thought prior to the founding of disciplinary psychology toward the end of the nineteenth century. The work of eighteenth-century theorist Giambattista Vico (2000) is often cited as an important precursor to such approaches. But as Jerrold Seigel (2005) convincingly demonstrates, Vico was not unique in exploring the sociocultural sources of mind and self. John Locke, and especially his successors David Hume (see also Murray 1993) and Adam Smith, actively sought a philosophy of psychology that emphasized the importance of "points of attachment offered by life with others" (Seigel 2005:43). Seigel cautions us not to confuse the recognition that modern psychology requires individuals themselves to participate in their own self-formation with the idea that modern individuals can look only to themselves to give their psychological lives coherence and stability. Indeed, a long line of Anglo-American and Continental thinkers have held that our social relations with others have primacy with respect to our psychological existence, being an indispensably necessary source for our thinking about the world and ourselves. Such individuals include not only the English descendants of Locke, but also many German scholars (e.g., Herder, Fichte, Hegel) who stressed our dependence on social and material existence, even as they advocated that knowledge of the self could serve as a model of the world. French-speaking thinkers, too (e.g., Diderot, Rousseau, Constant), recognized the inescapable influence of social forces on our psychological lives, even while cautioning that we must shield ourselves from some of society's more oppressive and distorting powers.

In fact, during and immediately following the founding of disciplinary psychology, this type of sociocultural and relational thinking was common to the thought of several influential psychologists and other seminal figures of early twentieth-century social thought. These include the experimental and social psychologist Wilhelm Wundt (1900–1920), developmental psychologists James Mark Baldwin (1897, 1911) and Heinz Werner (1948), psychiatrist Pierre Janet (1925, 1929), cultural-historical psychologist Lev Vygotsky (1978, 1986), social psychologist George Herbert Mead (1934), philosopher John Dewey (1939, 1987), sociologist Charles Cooley (1925), and many others. Later influences on sociocultural thought in psychology and social science more generally included the works of philosophers Ludwig Wittgenstein (1953), Hans-Georg Gadamer (1995), and Charles Taylor (1989); poststructuralist theorists Jacques Derrida (1978) and Michel Foucault (1980); and literary critic Mikhail Bakhtin (1986). The work of sociocultural psychologists is also related to other traditions in Euro-American social theory and philosophy, including those originating from the structuralist sociology of Emile Durkheim (Durkheim 1973; Mauss 1985; Durkheim and Mauss 1967) and Pierre Bourdieu (1972), the interpretive sociology of Max Weber (1958) and Clifford Geertz (1971), and even earlier contributions by Karl Marx, Wilhelm Dilthey, and others.

Since the middle of the twentieth century, there have been influential intellectual developments in sociology and anthropology that parallel or complement the sociocultural psychologies included in this book. In sociology, the writings of Erving Goffman (1959) and the ethnomethodologists (Garfinkel 1991) are relevant, along with that of contemporary theorists such as Judith Butler (2006). In psychological anthropology, the "cultural psychology" movement (Shweder 1990, 1991; Shore 1996; Holland, Lachicotte, Skinner, and Cain 2001) has helped to legitimize a view of persons as being constitutively intertwined with their cultural surround. Currently there is also a renewed interest on the part of cultural anthropologists in theorizing a socioculturally constituted subjectivity (Biehl, Good, and Kleinman 2007). Such a move is partly a reaction against the tendency among anthropologists and social theorists, during the past few decades, to give relatively short shrift to subjective experience, dismissing it as relatively unimportant or even epiphenomenal (Fox Keller 2007).

Nonetheless, despite a long history and the backing of so many influential scholars, sociocultural, relational approaches remain underdeveloped in psychology. This is especially the case for those perspectives that adopt a strongly constitutive stance that understands psychological phenomena (such as mind, self, and agency) to be "made up" from and largely to consist in the taking up of historically and culturally established forms of social practice, interaction, and coordinated conduct. For despite a promising beginning that followed the founding of disciplinary psychology, constitutive sociocultural theorizing in psychology per se was overcome, for the most part, by the new discipline's longing for scientific credibility, a desire that took the form of powerful methodological commitments to objectivist theories of knowledge (Bernstein 1983), operational definitions, and quantified measurements. Such ways of framing the subject matter and procedures of psychology left little room for the study of complex social and cultural phenomena and processes that could not easily be molded to fit such methodological penchants, at least as practiced by new generations of self-proclaimed psychological scientists.

However, by the last decades of the twentieth century, it was clear to most observers that the sociocultural, relational side of psychological science had been neglected to the extent that psychology was beginning to suffer from a detachment from the social, historical, cultural, and political contexts of human life. This detachment made many of its findings and prescriptions seem overly simplistic, excessively instrumental (even market driven, in a manner consistent with a technological, "quick fix" mentality), and only marginally connected to the real struggles and challenges of contemporary existence. The present volume deals specifically with the sociocultural turn in contemporary psychology that materialized during the final decades of the twentieth century and the first decade of the new century. During the past two decades in particular, various psychologists have further developed sociocultural visions of human nature and social life as means of exploring phenomena conventionally considered "psychological," and have done so along several distinctive lines. This book brings together the work of a number of these distinguished contemporary psychological theorists, who are the architects of many of the most influential current sociocultural perspectives. Their work is divided into four types: social constructionism/discursive psychology, hermeneutics, dialogical psychology, and activity theory.

For a number of reasons, both principled and pragmatic, we have limited the contents of this collection in two ways. First, unlike some types of psychology that study social and cultural influences on the mind, self, or development, the approaches contained herein do not conceive of self, mind, emotion, identity, and other psychological entities as variables that fluctuate systematically according to the effects of a particular context or environment or set of relationships. Rather, all of the perspectives included here take a more radical approach, framing these entities as emergent phenomena that are in no sense "prior" to their sociocultural surround. While there are undoubtedly additional influential theorists whose work also reflects this vision (e.g., Bickhard 2008; Slife 2004), the group included here is a good representative sample of such approaches. Second, we have chosen to include only those constitutive sociocultural approaches that were developed primarily in academic settings (although some of the approaches included here also are widely used in applied contexts, e.g., by psychotherapists and educators). Hence, we have not included relational psychoanalytic approaches (Stolorow, Brandschaft, and Atwood 2000; Stolorow and Atwood 2002; Mitchell and Aron 1999), even though they too envision the distinctive qualities of self and other as emerging out of a relational field. We have made this choice in part because these approaches often make use of metapsychological concepts and language that are not widely known or used, even by those psychologists who are familiar with sociocultural approaches.

Although this volume is thus not intended to be a comprehensive collection of all contemporary psychological theorists and approaches that might be called "sociocultural," even according to our definition of the term, it does provide an introduction to many of the most prominent and influential contemporary sociocultural perspectives. In the chapters that follow, each theorist discusses in depth his or her vision of how the mind or self emerges out of social life, and the type of research that is made possible by such an approach.

These four families of sociocultural perspectives do not espouse a single, unified vision. As the reader of this book will discover, they diverge from one another in some significant ways; even those authors grouped together under a single approach evince important differences among themselves. However, in this introductory chapter we focus mainly on what these authors—be they discursivist, hermeneutic, dialogical, or activity theorists—do hold in common, as well as the ways in which their approaches complement one another. In highlighting these overarching commonalities, we also make clear the ways in which all these approaches pose challenges to "conventional" or "mainstream" approaches to understanding and studying psychological phenomena. We discuss below three themes-and-variations that run through virtually all of the contributions to this volume: (1) undoing dualisms, (2) the emergence of agency, and (3) psychology as a human science (metatheoretical and methodological implications). We then briefly discuss some points of divergence, and end with an invitation to consider the current relevance of constitutive sociocultural perspectives within the broader context of contemporary psychology.[1]

Undoing Dualisms

Constitutive sociocultural approaches frame psychological phenomena in ways that call into question, and at least partly dissolve, conventionally theorized bifurcations that lie at the heart of much work in psychology. Such dualisms include the divides between the self and society, and between the individual and culture. Some of these authors frame such bifurcations in alternative terms: organism and environment, inner/private experience and outer/public action, or self and (both particular and generalized) others. Whatever terms are used, the conceptualization of subjectivity as emerging out of "otherness," and as enduringly permeated by it, is significantly different from how the subject is conceived in much psychological theory and research; the latter tends to frame mental phenomena as being (in the words of Harré, this volume): "*all and only* attributes of individual persons."

Constitutive sociocultural approaches problematize "self-contained" conceptions of the mind in a variety of ways. Thus, for discursivist/constructionists Shotter and Gergen—both strongly influenced by the later Wittgenstein—mind and self are discursive formations that emerge within a relational field of "joint action." The most extreme articulation of this notion of mind as a strategic performance is Gergen's; he believes that relationship is prior to essence, and argues that what we describe as the self or mind, along with its contents (emotions, thoughts, motives), only takes form within the context of a relational configuration. For him, when a person articulates such states, it is primarily a performative act, rather than expressive of some deep psychic interiority. The radical implication of this is that psychological research should be transformed into the study of social coordination and the ongoing relational construction of meaning. Like Gergen, Shotter emphasizes that we use our words (including our words about thoughts and feelings) to do things. Thus he too is concerned with the performative aspect of people's utterances, expressive behaviors, and responsive reactions. He also highlights the fact that since no two relational contexts are exactly alike, the (socially constructed) meanings generated in a given context are invariably going to be local and somewhat situation-specific. However, unlike Gergen, he does not aim to entirely jettison the notion of mind as interiority, or the study of how a self develops its distinctive and enduring tendencies.

Sociocultural psychologists do not only analyze psychological discourse's local and performative dimensions. They also study the ways in which the mind is constituted by more enduring cultural symbols and traditions, as well as by the relations of power within a society. In their chapter on the construction of gender identity, Magnusson and Marecek highlight the fact that the discursive construction of the individual involves both local/pragmatic interactions and performances, and institutionalized/epistemic (Foucault 1971) symbols and narratives. Discourse, as it is used in the latter sense, constructs more formal systems of knowledge that both produce and limit individuals' dispositions to act in particular ways. Magnusson and Marecek analyze aspects of "masculinity" and "femininity" that are often considered to be rooted in universal, probably biological, tendencies, and argue that they are actually configured by the sociocultural understandings shared by an entire community or society. These horizons of understanding, or structures of knowledge, set boundaries and limits on what can be conceived as "real," producing some distinctive realities and identities, and prohibiting others. Magnusson and Marecek, like many of the contributors to this book, are interested not only in the particular performances and activities authorized by discourse; they are interested also in how discourse engenders our experience of ourselves.

In thus facilitating analytic distance from what are generally considered (by psychologists as well as laypersons) to be taken-for-granted, essential realities, sociocultural approaches can illuminate the contingent nature of such socially produced identities. This, in turn, can lead to a recognition of the ways in which some of these identified "differences"—not only gender, but also race, class, ethnicity, and sexual orientation—reproduce and further extend relationships of inequality within a society. Thus sociocultural approaches can lead us to frame subjectivity as what Magnusson and Marecek call "subjectification." This term refers to the ways in which relations of unequal social and political power are not necessarily imposed from without, but relate to gender, class, ethnic, and other aspects of identity.

The dialogical psychologist Bhatia also argues for a more critical, self-consciously "transnational" sociocultural psychology, one that takes up issues of race, oppression, and power in the context of conflicting and contested perspectives on both culture and identity. In addition, Bhatia's analysis highlights the fluidity of identity—both self-identification and the (not unrelated) ways in which one is identified by others in one's society or community. In so doing, he makes explicit some fundamental complexities inherent in the concept and politics of identity itself. His analysis of the ways in which South Asian immigrants to North America evolve complex self-understandings in an equally complex and changing social field demonstrates how identity (and thus subjectivity itself) must be understood in terms of the interplay between self-identification and the ways in which one is identified (and thus "othered") by others. The identities of these postcolonial immigrants are revealed as transnational, hybrid, fluid, multivocal subjectivities that embody internal (and external) conversations and dialectics between oppression and resistance.

Reflected in such critical work is the basic idea that the sociocultural constitution of self and mind can be studied in terms of how an individual's sense of identity, and related phenomena such as memory and emotion, are patterned in terms of cultural narratives, symbols, and practices. The work of hermeneuticists Richardson and Fowers, along with that of Freeman, makes clear how cultural and historical forms shape psychological processes that are generally considered to be private, original, and (in many cases) unique. These theorists draw on ontological hermeneutics (the work of philosophers Heidegger, Gadamer, Taylor, and Ricoeur) to articulate a conception of human beings as, first and foremost, meaning-makers—self-interpreting beings who strive to make sense of themselves and the world, and whose interpretations always possess an evaluative dimension. According to hermeneuticists, humans' self-interpretations are derived from a shared background of meanings; thus subjectivity is constituted in terms of the cultural surround of beliefs and "visions of the good" into which one is born. In his work on cultural narrative and memory, Freeman offers some provocative illustrations of the ways in which psychological processes that are generally framed and studied as private and original can be fruitfully understood as culturally and historically constituted. He explores the "faux" autobiography of "Benjamin Wilkomirski," a pseudo-survivor of the Holocaust, and some early stories written by Helen Keller, to argue that both autobiographical memory and literary creation may be (and perhaps inevitably are) unwittingly emplotted in terms of a "narrative unconscious" that is laced with cultural and historical symbols.

As a number of these sociocultural theorists point out, the subject is not constituted by just one cultural discourse, or by a single relationship, but rather by a multiplicity of these sources of "otherness." Hermans and Salgado's chapter on the dialogical approach elaborates a model of thought in which both (internalized representations of) actual and imagined others populate the self. By exploring the dynamics of the relationship between these different inner others, sociocultural psychologists can study how the self is configured, how it develops over time, and how personality change might be facilitated (e.g., in psychotherapy) by means of modifying the relative prominence and influence of various inner voices. Moreover, in a world typified by increasing globalization and intercultural engagement, some sociocultural psychologists (e.g., Bhatia and Hermans and Salgado, this volume) have begun to theorize ways in which different cultural selves (or at least self positions), and dialogues among them, now often exist within the same person. Bhatia even points toward a radical retheorizing of concepts such as "culture, identity, diversity, and difference" based on this new understanding of the emerging global context. Of particular interest is the way in which these scholars continue to assert

the possibility of a substantial selfhood, possessed of an agency that matters, even within all of this multicultural multiplicity and fluidity. Where
some others worry about fragmentation and displacement, they see excit-
ing possibilities for truly transformative personal/cultural symbioses.
Indeed, emphasis on such symbiotic dynamics is symptomatic of the
broader assumption, apparently shared by many contributors to this volume, that persons and their societies are continuously emergent within
an ongoing co-constitutive process. Nonetheless, exactly how this process
of co-constitution is parsed differs across the sociocultural approaches
considered, with different contributors making more or less of various
social and psychological distinctions between persons and their contexts.

The formation of the mind through the internalization of cultural and
sociohistorical "otherness" is also explored by the activity theorists Cole and
Gajdamaschko and Stetsenko and Arievitch. These authors draw upon and
further develop the framework of Lev Vygotsky (1978, 1986), who was one of
the most influential early sociocultural psychologists. Vygotsky advanced a
view of the person as socially constructed through interactions with others.
For Vygotsky, the crucial step in the social formation of the person involved
the acquisition of capabilities of self-expression and self-reference. The psychological tools and discursive skills required for such capabilities develop
in interaction with others already skilled in speaking and acting within
relevant social contexts and linguistic (and other relational) practices. In
this context, whenever the infant appears to attempt some intentional act,
adults or older children supplement its efforts by interpreting and reacting
to the child's actions in ways that initiate the child into the social, linguistic practices and artifacts of the society. In this way, the unordered mental
activity with which infants are neurophysiologically endowed evolves into
the structured patterns of mature minds. Along with such socially spon-
sored development, the child acquires those discursive references, and lin-
guistically mediated means for responding to its own activity, that permit it
to experience and act in the world as an individual self.

At a more general level, Vygotsky (1978, 1986) distinguished human
beings from other animals in terms of the making and use of tools that
have radically altered their conditions of existence and their psychological
makeup. Such tools are socially spawned cultural artifacts that include
not only material creations such as rakes and utensils but, more importantly, social practices and language (the "tool of tools"). Such tools mediate between the functional capacities and capabilities of tool users and
their tasks and goals. In this sense, culture encompasses the pool of arti-

facts and practices accumulated by a social group during the course of its historical development. Human phylogeny, history, and ontogeny were understood by Vygotsky to turn respectively on the appearance of tool use among our primate ancestors, the emergence of labor and symbolic mediation in human history, and the acquisition of language as a transformative tool of individual development within a sociocultural context.

Cultural-historical activity theorists (CHAT) Stetsenko and Arievitch use an approach that is at once materialist and nondualist (yet also nonreductionist) by proposing that the mind exists at the "organism-environment nexus, rather than in organisms taken in isolation [from the environment]." Using the Soviet psychologist Galperin's metaphor of mind as "object-related action," they explore how the mind develops out of collaborative participation in goal-directed activities. Human subjectivity emerges out of such cooperative activity; at the same time, the mind that is thereby constituted plays an active role in constructing and reconstructing the world out of which it has emerged.

Yet another feature of the erosion of dualistic thinking evident in the various contributions to this volume is a tendency to consider persons acting in the world as the basic focus (unit of analysis) of psychological theorizing. Compared to most extant work in psychology, the reader will encounter relatively little in the way of "subpersonal" talk about brains doing things, emotions taking over, or attributions to particular cognitive abilities, personality factors, or neurophysiological mechanisms. Indeed, the holism evident in these sociocultural, constitutive accounts is highly reminiscent of that found in an earlier generation of sociogenetic thinkers (including Janet, Baldwin, Mead, and Vygotsky) in the first few decades of the twentieth century (see Valsiner and van der Veer 2000). To paraphrase Bennett and Hacker (2003), it is persons who think and act, not their various parts, as vitally required as these may be. None of this is to deny the importance (indeed the necessity) of our bodies, brains, and psychological capabilities to our worldly functioning—rather, it is to remind us that the primary object of psychological study is the person acting within the biophysical and sociocultural world.

The Emergence of Agency

If the self emerges out of its sociocultural contexts, then a major challenge arises: how are we to account for agency? If relational configurations, social structures, and cultural discourses constitute the self, then how are we to account for human beings' capacity to appraise, choose, resist, and innovate? How does the self position herself in relation to her external and internalized constituents such that she can affect her environment as much as the environment affects her? This issue is often framed in psychology as the problem of determinism (Slife 1994; Robinson 1985), and in sociology as that of structure versus agency (Giddens 1984). In psychology, determinism has not necessarily been considered something to be avoided. After all, the explicit goal of many psychologists has been (and continues to be) to predict and control behavior, and the existence of human freedom calls into question the viability of such a project. Yet in spite of such a widespread commitment to determinism, many applications of psychological theory and research in education, psychotherapy, and numerous other social institutions and situations tend to assume (at least tacitly) that human beings are capable of making choices and responding in creative and unforeseeable ways, and of asserting themselves in thought and action to improve their own lives and those of others. The general failure of disciplinary and professional psychology to reconcile the strongly deterministic, and sometimes reductive, assumptions of traditional psychological research with the seeming necessity of human agency demanded by the professional ministrations of psychologists stands as one of the most obvious difficulties currently faced by contemporary psychology and psychologists (Martin, Sugarman, and Thompson 2003). For without a viable, nonreductive, yet nonmysterious conception of human agency, psychology lacks the theoretical resources necessary to support not only its claims with respect to application and relevance, but also its status as the social science primarily concerned with an understanding of human experience and action. Even the word "action" denotes a kind of agentive intentionality that seems missing from much contemporary theory and inquiry in the discipline.

The sociocultural theorists included in this book mostly insist that meaningful human activity and experience are emergent levels of reality that cannot be reduced to a set of biological underpinnings, and therefore are not fully explicable in terms of mechanistic, cause-and-effect dynamics. They are equally adamant that the sociocultural perspective not lead to determinism of a sociological sort. That is, these theorists eschew a model of subjectivity in which the person is regarded as what Garfinkel (1991) called a "cultural dope"—someone whose mind is conceived as a passive recipient and regurgitator of relational scripts, social-structural forces, and cultural ideologies. Having said this, it must be noted that at least one contributor to the current volume, Kenneth Gergen, advocates a radically reformulated understanding of human emancipation that attempts to do away with the problem of agency altogether by diverting the field of inquiry away from individuals and interiority of any kind and toward social relational dynamics that are always ongoing, radically contingent, and shifting in ways that prevent any possibility of unambiguous, once-and-for-all answers either to our existence or to our condition.

Given their anti-deterministic commitments, it is hardly surprising that many of the sociocultural theorists represented here are explicit and emphatic about the possibility of human freedom and agency. Indeed, the matter of moral agency has been a mainstay of sociogenetic thought in psychology both currently and in the past (Valsiner and van der Veer 2000). Thus, for example, Magnusson and Marecek assert that, while hegemonic discourses of masculinity and femininity produce, and are reproduced by, individual identities, it is nonetheless true that "people are active agents who—although invited into certain subject positions by societal forces and conversational interventions—constantly navigate and negotiate these positions in order to relocate themselves in positions they find comfortable." They remind us that in social life, "people may take up a subject position or refuse it; they might take it up but enact it ironically." Similarly, hermeneuticists and dialogical theorists emphasize an agency that originates in the necessity of our acting. Because we have no choice but to act, we make use of whatever understandings and practices are available to us within the traditions and ways of life that we inhabit. Thus, for hermeneuts like Richardson and Fowers, human life is a constant flow of interpretation and reinterpretation within which we take up the understandings and practices available to us within our worldly milieus, and invest them with significance and concern by applying them in our own life projects and relations with others. For dialogical theorists like Hermans and Salgado, our acting in the world is necessarily perspectival, informed as it is by a variety of positions and possibilities for being and doing. Yet it is the human agent who selects from the interpretations, practices, positions, and possibilities available to her. Although some such selection is mandated by the human condition (i.e., the necessity to act in a worldly context experienced by entities who care about their own existence), any particular selections also reflect the life projects and concerns of those whose lives are enacted within this condition. As was noted earlier, activity theorists, too, depict the emergent and evolving self as an agent. Stetsenko and Arievitch argue that, in CHAT, organisms are attributed with an agentive power to actively shape their own development through their own activity rather than viewed as passive recipients of environmental influences (but without assuming any inherent or inborn properties of organisms, such as mental representations existing prior to their interaction with the world).

The most fully developed account of how the agentive self emerges out of a sociocultural matrix is provided by Sugarman and Martin, with their "levels of reality" approach. Drawing upon the work of Vygotsky, Mead, and the Scottish philosopher Macmurray, they propose a model of agency as an emergent property that develops within relational fields of activity that are embedded within biophysical and sociocultural levels of reality. In social relationships, an individual learns to play many different roles, and thereby to take a variety of perspectives. One witnesses and reacts to the responses of others and learns to see and act toward oneself as others do, thus coming increasingly to know oneself as both object and subject, and to build up a repertory of perspectives that may be further coordinated, refined, and applied in ongoing interaction with others, especially in the face of challenges, problems, and conflicts. Understood in this way, agency is conditioned but not fully determined by interactions and interrelations within biophysical and sociocultural contexts, yet is constantly emergent in interaction with problems and concerns of living that resist structures, processes, practices, and understandings drawn solely from the past. In this way, agency is a conditioned, yet partially self-determined, reactivity that enables an immediate future—a future that flows not from the past alone, but also from the ongoing interactivity and reactivity of persons (who care about themselves and others) acting together.

Psychology as a Human Science: Metatheoretical and Methodological Implications

According to sociocultural theorists, a defining feature of humans is that they are self-interpreting beings whose psychological properties emerge out of particular relational contexts. Thus the aims and methods of sociocultural inquiry diverge significantly from those championed by psychologists who desire to emulate what they call the "natural sciences"—this in spite of the fact that these natural sciences are far more diverse and heterogeneous than is generally clear from the image of them that circulates in the cultural imagination (see Geertz 2000; Rorty 1991; Shweder 2001; Toulmin 1987). Rather than seeking to construct cause-and-effect models, to predict and control behavior, or to "carve nature at its joints" (a phrase generally attributed to Plato, and also found in Bacon [1955]), sociocultural theorists are more likely to envision their purpose as the achievement of an increasingly adequate (though never perfect, timeless, or completely unambiguous) understanding of phenomena of interest. Such understanding is often framed as the development of the capacity to communicate with those whom one is studying (Geertz 1971), and to participate in their forms of life (Wittgenstein 1953). For discursive and constructionist psychologists such as Harré, Shotter, and Gergen, this might mean acquiring the ability to take part in language games or ritualized joint action. Hermeneuticists such as Richardson and Fowers, and Sugarman and Martin, frame the aim of such inquiry in terms of the fusion of the researcher's own situated, culturally constituted horizon of understanding with the life-world of the other, such that an enhanced (but still situated) appreciation of the phenomena under scrutiny is achieved. Many sociocultural theorists, including activity theorists, agentive herme-neuts, and dialogical psychologists, also pay explicit attention to the gen-esis of the mind and self—to the developmental processes and dynamics by which subjectivity comes to be constituted out of micro- and macroso-cial relationships.[2]

A second metatheoretical theme that runs through these sociocultural approaches is that all knowledge about humans is situated and perspec-tival. Just as the mind is constituted by the social, cultural, political, and historical contexts in which it emerges, so also is this true of the mind's products, including psychological knowledge itself. As Magnusson and Marecek put it, "Knowledge is always perspectival, always situated in some way. Knowers necessarily see from a particular angle of vision. They are always located in social and cultural forcefields. For example, we see history from our standpoint in the present and we necessarily bring pres-ent concerns and meanings to our analyses of the past. Moreover, knowl-edge is 'interested': that is, there is a reason why a particular question is of interest." Of course, sociocultural theories themselves are no excep-tion to this rule: they, too, emerge out of particular sociocultural contexts. Both the relational theorist Gergen and the hermeneuts Richardson and Fowers make this point when they illustrate the affinities between the concepts and methods of modern psychology and the contours of mod-ern life itself (Toulmin 1992, 2001). Activity theorists also contend that all knowledge—be it the everyday "knowing how" of laypersons in everyday life, or the formal systematic theories and methods developed by social researchers themselves—is produced within particular sociocultural fields. For Stetsenko and Arievitch, this means that all knowledge serves as an adaptation to social and material environments. Cole and Gajdamaschko make a somewhat different point about the sociocultural embeddedness of activity theory: they demonstrate how the "cultural borrowing" of the original Vygotskian notion of "context" by North American psychologists resulted in a significant alteration of its meaning and use by researchers.

Related to this awareness of the inevitably situated and "interested" dimension of knowledge is the recognition that sociocultural theory and research (indeed, all psychological and social research) must be appreciated not only as theory, but also as practice. The ways in which we theorize the mind, the self, and the world inevitably have practical effects, delineating and legitimizing certain realities and forms of identity while obscuring or delegitimizing others. For example, the very idea that psychological entities like mind and self emerge through interactions with others suggests the possibility of constructing modes of psychological being and acting capable of supporting valued communal goals and goods, as opposed to passively accepting current states of affairs as somehow unavoidable because of essential aspects of our natures that are pre-given and immutable. Gergen even goes so far as to argue that the consequences of a particular theory—its practical outcomes—should replace "traditional issues of truth and objectivity" as the criteria of a theory's validity. This is a controversial pronouncement, one with which many of the other contributors to this book would not fully agree. But all of these authors do share the view that, like the mind itself, sociocultural theories are the products of multiple contexts, and in turn produce effects on those contexts. In addition, they are in accord that it is essential that psychologists build an awareness of such contexts into all aspects of their work.

Another sensibility shared by sociocultural psychologists is an aversion to foundational metadiscourses (theories that analyze all psychological phenomena in terms of a single metaphor, or reduce them to some deep structure). There is a similar rejection of the search for general laws or universal principles of human nature. Thus, Shotter's Wittgensteinian sensitivity to the contingency of all discursive practices leads him to assert that there should be no "prior system or framework of foundational propositions in terms of which to conduct investigations." For him, the aim of sociocultural inquiry is to articulate the shared conventions (and improvisations) by means of which social life is lived in particular, local contexts. What has merit is what functions to illuminate and further our lives as understood and enacted within particular contexts and ways of being. There is no need in any of this to assert general truths that go beyond our discursive practices and conventions. Once progress in advancing our projects and moving beyond particular difficulties is achieved, nothing is gained by adding superfluous statements such as "and that's the truth." Along similar lines, the hermeneuts Richardson and Fowers suggest that sociocultural psychologists eschew general laws of human nature, motivation, and development. Their rationale for this is that human nature and selfhood vary depending on the historical and sociocultural contexts out of which they emerge. As Sugarman and Martin put it, "much of what we humans share in common is not a definable essence or a discoverable nature, but rather the existential condition of preexisting societies and cultures into which we are born, develop, and act."

Some Points of Divergence

In this chapter we have introduced constitutive sociocultural perspectives by emphasizing the themes and commitments that they share. There are undoubtedly many ways in which the approaches presented throughout this volume could be compared and contrasted. We hope that readers will actively engage with the rich array of ideas that follows, in order to draw their own conclusions regarding whether, or in what ways, these approaches might be integrated, or viewed as complementary or supplementary to one another. Here in this section we highlight just a few of the ways in which they diverge from one another. In particular, we note that theorists deal with the themes of "meaning" and "culture" in several different ways. We also note that they vary in the degree to which they emphasize humans' embodiment, and that they are not of one mind in their treatment of political or ethical themes.

As we have discussed, these sociocultural psychologies are characterized by efforts to undo the conventionally accepted, strong distinction between "self" and "otherness." But exactly what that "otherness" consists of, and in what sense it pervades the self, varies depending on the theory. Thus, for example, discursivists exhibit a tendency to dissolve the self-other bifurcation by envisioning "mind" and "self" as performances that function to promote social coordination, rather than as entities or experiences located inside some interior mental space. By contrast, most of the other theorists writing for this volume (and even some discursive psychologists) do retain some version of an interiorized subject, albeit a subject that is populated by actual and imagined others (which may be framed in terms of relationships, cultural traditions, or additional forms of "otherness").

As has also been noted, "meaning" is a core theme for sociocultural psychologists. Some of these theorists study "discourse," while others focus on "activity." In either case, a diagnostic feature of the phenomena under consideration is that they are both social and meaningful. But just as philosophers and others who study language do not unanimously endorse a particular theory of meaning, so also are there differences among some of the theorists represented in this book. For a neo-Wittgensteinian such as Shotter, cultural meanings are local, and often fleeting or ephemeral. For Gergen, who also makes use of Wittgenstein (though not in exactly the same way), stability and transparency of meaning are beside the point: communication between two discrete selves, in the conventional Cartesian sense, is not what language is for. By contrast, the ontological hermeneuts (Richardson and Fowers) and narrative theorists (Freeman)—who draw upon Gadamer as opposed to Wittgenstein—tend to associate cultural meanings with shared traditions. Hence the well-known hermeneutic likening of culture to a "text," with its connotations of stability and coherence, as well as the possibility of some degree of intersubjective understanding. The mind or self that has internalized cultural symbols and patterns, therefore, is likewise considered to possess a narrative and ethical coherence. (It should be acknowledged, however, that for hermeneuts, too, meaning is always considered to be indeterminate, in the sense that it arises out of the interaction between a "positioned" reader and the text.). Dialogical theorists (Hermans and Salgado, Bhatia) also envision subjectivity in terms of a socially spawned interiority, but they are less concerned than ontological hermeneuts with envisioning that subject in terms of an integrated coherence. For dialogical theorists, a defining feature of the subject is its multiplicity and heteroglossia. They consider this multiplicity to be an essential, and quite positive, feature of subjectivity, since it is what enables all manner of individual and sociocultural change.

Finally, activity theorists (Cole and Gajdamaschko, Stetsenko and Arievitch) have their own way of reconciling the tensions between meaning-located-in-an-interiorized-subject and meaning-as-performance, and between subjectivity-as-coherence and subjectivity-as-multiplicity. For these neo-Vygotskians, the interactions and collaborative activities out of which the self develops are certainly routinized and ritualized. Hence they are, in a sense, cultural "texts." But there is also an awareness that improvisation and innovative performances are both inevitable and essential. For example, Cole and Gajdamaschko take issue with understandings of Vygotsky's developmental theory as involving "a kind of 'social learning,'" pointing out that it is the child's active and dynamic participation and problem-solving within social situations that creates the "social situation of development." This is a theme echoed in Stetsenko and Arievitch's rendering of cultural-historical activity theory (CHAT)—"the *evolving dynamics of activity* that connects the two [individual organisms and their environments] in a constantly unfolding, ever-shifting, give-and-take, dynamical interaction."

Another way of parsing the differences among these four approaches is to note that some of them are less inclined than others to emphasize human embodiment. Hermeneutic approaches, as well as at least some of the discursive/constructionist theories, tend to emphasize language and related symbolic forms of social coordination to such a degree that they sometimes seem to suggest that we really are language "all the way down." By contrast, dialogical and activity theories—while in no way denying the importance of linguistic and interpretive processes of psychological constitution—also place considerable emphasis on our embodiment. Our bodies are the sites at which particular modes of psychological being are taken up. It is because we act and interact in the biophysical and sociocultural world through our bodies that we are able to become objects to ourselves once we have been so constituted by our engagements with others in sociocultural practices that define mind and self at different historical times and places. As has been noted, most activity theorists are heavily influenced by the writings of Lev Vygotsky and the broader Russian tradition of dialectical materialism, so that they also highlight, in addition to our biophysical and sociocultural embodiment, the importance of our active engagement with those material artifacts of a culture that serve particular social and psychological functions. Dialogical theorists, on the other hand, tend to be more interested in the ways in which we embody positions and practices of mind- and self-making that we encounter through our interactions with a diversity and plurality of others. A strong emphasis is placed in these approaches on the multiplicity of voices and perspectives readily evident in contemporary multicultural existence.

Finally, all the positions presented in this volume embrace some significant possibility for enhancing personal and collective well-being. However, they are not of one mind regarding exactly what such well-being entails, or how it might best be promoted. In particular, there are some interesting differences of emphasis when it comes to how these various theorists appraise the ethical or political effects of the sociocultural constitution of identity. While all consider our emergence out of a sociocultural medium to be a fundamental and inescapable aspect of the human condition, some theorists focus on the ways in which this situation enhances human well-being, whereas others are more concerned with demonstrating how the sociocultural constitution of meaning and subjectivity also serves as an oppressive force. This issue is related to (yet not identical with) the question of how humans can possess free will and exert agency if self and mind emerge out of a sociocultural matrix. Although all of these theorists consider human freedom, choice, and responsibility to be indispensable, the question of how much, and in what ways, humans should be critical of their culture or society is more contentious. For example, ontological hermeneuts emphasize how the long-standing cultural traditions that live within us sustain structures of meaning and morality that are required for both individual virtue and social harmony. Modernity and postmodernity thus come under criticism from some hermeneuts, precisely because those forms of social life may have less to offer when it comes to promoting a shared vision of the good. Moreover, even as they attempt to straddle the tension between the need for cohesion and intelligibility served by shared sociocultural traditions, on the one hand, and the desire to foster mutually enriching openness to dialogue between divergent moral visions, on the other, theorists like Richardson and Fowers nonetheless tend to privilege cultural tradition in ways that may lessen the transformative potential of critical cultural analysis. By contrast, the feminist discursivists Magnusson and Marecek and the dialogical theorist Bhatia highlight some oppressive aspects of cultural discourses (both traditional and contemporary) that inescapably shape the self. They emphasize that sociocultural analysis should serve a different kind of critical function: it should raise our consciousness about the fact that some social groups are not as free and equal as contemporary democratic ideology would have us believe, and that resistance to the status quo (which exerts its hegemony largely through the way it shapes our subjectivity) may be both possible and necessary.

A somewhat different rendering of this basic democratic ethical stance is detectable in the developmentalist visions present in agentive hermeneutics and in CHAT. While neither of those approaches posits a specific, substantive endpoint toward which all humans, and all cultures, move, both do suggest a natural tendency to evolve toward higher and "better" ways of being. For the agentive hermeneuts, this is a movement toward individual and communal agency (with goals and goods emerging within collective engagement and problem solving with others), whereas for CHAT theorists, it is a movement toward a society built on "a foundation of social justice and equality."

An Invitation

All of the sociocultural perspectives discussed in the various chapters of the current volume envision human beings' basic condition as one in which we act, and are formed, within practices and traditions of living; thus, they consider psychological persons to be contingently constituted through relations and interactions with others. Such an orientation and emphasis should not be confused with strong forms of social determinism, and they certainly are incompatible with attempts to reduce our psychological being to our biological bodies and brains. Both society and biology are absolutely necessary conditions for human activity in the world, and therefore for the sociocultural, relational constitution and emergence of psychological being and understanding. However, such conditions stop well short of full determination, and the emergence that continually characterizes our ongoing worldly interactivity is transformative of both our selves and our societies. Nonetheless, the sociocultural practices and traditions within which we develop as psychological beings provide pragmatic warrants for our understandings of our selves, our experiences, and our condition.

Surely it is not mere coincidence that these sociocultural perspectives have become elaborated in new ways, and sparked intensified interest, at a time when biological approaches to psychology are in greater ascendance than ever before. Although neuroscience and behavior genetics, along with the methods and technologies that accompany these endeavors, hold enormous promise for the advancement of knowledge, and for human betterment, they also engender concern on the part of psychologists and many others. In part this is due to their association, both in the public imagination and in the minds of at least some scientists, with reductionism and strong versions of determinism that discount the possibility of a human agency that matters. But even more worrisome is the prospect that the increasing visibility and power of such approaches will erode awareness that there are viable and robust perspectives on human being and social life that are fundamentally compatible with materialism yet also do justice to humans' deeply sociocultural and historical nature (Harrington, Deacon, Kosslyn, and Scarry 2001; Kirschner 2006; Martin 2000; Shweder 2001). Thus it has never been more important to promote conversation about what kind of beings we are, and what kind (or kinds) of psychology are most adequate to study, understand, and support human flourishing.

As was noted in the preceding section, across the various approaches discussed in subsequent chapters, there exist disagreements about the extent and exact manner of our ability to interpret and transform our lives. But whether formulated explicitly in terms of discursive/constructionist, hermeneutic, dialogical, or activity theorizing, all of the perspectives presented are, at least implicitly, morally, politically, and socially concerned in ways that go well beyond what is typically the case in much extant psychological theory and practice. At the same time, such concerns are not addressed with the goal of achieving once-and-for-all conclusions, but instead take much more situated, contextualized, particular, and tentative forms. It is far from clear how satisfactory all of this is, and obviously has a great deal to do with the expectations that we might reasonably hold about psychological theory and inquiry. Thus, in inviting readers to consider critically the various perspectives that follow, we also encourage reflection on what it is possible to expect of psychological theory and how it relates, and ought to relate, to our lives as psychological persons in interaction with others.

Notes

1.   We must emphasize that our purpose is not to squeeze all of the approaches discussed in our volume into a single theoretical framework. Rather, our goal is to present a variety of social and cultural perspectives within psychology in the words of their leading proponents. Our discussion of areas of convergence and divergence in the remainder of this introduction is consistent with this aim, as is our classification of the approaches discussed as social contructionist/discursive, hermeneutic, dialogical, and activity theory. In no way do we want to either over-

or underemphasize commonalities or distinctions within and across these classifications. What we do want is to allow the authors of the chapters that follow the freedom to present their work and ideas in the ways they deem most appropriate. Our commentary in this introduction (along with our organization of the essays and approaches included) is intended only to assist the reader in grasping the breadth and power of contemporary sociocultural approaches in psychology.

2.   In accord with these somewhat diverse aims, the sociocultural psychologists included in this book make use of a plurality of methods, including discursive, interpretive, ethnographic, literary, critical-psychological, poststructuralist, and other types of social and cultural analysis. It will be clear from this list that the metatheoretical vision articulated here leads to a favoring of qualitative methods. Nonetheless, at least some of these writers do not categorically reject the use of quantification as well, if such methods are deemed useful for particular purposes.

References

Arendt, H. 1958. *The Human Condition.* 2nd ed. Chicago: University of Chicago Press.

Atwood, G. E., and R. D. Stolorow. 1999. *Faces in a Cloud: Intersubjectivity in Personality Theory.* Northvale, NJ: Jason Aaronson.

Bacon, F. 1955. *Selected Writings of Francis Bacon.* Ed. H. G. Dick. New York: Random House.

Bakhtin, M. M. 1986. *Speech Genres and Other Late Essays.* Ed. C. Emerson and M. Holquist. Trans. V. W. McGee. Austin: University of Texas Press.

Baldwin, J. M. 1897. *Social and Ethical Interpretations in Mental Development.* New York: Macmillan.

———. 1911. *The Individual and Society.* Boston: Richard G. Badger.

Bennett, M. R., and P. M. S. Hacker. 2003. *Philosophical Foundations of Neuroscience.* Oxford: Blackwell.

Bernstein, R. J. 1983. *Beyond Objectivism and Relativism: Science, Hermeneutics, and Praxis.* Philadelphia: University of Pennsylvania Press.

Bickhard, 2008. Are you social? The ontological and developmental emergence of the person. In U. Müller, J. I. M. Carpendale, N. Budwig, and B. Sokol, eds., *Social Life and Social Knowledge: Toward a Process Account of Development,* 17–42. New York: Erlbaum.

Biehl, J., B. Good, and A. Kleinman. 2007. *Subjectivity: Ethnographic Investigations.* Berkeley: University of California Press.

Bourdieu, P. 1972. *An Outline of a Theory of Practice.* Trans. R. Nice. Cambridge: Cambridge University Press.

Bronfenbrenner, U. 1979. *The Ecology of Human Development.* Cambridge, MA: Harvard University Press.

Bruner, J. 1990. *Acts of Meaning.* Cambridge, MA: Harvard University Press.

———. 1996. *The Culture of Education.* Cambridge, MA: Harvard University Press.

Butler, J. 2006. *Gender Trouble: Feminism and the Subversion of Identity*. New York: Routledge.

Cahan, E., and S. White. 1992. Proposals for a second psychology. *American Psychologist* 247:224–235.

Cole, M. 1996. *Cultural Psychology: A Once and Future Discipline*. Cambridge, MA: Harvard University Press.

Cooley, C. H. 1925. *Social Organization: A Study of the Larger Mind*. New York: Charles Scribner's Sons.

D'Andrade, R. 1990. Some propositions about the relations between culture and human cognition. In J. W. Stigler, R. A. Shweder, and G. Herdt, eds., *Cultural Psychology*, 65–129. New York: Cambridge University Press.

Dasen, P. R., ed. 1977. *Piagetian Psychology: Cross-Cultural Contributions*. New York: Gardner.

Derrida, J. 1978. *Writing and Difference*. Trans. A. Bass. Chicago: University of Chicago Press.

Dewey, J. 1987. *Psychology*. New York: American Book Company.

——. 1939. *Freedom and Culture*. New York: G. P. Putnam's Sons.

Durkheim, E. 1973. Individualism and the intellectuals. In R. Bellah, ed., *On Morality and Society: Selected Writings*, 43–57. Chicago: University of Chicago Press.

Durkheim, E., and M. Mauss. 1967. *Primitive Classification*. Chicago: University of Chicago Press.

Engeström, Y. 1990. *Learning, Working, and Imagining: Twelve Studies in Activity Theory*. Helsinki: Orienta-Konsultit.

Foucault, M. 1971. *The Order of Things: An Archeology of the Human Sciences*. New York: Pantheon.

——. 1980. *Power/Knowledge: Selected Interviews and Other Writings*. Trans. C. Gordon. New York: Pantheon.

Fox Keller, E. 2007. Whole bodies, whole persons? Cultural studies, psychoanalysis, and biology. In J. Biehl, B. Good, and A. Kleinman, eds., *Subjectivity: Ethnographic Investigations*, 352–361. Berkeley: University of California Press.

Gadamer, H. G. 1995. *Truth and Method*. Trans. J. Weinsheimer and D. G. Marshall. 2nd rev. ed. New York: Continuum.

Garfinkel, H. 1991. *Studies in Ethnomethodology*. New York: Polity.

Geertz, C. 1971. *The Interpretation of Cultures: Selected Essays*. New York: Basic Books.

——. 1984. From the native's point of view: On the nature of anthropological understanding. In R. A. Shweder and R. LeVine, eds., *Culture Theory: Essays on Mind, Self, and Emotion*, 123–135. New York: Cambridge University Press.

——. 2000. *Available Light: Anthropological Reflections on Philosophical Topics*. Princeton: Princeton University Press.

Giddens, A. 1984. *The Constitution of Society: Outline of a Theory of Structuration*. Cambridge: Polity.

Goffman, E. 1959. *The Presentation of Self in Everyday Life*. New York: Anchor.

Goodnow, J. J., P. Miller, and F. Kessel, eds. 1995. *Cultural Practices as Contexts for Development*. San Francisco: Jossey-Bass.

Greenfield, P. M. 1984. *Mind and Media: The Effects of Television, Video Games, and Computers.* Cambridge, MA: Harvard University Press.

Guignon, C. 2004. *On Being Authentic.* London: Routledge.

Harkness, S., and C. M. Super. 1992. Parental ethnotheories in action. In I. E. Sigel, V. McGillicuddy-Delisi, and J. J. Goodnow, eds., *Parental Belief Systems,* 373–391. 2nd ed. Hillsdale, NJ: Erlbaum.

Harrington, A., T. Deacon, S. Kosslyn, and E. Scarry. 2001. Science, culture, meaning, and values: A dialogue. In A. Damasio et al., eds., *Unity of Knowledge: The Convergence of Natural and Human Science,* 217–232. New York: New York Academy of Sciences.

Holland, D., W. Lachicotte, D. Skinner, and C. Cain. 1998. *Identity and Agency in Cultural Worlds.* Cambridge, MA: Harvard University Press.

Hoshmand, L. T., ed. 2006. *Culture, Psychology, and Counseling: Critical and Integrative Perspectives.* Thousand Oaks, CA: Sage.

Hutchins, E. 1991. The social organization of distributed cognition. In L. B. Resnick, J. M. Levine, and S. D. Teasley, eds., *Perspectives on Socially Shared Cognition,* 282–307. Washington, DC: American Psychological Association.

Janet, P. 1925. *Psychological Healing.* New York: Macmillan.

——. 1929. *L'evolution psychologique de la personalité.* Paris: Cahine.

John-Steiner, V. 1985. *Notebooks of the Mind: Explorations of Thinking.* Albuquerque: University of New Mexico Press.

John-Steiner, V., C. Panofsky, and L. W. Smith, eds. 1994. *Sociocultural Approaches to Language and Literacy: An Interactionist Perspective.* Cambridge: Cambridge University Press.

Kirschner, S. R. 2006. Psychology and pluralism: Towards the psychological studies. *Journal of Theoretical and Philosophical Psychology* 26:1–17.

Kozulin, A. 1998. *Psychological Tools: A Sociocultural Approach to Education.* Cambridge: Cambridge University Press.

Lave, J. 1988. *Cognition in Practice: Mind, Mathematics, and Culture in Everyday Life.* Cambridge: Cambridge University Press.

Lave, J., and E. Wenger. 1991. *Situated Learning: Legitimate Peripheral Participation.* New York: Cambridge University Press.

Leontiev, A. N. 1981. *Problems of the Development of Mind.* Trans. M. Koplova. Moscow: Progress.

Luria, A. R. 1979. *The Making of Mind.* Cambridge, MA: Harvard University Press.

Markus, H., and S. Kitayama. 1991. Culture and the self: Implications for cognition, emotion, and motivation. *Psychological Review* 98:224–253.

Martin, E. 2000. Mind-body problems. *American Ethnologist* 27:569-690.

Martin, J., J. Sugarman, and J. Thompson. 2003. *Psychology and the Question of Agency.* Albany: State University of New York Press.

Mauss, M. 1985. A category of the human mind: The notion of Person, the notion of Self; trans. W. T. Halls. In M. Carrithers, S. Collins, and S. Lukes, eds., *The Category of the Person: Anthropology, Philosophy, History,* 1–25. Cambridge: Cambridge University Press.

Mead, G. H. 1934. *Mind, Self, and Society from the Standpoint of a Social Behaviorist.* Chicago: University of Chicago Press.

26   THE SOCIOCULTURAL TURN IN PSYCHOLOGY

Mitchell, S. A., and L. Aron, eds. 1999. *Relational Psychoanalysis: The Emergence of a Tradition*. Hillsdale, NJ: Analytic Press.

Murray, D. M. 1993. What is the Western concept of the self?: On forgetting David Hume. *Ethos* 21:3–23.

Newman, F., and L. Holzman. 1993. *Lev Vygotsky: Revolutionary Scientist*. New York: Routledge.

Ratner, C. 2002. *Cultural Psychology: Theory and Method*. New York: Springer.

Richardson, F., B. Fowers, and C. Guignon. 1999. *Re-envisioning Psychology: Moral Dimensions of Theory and Practice*. San Francisco: Jossey-Bass.

Robinson, D. N. 1985. *Philosophy of Psychology*. New York: Columbia University Press.

Rogoff, B. 2003. *The Cultural Nature of Human Development*. New York: Oxford University Press.

Rorty, R. 1991. *Philosophical Papers*. Cambridge: Cambridge University Press.

Saxe, G. B. 1991. *Culture and Cognitive Development: Studies in Mathematical Understanding*. Hillsdale, NJ: Erlbaum.

——. 1994. Studying cognitive development in sociocultural contexts: The development of practice-based approaches. *Mind, Culture, and Activity* 1:135–157.

Scribner, S., and M. Cole. 1981. *The Psychology of Literacy*. Cambridge, MA: Harvard University Press.

Seigel, J. 2005. *The Idea of the Self: Thought and Experience in Western Europe Since the Seventeenth Century*. Cambridge: Cambridge University Press.

Serpell, R. 1976. *Culture's Influence on Behaviour*. London: Methuen.

Shore, B. 1996. *Culture in Mind: Cognition, Culture, and the Problem of Meaning*. New York: Oxford University Press.

Shweder, R. 1990. Cultural psychology: What is it? In J. Stigler, R. A. Shweder, and G. Herdt, eds., *Cultural Psychology*, 1–43. New York: Cambridge University Press.

——. 1991. *Thinking Through Cultures: Expeditions in Cultural Psychology*. Cambridge, MA: Harvard University Press.

——. 2001. A polytheistic conception of the sciences and the virtues of deep variety. In A. Damasio et al., eds., *Unity of Knowledge: The Convergence of Natural and Human Science*, 217–232. New York: New York Academy of Sciences.

Slife, B. D. 1994. Free will and time: That "stuck" feeling. *Journal of Theoretical and Philosophical Psychology* 14:1–12.

——. 2004. Taking practice seriously: Toward a relational ontology. *Journal of Theoretical and Philosophical Psychology* 24:147–178.

Sorabji, R. 2006. *Self: Ancient and Modern Insights About Individuality, Life, and Death*. Chicago: University of Chicago Press.

Stigler, J., S. Lee, and H. W. Stevenson. 1990. *Mathematical Knowledge of Japanese, Chinese, and American Elementary-School Children*. Reston, VA: National Council of Teachers of Mathematics.

Stigler, J. W., R. A. Shweder, and G. Herdt, eds. 1990. *Cultural Psychology: Essays on Comparative Human Development*. New York: Cambridge University Press.

Stolorow, R. D., and G. E. Atwood. 2002. *Contexts of Being: The Intersubjective Foundations of Psychological Life*. New York: Analytic Press.

Stolorow, R. D., Brandschaft, B., and G. E. Atwood. 2000. *Psychoanalytic Treatment: An Intersubjective Approach.* New York: Analytic Press.

Super, C. M. 1981. Behavioral development in infancy. In R. H. Munroe, R. L. Munroe, and B. B. Whiting, eds., *Handbook of Cross-Cultural Human Development,* 181–270. New York: Garland.

Taylor, C. 1989. *Sources of the Self.* Cambridge, MA: Harvard University Press.

Tomasello, M. 1999. *The Cultural Origins of Human Cognition.* Cambridge, MA: Harvard University Press.

Toulmin, S. E. 1987. On not oversimplifying psychology: A response to Krantz. *New Ideas in Psychology* 5:351–353.

——. 1992. *Cosmopolis: The Hidden Agenda of Modernity.* Chicago: University of Chicago Press.

——. 2001. *Return to Reason.* Cambridge: Harvard University Press.

Valsiner, J. 1998. *The guided mind: A sociogenetic approach to personality.* Cambridge, MA: Harvard University Press.

Valsiner, J., and R. van der Veer. 2000. *The Social Mind: Construction of the Idea.* Cambridge: Cambridge University Press.

Vico, G. 2000. *New Science.* 3rd ed. Trans. D. Marsh. New York: Penguin.

Vygotsky, L. S. 1978. *Mind in Society: The Development of Higher Psychological Processes.* Ed. M. Cole, V. John-Steiner, S. Scribner, and E. Souberman. Cambridge, MA: Harvard University Press.

——. 1986. *Thought and Language.* Trans. A. Kozulin. Cambridge, MA: MIT Press.

Wagner, D. A. 1993. *Literacy, Culture, and Development: Becoming Literate in Morocco.* New York: Cambridge University Press.

Weber, M. 1958. *From Max Weber: Essays in Sociology.* Ed. H. Gerth and C. W. Mills. New York: Scribner's.

Werner, H. 1948. *Comparative Psychology of Mental Development.* New York: International Universities Press.

Wertsch, J. V. 1998. *Mind in Action.* New York: Oxford University Press.

Wittgenstein, L. 1953. *Philosophical Investigations.* Trans. G. E. M. Anscombe. Oxford: Blackwell.

Wundt, W. 1900–1920. *Völkerpsychologie: Eine Untersuchung der Entwicklungsgesetze von Sprache, Mythus und Sitte,* vols. 1–10. Leipzig: Wilhelm Englemann.

Part I

Discursive and Constructionist Approaches

Public Sources of the Personal Mind

Social Constructionism in Context

Rom Harré

Social constructionism has emerged as the generic name for a cluster of ways of conceptualizing the projects of psychology and sociology. It includes certain recommendations about the methodology appropriate to attaining an understanding of the mental and social lives of human beings, by human beings. While it shares some insights with postmodernism, there are important ways in which the social constructionist viewpoint is very different. Two, in particular, stand out. It is no part of the social constructionist approach to deny that there are any universal aspects of human life, or that, in a certain sense, there are some essential attributes of persons and processes. Nor is it any part of the social constructionist approach to deny that there are better and worse representations of the social world and of human psychology. In short, social constructionism, while at a very great remove from positivistic mainstream psychology, is not radically relativist.

Social Constructionist Contributions to Developmental and Cognitive Psychology

There are major social constructionist contributions to two different but interconnected domains of psychology, developmental and cognitive. The way the social constructionist thesis is applied and developed is rather different in each. In the former, the results of construction are fairly long-term and stable attributes of individual persons. In the latter, the results of construction are ephemeral attributes of the flow of jointly created sequences of meaningful actions. There is a link: only if the individuals who are members of a certain social/cognitive world are so formed as to be capable of certain kinds of joint action are collective expressions of psychological phenomena possible. There can be a winning goal only if the members of the club can play football, and that requires that football be a culturally recognized activity.

The Social Construction of Minds

In the context of developmental psychology, we can easily discern a movement one might call "psychologists against biological determinism." Whence come our cognitive skills, emotional propensities, and repertoires of personality displays? Following Vygotsky, social constructionists believe that it has already been empirically demonstrated that such cognitive skills as remembering, deciding, and such social propensities as the tendency to put on an angry display in certain situations, to organize one's sense of individual identity in a certain way, and so on, are appropriated and privatized by individuals from patterns of intimate social interactions. There are both local and universal features of social processes from which higher mental functions are appropriated.

The first basic thesis of the social constructionist point of view is simply stated: individual psychological skills and capacities are derived from participation in collective psychological phenomena, in the manner described by Vygotsky (1962). Insofar as social practices are culturally and historically diverse, there will be local variations in such individual skills. As Wittgenstein (1953) emphasized, there is a human form of life, however various are the tribal variations on it. A person is necessarily *embodied*, though what forms of embodiment are regarded as acceptable vary widely.

According to social constructionists, the human brain is one of the tools people use to accomplish their cognitive projects, just as a spade is one of the tools people use to accomplish their horticultural projects. As Luria (1981), Tsunida (1985), and others have demonstrated, the brain is shaped up for the tasks it is used to perform.

There are two kinds of constraints on the kinds of minds that Vygotskian processes can induce in a human being. The human brain does have an inherited architecture, the importance of which has become very clear against the background of attempts to construct machines capable of artificial intelligent action. The way vast amounts of data are maintained in each type of system is evidently completely different. While human beings, confined to using their brains as the computational device, cannot perform certain kinds of information processing that are performed by machines, it has proved impossible so far to build a machine that performs creative cognitive tasks as a human being does. The other limiting factor is set by the history of a culture. What kinds of cognitive practices and affective reactions are implicit in the legitimate practices of a social order? There are limits to the sort of being that can be created by Vygotskian appropriation from this cultural and anatomical here-and-now.

The Social Construction of Psychological Phenomena

In the context of cognitive psychology and the psychology of emotional displays and feelings, there is another movement, one we could call "psychologists against radical individualism." The origin of this movement is different from that of the Vygotskian developmentalist school. It arises from asking the question: Are cognitive and emotional phenomena *all and only* attributes of individual persons? For the phenomenologically inclined, psychological phenomena might be sequences of mental states, or even, for some reductionists, sequences of material states of the brains and nervous systems of individual organisms. Commonsense reflection on what ordinary psychological descriptive terms refer to can start one thinking along constructionist lines. Do we not sometimes come to a decision in the course of a public conversation? Surely jealousy is often part of a complex pattern of interpersonal actions and relationships? The theoretical identification of a domain of psychological phenomena that are neither patterns of large-scale collectivities, such as revolutionary movements, nor attributes of individuals, such as disloyal thoughts kept to oneself, has been a major achievement of authors like Shotter (1990). In this sense, psychological phenomena are socially constructed.

Once this idea has taken root new research dimensions are opened up. Studies of remembering as an interpersonal phenomenon have proliferated in recent years; these include the work of Middleton and Edwards, reported in their *Collective Remembering* (1990), and the remarkable studies by Dixon (1996) on the difference in success levels in recalling events by older people when they are required to recall individually, from their success in similar tasks when carried on collectively. In the collective condition older people fared as well as younger folks. These studies have shown empirically that the constructionist point of view is certainly vindicated for the psychology of remembering. Mapstone (1996) has explored the patterns of problem-solving techniques that are to be seen in joint action when two people collaborate in attacking a challenge.

Further developments along these lines have forged a close link between discourse analysis and psychology. If some substantial part of our cognitive activities is conducted collectively, the natural place to look for evidence of this is in conversations. A valuable methodology has emerged from taking up Austin's (1962) performative account of language use and the various analytical concepts he developed, such as the illocutionary and perlocutionary effects of saying as doing. Since narrative conventions often shape conversations into stories (Bruner 1990), there is a good case for merging narratological analysis and cognitive psychology, for example in studying how patterns of reasoning are rendered more or less acceptable, and how beliefs are induced (Harré, Brockmeier, and Mühlhäusler 1999).

Social and Semantic Conventions Replace Laws

The social constructionist take on such topics as the psychology of the emotions is just one of the paradigm shifts that follow from a fundamental change of theoretical orientation. For nearly a century psychologists framed their theories, their methodologies, and their interpretative and explanatory discourses exclusively in terms of cause and effect. For the most part this was not the concept of "causality" as it is used in the natural sciences, but a philosophical innovation from the eighteenth century, causality as regular concomitance; this is the analysis proffered by David Hume (1748). A sequence counts as causal in the natural sciences only if a causal mechanism can be found or, when unobservable, plausibly modeled. Correlations are not causes! Physicists postulate active agents, such as charges, as the sources of dynamic processes. Positivists, determined to eschew anything that seemed speculative, gave a new impetus to the use of the Humean conception of causality in the first half of the last century. The most important step in the move to a social constructionist point of view has been to drop the Humean causal metaphysics of the positivist school in favor of normative explanations. This means that psychological processes are to be interpreted largely as the result of the management of meanings in accordance with the rules and conventions of the relevant practice. Intentionality (meaning) and normativity (conformity to rules and conventions), not cause and effect, need to be adopted as the framing concepts of psychological studies. This leads us back again to the root metaphor of cognition as conversation.

These points have been made many times in recent years, notably by Billig (1987), Edwards and Potter (1992), Moghaddam (1998), Nightingale and Cromby (1999), Radden (1996), Searle (1995), Shotter (1990), and a number of others. Such is the power of selective filtration in defense of a dying paradigm, however, that it is only a mere caricature of social constructionism that has been taken up and then rejected by many psychologists, comfortably established in the old paradigm. The fault is not only with the defenders of the old scientistic paradigm, however. Some authors have interpreted social constructionism as being more or less identical with postmodernism. While both movements are set against positivism in any form, and rightly suspicious of the scientistic character of a good deal of mainstream psychology, the positive claims of social constructionism fall short of the radical relativism of postmodernism.

What Social Constructionism Is Not

What anchors a social constructionist analysis? Surely a great many storylines could be offered as hypotheses about the possible organizing principles of some stretch of social interaction? Which is the correct one? Before that question can be asked, or even made intelligible, the very idea of alternatives presupposes that something is common to both. What criteria determine that two or more narratological analyses of what happens when some people getting together at some time and place are in fact referring to something that retains its identity through different interpretations? If the phenomena are the meanings, and the meanings are the products of interpretations, does not the diversity of actual and possible interpretations entail that a like diversity of phenomena could be created at that time and place?

Even if a good account of what the common bearer of different interpretations is could be given, another conundrum would emerge. Bearing in mind that the analysis offered by a social psychologist of some incident—say, by using the concepts of cognitive dissonance—is also a story, on what basis can this claim to be a privileged account? Surely the accounts offered by the actors are equally worthy of our attention? What then becomes of the idea of "scientific truth" and of the best representation of the phenomena and their mode of genesis?

Postmodernists would say that no account available from whatever source is more worthy of the attention of those who study social life than any other. Social constructionists, for the most part, would say that some accounts capture psychological reality better than others, all the while conceding that more than one psychological reality may be created in some sequence of actions, and that each of these can nevertheless be psychologically and socially real. On what would such a claim be based? Choice among putative explanatory storylines can be made only through attention to the further unfolding of psychologically relevant social interactions. For example, how do we decide which version of the past is the more robust for a family, given that several versions of the past are offered by differently situated family members? What the family does next will throw light on that question, even though *what* they do next is as much a product of interpretative procedures as anything else. The range of interpretations is constrained by all sorts of factors, one of which is the collectively arrived-at version of the past. "Going to the match" may have all sorts of interpretations, but "visiting Florida Disneyland" is not one of them.

An ingenious observer could discern many possible storylines in some strip of life. However, the people living that strip may take themselves to be following only one. Mere ingenuity of interpretation does not inflate psychological reality; however, in any given strip of life there may be more than one reality produced. It is important to emphasize the insight that the same sequence of actions, for which certain criteria of identity can be drawn on, may be the bearer of more than one psychological reality. The action of kissing can be used to perform all sorts of acts, from displays of affection to betrayal in the garden of Gethsemane. Actions and acts are not in one-to-one correspondence. If meanings—that is, acts—are constitutive of social and psychological reality, then the same action sequence may be the bearer of more than one act sequence, and so of more than one social and psychological reality.

Illustrations of Social Constructionist Research

In the remainder of this paper I shall set out the Vygotskian the-sis in more detail, and follow up with some illustrations of researches into the social construction of some common psychological phenomena. It will become evident, I hope, that neither the simplistic universalism of "mainstream" positivistic psychology nor the extreme relativism of some recent distorted expositions of the constructionist point of view can be sustained. Psychology is a hybrid science in two ways. First, it must find metaphors for bringing together the exploration of the intentionality of human action, be it private or public, with studies of the neurophysiology of the human brain and nervous system, by means of which such action is accomplished. It must also seek the universal in the local and the particu-lar, without achieving a false generality by developing concepts of a higher and higher order of abstraction, and without elevating the local and the particular to the exclusive status of all that there is.

The Paradox of Statistical Methods

One of the problems with the old-paradigm psychology that social constructionist theory and its associated analytical methodology replace is the use of statistical methods, applied to mass data. It is close to a neces-sary condition for the publication of a psychological study in the majority of journals that there be a statistical analysis of "results," as a proof of a *psychological* hypothesis. This is very strange.

Why? The basic metaphysics of old-paradigm psychology requires that psychological processes be attributes of individuals, *and* that sequences of states, actions, or whatever be interpreted within a cause-and-effect framework. As mentioned above, the causal concepts that seem to be in use in most published interpretations of results are dominated by a long-abandoned philosophical theory, the regular concomitance theory of David Hume.

Enter statistics (Danziger 1990). A statistical analysis is supposed to reveal the most likely causal hypothesis, that is, the best-supported cor-relation between "variables." Variations among individuals are excluded. However, herein lies the snag. A statistical analysis cannot—that is, *logically cannot*—be used to ascribe a corresponding propensity to any individual who was a member of the reference class. To take a very simple case: if the proportion of people doing something X, in a sample population, is 6/10, the probability of a randomly selected individual doing X is 0.6. However, this index must not be interpreted as a propensity. The selected individual either will do X or will not do X. The probability simply means that there is a 0.6 chance that the selected individual will fall in the "will do X" group, given that all we know about him/her is membership in the reference class. Statistical analysis shunts one's work off the line of psychology as a science of individuals onto another track, demography. One cannot consistently insist that psychological phenomena occur at the level of isolated individuals and then use statistical methods to try to find out what those phenomena are!

Vygotsky's Thesis: The Social Construction of Persons

Vygotsky's work in the 1930s was motivated to some extent by a deep-seated disagreement with the universalist scope and the metaphysical individualism of Piaget's famous sequential schedule of stages of development. Cognitive skills were first acquired in the domain of public, interpersonal joint action in the zone of proximal development, and then later appropriated as the capacities of a freestanding psychological individual.

What is it like in the "zone of proximal development?" The performances of an unskilled actor are interpreted by a more skilled actor as attempts at some well-defined skilled activity. The deficits in the performance are made up for by contributions from the more skilled members of the group, though often the group consists of just two people. The joint performance, meeting local standards of adequacy, has been called "psychological symbiosis." The developmental process is furthered by the unskilled member of the dyad taking over some of the supplementary contributions of the more skilled. The skill moves then from the zone of *proximal* development to a permanent attribute of the learner, in the zone of actual development.

Thus, there is a collective or social construction of a person, an embodied being with cognitive skills and capacities and with a form of consciousness shaped by local conventions. I will return to the issue of the social shaping of consciousness.

A Schematic Representation

If we imagine that these are the successive locations of cognitive processes, we can express Vygotsky's point of view in the claim that development of cognitive capacities—or "higher-order mental functions," as Vygotsky called them—follows the order set out below. For example, a cognitive skill is first entered into symbiotically in the collective/public domain (1), as in a conversation with colleagues. One picks up the discursive conventions in collective/private (2), perhaps via sotto voce reasoning discursively to oneself. These conventions may be transcended or supplemented in the individual/private domain (3), for instance in the development of some idiosyncratic cognitive device, such as a new metaphor. This device may be given an individual/public presentation (4), for example by trying out that metaphor in a public discussion. It becomes part of the collective/public domain as and if the new metaphor catches on.

1. Collective/Public	→	2. Collective/Private
↑		↓
4. Individual/Public	←	3. Individual/Private

Assignments of Rights: Micromoral Orders

A new twist to the Vygotskian cycle has come from "positioning theory." Contributions to episodes of joint action are not necessarily determined by the skills, capacities, or relevant knowledge of the individual actors. What happens depends, very often, on how rights and duties to introduce topics, to confirm or deny the actions of others, and so on are distributed. To position someone or to be positioned is to implicitly (and sometimes explicitly) to assign or remove contributing rights. People are also positioned by virtue of attributions of personality and character. Someone may be treated as unreliable, dishonest, ill-informed, and so on. Those who are unreliable do not have the right to make promises on behalf of others, and so on.

There are many applications of positioning theory in social and cognitive psychology (Harré and van Langehove 1999). However, in this context it is important to attend to the distributions and redistributions of rights and duties in relations of psychological symbiosis. Who has the right to contribute to "beef up" an inadequate performance may be an important issue that has consequences for the development of the less skilled.

Here we a have well-established paradigm for research into the social construction of persons.

How much room for variety is there in the kind of beings that can be so produced? We do know that, as Giddens (1986) has stressed, person-making generally results in beings well fitted to reproduce the society in which they were manufactured. Once she has been created, it seems to be very hard to recreate that human being. Yet it is equally evident that the production process is imperfect, and that new types of people do come forth within the continuous history of a well-defined and demarcated social and cultural order. A close study of the history and fact of attempts to create wholly new social orders shows that there are very definite limits on how far people created within an existing social order can be reshaped to live comfortably within something very different. As Hoffer (1966) showed, conversion involves shifts within an overarching framework rather than a radical departure.

The fact of embodiment is equally important in setting limits to how far new forms of person can be constructed. Each person has a singular trajectory through space and time, and one and only one consciousness, tied in many ways to the fact of singular embodiment. No doubt, beliefs about what sort of person one is, what sort of life one has led, and so on are variable, depending on the circumstances that have brought on a moment of self-attention and self-reflection. However, variations in these beliefs make sense only against the stable background of singular embodiment. Let us follow up these brief remarks with a close look at the sense of self and how it can be studied.

Expression and Description

When I say that "You are in pain, you poor thing!" I am describing your feelings, and I may be right or wrong about them. However, when I say "I am in pain," should this remark be treated as a self-description? Wittgenstein argued that describing is the speech act appropriate to cases in which the speaker could be mistaken. The phenomenon and the act of describing are independent of one another. In the case of reporting my feelings to someone else, there is no gap between my report and my feeling. Part of what it is to be in pain is to be ready to make such reports and to do other appropriate things, like groaning. "I am in pain" expresses my feeling. It does not describe it.

Could we make a similar analysis of the uses of the word "I?" Descartes treated "je" in "Je pense, donc je suis" as if it referred to an inner being, an immaterial component of the whole person. He treated the statement "Je pense" as if it described what he was doing, and about which he could have been wrong. Yet Descartes was far from conceding that he could have been mistaken in thinking that he was thinking, since even to doubt that he is thinking is to think.

The Expression of Selfhood in Grammar

Wittgenstein's resolution of the description/expression puzzle works very nicely here too. Let us ask what we actually do with the first-person voice. In many common cases, the word "I" serves to index the content of what has been said within the spatio-temporal location of the embodied speaker. If someone says "I can smell gas!!!" we take it for granted that the smell is where the speaker is then and there. Using the first person also indexes the social force of the utterance with the moral standing of the speaker. The use of the first-person voice commits the speaker to whatever the utterance involves. And so on. The point is that this potent word expresses aspects of personhood.

Language has to be learned. Learning the discursive conventions for the use of the first-person voice may be a Vygotskian vehicle for the acquisition of the local reflexive concept of person. Do people of our sort take individual responsibility for our actions? Alternatively, do we experience our actions as deriving from and reflecting back on some collective, such as the family? The social constructionist position would be that the moral style of the community is displayed in discourse. It is a product of the expressive repertoires of the culture. One important vehicle for the acquisition of the relevant practices is the pronoun system through which important aspects of personhood are manifested.

It is evident that personhood has several components. There is a universal feature of all person concepts: the singular trajectory through space and time of the embodied human being. Even when there seem to be multiplicities of personhood, each has a unique share of the spatio-temporal path. Whatever else there is in MPD (multiple personality disorder), it is evident that the alternative persons are sequentially present, not simultaneously.

Holiday's Paradox: Moral Universals and the Conditions for Communication

The advent of positioning theory has led to the realization that moral principles cannot be ignored in psychology. The same insight has emerged from more realistic studies of the emotions, such as envy and jealousy, anger, and embarrassment. The very identifying description of these emotions requires attention to the moral judgments that are implicit in their display.

Holiday (1988) has presented a detailed analysis of the conditions of linguistic communication that highlights the necessary shared moral underpinnings of the very possibility of using language in concert with others. For example, the presumption that what one has said can be understood by the one addressed presupposes not only competence but also a certain pattern of rights to exercise that competence. In the light of his analysis, the postmodern claim, expressed in language and meant to be understood, that there are no moral universals is self-refuting. In order for the claim to be intelligible, certain conditions must already be satisfied, and these are the necessary conditions for the possibility of *any* use of language.

Critical Realism

At the other extreme from postmodernism lies "critical realism." This movement arises at two removes from the realist philosophy of the physical sciences. Scientific realism is based on two main theses:

1. Models are imperfect but improvable representations of natural structures and processes that exist independently of human beings.
2. There is more to material reality than has been represented by scientific models.

The first principle requires that there be some way in which the natural objects represented by models can be employed independently of existing models to assess the verisimilitude of those models. How can we know about them? The secret is simple: we can know how whatever occupies deeper levels of reality behaves, at the same time as we do not know what its constitution is and even if it can be properly to referred to as an "it." The models we construct must behave in a way similar to how the hidden beings in material reality behave. We can then infer, sometimes, that they are similarly constituted. The second principle requires that there be ontologies that are not reducible to extensions of the substance/property metaphysics of what can be perceived.

Critical realists have tried to extend scientific realism to social and psychological research paradigms (Bhaskar 2001). Since the social world and the human psyche consist entirely of meanings, there can be no reality beyond another discourse against which the relevant discourses could be corrected. As Wittgenstein remarked, this is like buying several copies of the morning paper to see if what it says is true. The first principle of natural scientific realism cannot be transferred to social and psychological research paradigms. However, just as there is more to the material world than we can currently represent, there is more to the human world than we currently bring into being by our meaning-giving procedures and customs. We may not have exhausted possible human powers and capacities, nor yet fully realized the possibilities inherent in those powers and capacities we have brought into being by psychological symbiosis.

It should now be quite clear that the discursive turn and the adoption of a generally constructionist orientation in psychology does not license a slide into radical relativism. There is a thread of continuity—the embodied person—on which the multicolored garments of the many possibilities of self-presentation to oneself and to others are hung. That different discourse genres disclose different aspects of material reality is no ground at all for denying that it is that very material reality, never fully explored through any of them, that is involved in our adherence to some and abandonment of others.

There surely are many interpretations of some given sequence of actions, identified and individuated by some commonly agreed criteria. However, one of these interpretations will be dominant in the interpretation of subsequent events, as this or that storyline. This will *be* the social/psychological reality. There is nothing else to which this story might or might not correspond. The social scientist or psychologist who notes down the dominant storyline has the truth of the matter.

References

Austin, J. L. 1962. *How to Do Things with Words*. Oxford: Clarendon Press.

Bhaskar, R. 2001. How to change reality: Story vs. structure. In J. Lopez and G. Potter, eds., *After Postmodernism: An Introduction to Critical Realism*, 28–39. London: Athlone.

Billig, M. 1987. *Arguing and Thinking: A Rhetorical Approach to Social Psychology*. Cambridge: Cambridge University Press.

Bruner, J. S. 1990. *Acts of Meaning: Four Lectures on Mind and Culture*. Cambridge, MA: Harvard University Press.

Danziger, K. 1990. *Constructing the Subject: Historical Origins of Psychological Research*. Cambridge: Cambridge University Press.

Dixon, R. A. 1996. *Interactive Minds: Life-Span Perspectives on the Social Foundation of Cognition*. New York: Cambridge University Press.

Edwards, D., and J. Potter. 1992. *Discursive Psychology*. London: Sage.

Giddens, A. 1986. *The Constitution of Society: Outline of the Theory of Structuration*. Cambridge: Polity Press.

Harré, R., and L. van Langenhove. 1999. *Positioning Theory: Moral Contexts of Intentional Action*. Oxford: Blackwell.

Harré, R., J. Brockmeier, and P. Mühlhäusler. 1999. *Greenspeak: A Study of Environmental Discourse*. Thousand Oaks, CA: Sage.

Hoffer, E. 2002. *The True Believer: Thoughts on the Nature of Mass Movements*. New York: Harper Perennial Modern Classics.

Holiday, C. A. 1988. *Moral Powers: Normative Necessity in Language and History*. Brighton: Harvester.

Hume, D. 1748 [1960]. *An Enquiry Concerning the Human Understanding*. Oxford: Clarendon Press.

Luria, A. R. 1981. *Language and Cognition*. New York: Wiley.

Mapstone, E. 1999. *Wars of Words: Men and Women Arguing*. London: Vintage.

Middleton, D., and D. Edwards. 1990. *Collective Remembering*. London: Sage.

Moghaddam, F. M. 1998. *Social Psychology: Exploring Universals Across Cultures*. New York: Freeman.

Nightingale, D. J., and J. Cromby. 1999. *Social Constructionist Psychology: A Critical Analysis of Theory and Practice*. Buckingham: Open University Press.

Radden, J. 1996. *Divided Minds and Successive Selves: Ethical Issues in Disorders of Identity and Personality*. Cambridge, MA: MIT Press.

Searle, J. R. 1995. *The Construction of Social Reality*. London: Penguin.

Shotter, J. 1990. *Knowing of the Third Kind*. Utrecht: ISOR.

Tsunida, T. 1985. *The Japanese Brain*. Trans. Yoshimori Oiwa. Tokyo: Tashiker.

Vygotsky, L. S. 1962. *Thought and Language*. Cambridge, MA: MIT Press.

Wittgenstein, L. 1953. *Philosophical Investigations*. Oxford: Blackwell.

The propositions describing this world-picture might be part of a kind of mythology. And their role is like that of rules of a game; and the game can be learned purely practically, without learning any explicit rules. It might be imagined that some propositions, of the form of empirical propositions, were hardened and functioned as channels for such empirical propositions as were not hardened but fluid. . . . But I distinguish between the movement of the waters on the river-bed and the shift of the bed itself; though there is not a sharp division of the one from the other.
—Ludwig Wittgenstein, On Certainty

It is in language that an expectation and its fulfilment make contact.
—Ludwig Wittgenstein, Philosophical Investigations

2   Inside Our Lives Together

A Neo-Wittgensteinian Constructionism

JOHN SHOTTER

This book is concerned with the degree to which sociocultural surroundings, which we grow into as we grow up, affect the constitution of the psychological processes and structures occurring in us as individuals. Although I think their impact is considerable, a major difficulty arises in identifying precisely in what such influences might consist, and the spheres of human activity within which they might be exerted and their impacts expressed. In line with the image of the river and the riverbed outlined by Wittgenstein (1969: nos. 95, 96, 97) above, I think that it is in "the inherited background against which I distinguish between true and false" (no. 94)—i.e., in the background riverbed—where we can find the character of these influences and the processes by which they are most powerfully at work. But—precisely because it is the *medium* within which we have our being as individuals, and are able to mean things to each other—the task of spelling out the features of this background in detail is not an easy one. We cannot simply turn ourselves round on it, to specify it simply as an object in itself. This would be as if we were seeds growing in a certain soil and climate, and must try to specify which aspects of that soil and climate were important to us while still ourselves growing within them—not an easy task. "Perhaps what is inexpressible (what I find mysterious and am not able to express)," said Wittgenstein, "is the background against which whatever I could express has its meaning" (1980:16).

In other words, because they involve the very medium within which we have our being as the kind of people we are, if we are to fashion an appropriate approach to sociocultural issues, we cannot simply set to and apply to them the same empirical methods of research we have routinely applied to other problematic spheres of inquiry in psychology. We must acknowledge that a quite different approach is required. Although I will draw upon important conceptual resources provided by Vygotsky (1966) and Bakhtin (1981, 1984, 1986, 1993), the main methodological influence in the approach I will outline below is Wittgenstein's, as set out in his later philosophy (1953). For, as we shall see, although the task we face is of the "fish discovering water," or the "seed discovering soil," variety, Wittgenstein nevertheless manages—not so much by himself noticing unique events others have failed to notice,[1] but in the *philosophical methods* he offers us—to provide us with ways to bring to our own attention certain crucial but unique relations between our own conduct and its surroundings that we would not otherwise notice.

This is in stark contrast, of course, to many of our more empirical approaches to psychological research. There, we feel, it would be good if we could replace the seeming "inadequacies" of our everyday talk with an ideal language, a closed, logical system in which misleading talk was rendered impossible—but this would also render impossible our own unique expressions indicative of unique aspects of our own unique lives. Such "pictures" are a crucial part of the workings of our everyday talk and cannot, Wittgenstein realizes, simply be eliminated. "It is not our aim," he says, "to refine or complete the system of rules for the use of our words in unheard-of ways" (1953: no. 133). Instead, he says, he is aiming at *complete clarity . . . [which] simply means that the philosophical problems should completely disappear*" (no. 133), i.e., we should no longer feel that certain puzzling, mysterious entities radically hidden from us "must" nonetheless exist somewhere and be responsible for what is not hidden from us. Such complete clarity would reveal to us both how we have been deceiving ourselves, and that other, more readily accessible ways of making sense to each other are in fact open to us. "The real discovery," he says, "is the one that makes me capable of stopping doing philosophy when I want to" (no. 133). In other words, the real discovery is the one that releases us from feeling the need to set up a prior system or framework of foundational propositions in terms of which to conduct investigations. As he sees it, our task is simply to describe how we do in fact manage to achieve what we do achieve.

Thus, while those doing empirical research seek evidence in support of certain theoretical propositions—ones they feel are more accurate, adequate, or general than those proposed by their competitors— Wittgenstein's aim is quite different. All his later works consist not in arguments for general claims, nor in a body of finalized results, but in exemplary investigations into this, that, or some other kind of concrete, everyday circumstance. His strategy in doing this is clear: "As soon as I think of an everyday use of [a puzzling] sentence instead of a philosophical use, its meaning becomes clear and ordinary" (1969: no. 347). In other words, as he puts it, instead of feeling the need to lay down a preliminary, metatheoretical framework for one's inquiries, "we now demonstrate a method, by examples; and the series of examples can be broken off.— Problems are solved (difficulties eliminated), not a single problem" (1953: no. 133). His aim is to bring to our notice the actual facts of our ways of interacting with each other, and how our "children are brought up to perform *these* actions, to uses *these* words as they do so, and to react in *this* way to the words of others" (1953: no. 6).

The Role of Unique, First-Person Utterances in Learning Generalities

In seeking to show us the actual facts of our ways of interacting with each other, Wittgenstein wants to go further than merely displaying a set of particular investigations—he wants to teach us, in just the same way that anyone (an adult) might try to teach another (a child) a practice, the *practice* of his kind of philosophical investigation. And he doesn't try to do this by impersonally giving us any foundational rules or principles. As a unique first-person, an individual "I" (as Ludwig Wittgenstein), he proceeds by continually providing us with appropriate examples at appropriate moments—to draw our attention to unnoticed features in our own actions, in our surroundings, etc., or to suggest alternative ways of "going on" to us, and so on. In such circumstances, he notes, "giving examples is not an indirect means of explaining—in default of a better. For any general definition can be misunderstood too" (1953: no. 71).

But what has he in mind in making this suggestion? How can what scientific psychologists usually dismiss as "mere anecdotes" be of any use to us in our inquiries? How can general definitions be misunderstood, and if so, why don't we notice this and give up still trying to use them? Here we must go back to his remarks on the crucial role played by being "struck," on the importance of spontaneous reactions in originating language-games, to see how a language-game can be based *on* a reaction, how a reaction can be, not the result of thought, but the prototype for a way of acting and thinking. "Not only rules, but also examples are needed for establishing a practice. Our rules leave loop-holes open, and the practice has to speak for itself," he remarks (1969: no. 139). "I shall teach him to use the words by means of examples and by practice.—And when I do this I do not communicate less to him than I know myself" (1953: no. 280). Thus, when a parent says to a young child who has just, thoughtlessly, walked in out of the garden, leaving a trail of muddy footmarks across the kitchen floor: "Stop! Look what you've just done! . . . Behind you . . . your feet . . . Wipe them next time . . . Look, like THIS!!!," the parent hopes that the child's reactions to these instructive remarks and example will become interwoven into the child's future entries into the kitchen from the garden, thus to refine them. The parent also hopes that, at the appropriate moment in subsequent trips into the kitchen (just as we might be reminded of "what comes next" in the unfolding movement of a piece of music), the child will also be reminded to stop, and to check his or her feet for mud in the future.

The very central role played in Wittgenstein's later philosophy by people's spontaneous, living, embodied reactions is often ignored by many claiming to be followers of his philosophy.[2] Central to it, however, is his emphasis on the fact that it is the existence of certain unlearned reactions that makes the process of training possible in the first place—a central aspect of which he calls "the ostensive teaching of words" (no. 6). Without that shared background of shared reactions in shared circumstances, it would be impossible for us to draw any distinctions between correct and incorrect uses of language in our practices. It is our shared (or sharable) spontaneous reactions to examples that make the teaching of sharable practices possible. Indeed, as Wittgenstein (1953) notes, if we are to teach our children anything, we must rely on their being spontaneously responsive in a differential manner to our evaluative reactions, to our smiles of encouragement and frowns of disapproval. We cannot teach simply by stating rules and principles to them. "[I]f a person has not yet got the *concepts*" says Wittgenstein, "I shall teach him to use the words by means of *examples* and by *practice.*—. . . I do it, he does it after me; and I influence him by expressions of agreement, rejection, expectation, encouragement. I let him go his way, or hold him back; and so on" (1953: no. 208). Here, "the teaching of language is not explanation, but training" (no. 5).

But much more than this, Wittgenstein's emphasis on people's spontaneous responsive reactions to events occurring around them also gives us a whole new approach to understanding the nature of what we call people's "inner" lives (Johnston 1993; Mulhall 1990), to understanding what we talk of as being "in" other people's minds. We notice a person grimacing at a noise, or people saying things like "I'm puzzled," "I'm in pain," "I don't like that music," while another makes a welcoming gesture, or whatever. As Johnston notes, irrespective of whether these first-person expressions are accurately linked to a mysterious inner realm or not, the fact is that "the account [i.e., the expression] has a use quite independently of whether or not it accurately reproduces some supposed inner event" (1993:14). "The notion of the Inner does not refer to some separate reality but expresses our relation to each other and a particular way of understanding human action" (p. 28). Such first-person avowals (especially if spontaneously expressed) tell us what that other person's expectations and anticipations are as to how we should "go on" with them, how we might respond to them, how they expect us to treat them. In other words, the importance of people's inner-talk in our shared lives is not in giving each other retrospective third-person *reports* on already completed events that occurred in the inner workspace of our minds, but to *tell* each other, as first-persons, something about ourselves, prospectively, something that—at the moment of telling—will help us to relate ourselves to what uniquely the other has it in mind to do in the (often immediate) future.[3] An individual's meanings are not hidden inside that person geographically, in a private inner space, but are "hidden" in time, in that their reference is to possibilities whose realization is still in the future.

Indeed, without the unique individualized understandings occurring at crucial moments in our particular exchanges with our children (and others), our attempts to train them to be active participants in the shared forms of responsive expression prevalent in our culture would be impossible. For our task in teaching them language is only marginally to teach them "aboutness" or representational talk. As I suggested above, we can find the beginning of new language-games in people's spontaneous reactions to events occurring around them. And as parents, we rely on our children responding in this spontaneous way to our expressions in our teaching them what, theoretically, we think of as rule-governed practices. By relying on the directionality inherent in the temporally unfolding of living activities, we utter at certain crucial moments in the course of this teaching, along with a whole set of exaggerated facial expressions and other bodily gestures, such verbal expressions as "Stop!," "Look," "Listen," "Look at that," "Listen to this," "Do it like this," "Do it like that," and so on.

The crucial importance of the *moment of utterance* in all of this cannot be overemphasized: in coming at a particular moment in the already ongoing flow of contingently intertwined activity occurring between them and us, in pointing in their gestural expressiveness from "*this* past" toward "*that kind* of future," our children's activities allow us to intervene at *that* moment and, in doing so, to point them toward "*another kind* of future," toward seeing a connection between events of a previously unnoticed kind. More than using words to *talk about* something, the child must learn to use words to arouse anticipations in others and to make (create or construct) connections and relations.

Our first-person expressions are crucial, then, not only in initially establishing but also in sustaining our shared forms of life. Indeed, they are crucial not only in our teaching of our infants to be participants in the language-intertwined practices of our social group, but in fact in almost all our ordinary everyday interactions. People want to know what we are trying to do in what we are saying, the "point" of our talk. In other words, in my first-person expressions, here and now, I am not in fact giving anything like a third-person description of, or a report on, my inner state(s) of mind (which could, if the need arose, be checked for its accuracy), but doing something like expressing a first-person appeal to those around me for help in interlinking their actions with mine, or, perhaps, appealing for sympathy, affirmation, or suchlike. To express such relational initiatives, we choose specific words that—in the circumstances of their use, in their gestural expressiveness—"point" for us "from this past toward that kind of future."

Thus, as Johnston remarks, in the context of our "inner-talk," the "use of a word does not involve learning rules; rather it builds on a natural reaction," and, on the basis of the embodied responses to the events occurring around us into which we have been trained, we "go on spontaneously to develop new possibilities of self-expression" (1993:25).

Two Realms of Activity Within a Third—
the Dialogical

Above, then, I began to place our difficulties in academic psychology in a new realm: in the realm of our everyday practices rather than in the realm of thinking and theorizing, and to suggest that the beginnings of new ways forward could be found in our uniquely novel, spontaneously responsive, embodied reactions to events occurring around us. I now need to outline in more detail the nature of the different realms of activity within which Wittgenstein's more practical approach to the resolution of our difficulties makes sense, and our different orientations toward them.

Central to the Wittgensteinian approach that I am adopting toward these issues, then, is a distinction between two very different realms of activity: the realm of our more deliberately conducted acts that, within the flow of interactivity occurring between us as individuals and the others and othernesses around us, constitutes the river, and the realm of our more spontaneously performed acts constituting the riverbed of that flow. Associated with these two realms of activity are two very different kinds of difficulty that we may face: those within the flow of the river we can call *problems*, because they are difficulties we can solve by applying to them a method or process of reasoning (often conducted within a theoretical framework or schematism of some kind); those of the riverbed, the difficulties that in the past have lain unnoticed in the background of our more deliberate and self-conscious activities, we can call here *difficulties of orientation* or *relational difficulties*, for they are difficulties in which we need to *resolve a line of action*, or a style or way of approach—they are difficulties that, Wittgenstein suggests, have the form "I don't know my way about" (1953: no. 123), i.e., they are difficulties of a *philosophical* kind as opposed to the empirical difficulties we call problems, which are solved within the guidelines provided to us by the riverbed itself.

It is important to distinguish between these two very different kinds of difficulty straightaway, for procedurally, the steps we take in coping with them are themselves quite distinct—and will become even more starkly so as my account of Wittgenstein's work develops.

For those difficulties we call *problems*, it must be possible to describe the initial state of affairs we confront in terms relevant to an already well-known process of reasoning, and to "work out" a clear link between the already known and the unknown states of affairs desired. We can then act in terms of a "plan of action." Relational or orientational difficulties, on the other hand, present themselves as almost the reverse of this situation—for it is only *after* we have discovered or, better, created a way of *relating* ourselves to our surroundings, and of finding a way to attend to certain aspects of our surroundings rather than to others, that the data relevant to our achieving our goal can be brought to light (and only after that can our problem-solving reasoning, if still necessary, be applied).

Two kinds of difficulties outlined above are termed by Wittgenstein (1980:17) difficulties of the intellect and difficulties of the *will* (as I have termed them, orientational or relational difficulties). It is perhaps worth noting at this stage that Vygotsky raised the importance of attending to matters of the will in relation to our spontaneous reactions to events around us: "It is surprising to us," he remarks, "that traditional psychology has completely failed to notice this phenomenon which we can call *mastering one's own reactions*. In attempts to explain this fact of 'will' [traditional] psychology resorted to a miracle, to the intervention of a spiritual factor in the operation of nervous processes, and thus tried to explain the action by the line of most resistance, as did, for example, James in developing his theory of the creative character of the will" (1966:33–34, my emphasis). Vygotsky, like Wittgenstein, sees the issue as a practical matter to do with the "instruction" the child receives from others.[4]

In the past, however, influenced by the privileging in Descartes' philosophy of mind over body, and of thought over practical action, we have tended to think of *all* of our difficulties as problems, as difficulties to be solved by the application of rational thought. But, as Wittgenstein (1953) makes clear, our bewilderment in many situations is often of a much more practical-relational or orientational kind than theoretical. Often, our real need is not a matter of simply being able to say, "Now I see it" (i.e., arriving at the solution to a problem of reasoning), but of being able *both* to declare to others, "Now I know how to go on" (no. 154), while in fact being able to "go on" in practice. Simply "to see" something is to be able to assimilate it to an already existing and well-known category; whilst being able to "go on" in practice is being able to do something unique in a unique, never before encountered situation, i.e., to be able continually to do something for yet another first time. Thus, the resolution of an orientational difficulty is something manifested or displayed at a practical level in one's unique way of being *responsive* to the unique details of a situation by one's actual actions within it—not by categorizing it at an intellectual level, which often involves ignoring its uniqueness in its important deviations from what is already well known.

Nowhere is this, perhaps, more obvious than in our relations to the others and othernesses around us. For we orient toward dead things in a way quite different from that toward living things. Indeed, as Wittgenstein puts it: "Our attitude to what is alive and to what is dead, is not the same. All our reactions are different" (1953: no. 284).

Living movement, motility, is utterly different, qualitatively, from the spatial displacements suffered by dead things. All living movement unfolds (grows, develops) in irreversible time. Indeed, the time-contouring of such movements is often—especially, for instance, in our voiced utterances—of much more significance than their spatial extent (if any). Furthermore, not only is there a kind of *developmental continuity* involved in the unfolding of all living activities, such that earlier phases of the activity are indicative of at least the *style*, the *physiognomy*, or the unique living identity of what is to come later, but the activities of all living beings also, so to speak, *imply* their surroundings. In their very nature, they come into existence ready to *grow into* their own appropriate environment, or *Umwelt* (von Uexkull 1957). Yet they do not become wholly absorbed into it. Even though they and their "parts" are always "on the way" to becoming more than they already are, there is what we might call an *identity-preserving* character to almost all the changes we observe in them. There is a characteristic "shape" to their unfolding in time such that their possible ends are already "there" in their beginnings. As a result, there is (or can be) a distinctive "inner dynamics" to our living relations with living wholes not manifested in those with dead, mechanical assemblages, such that *from within* those dynamics not only can the earlier phases of their activity be indicative to us of at least the style of what is to come later—such that we can respond to their activities in an *anticipatory* fashion—but we can also sense in their actions their relations to events in their surroundings.

Given that living beings are spontaneously responsive, in certain characteristic ways, to events occurring in their surroundings, these naturally occurring characteristics of living activities entail the existence of a third realm of activity that contains the other two realms outlined above. In the past I have called this realm of activity "joint action" (Shotter 1980, 1984), and more recently, following Bakhtin (1981, 1984, 1986), "the dialogical" (Shotter 1993a and 1993b), and, following Merleau-Ponty (1968), "the chiasmic" (Shotter 2003).[5]

This realm of activity arises out of the following facts: In such a spontaneously responsive sphere of living activity as this, instead of one of us first acting individually, self-consciously, and independently of an other, and then a second replying, by acting individually and independently of the first, a great deal of what occurs between us just *happens* as we act jointly, as a collective "we." And it happens to us bodily, in a "living" way, as we spontaneously respond to each other, without our having first to "work out" such ways of responding to each other. Thus as we grow and develop into the cultural world of those around us, and learn to attend to *these* identifiable details but not to those, we retain only a *subsidiary awareness* (Polanyi 1958, 1963)[6] of the voices and other expressions of those who directed our looking and listening in this way; and in our acting too, we easily forget the instructions—"Do it like *this*, not like *that!*"—given us by others in helping us to develop our skilled ways of acting. For on each occasion, these voices exerted a unique influence on us in a passing moment. But what kind of influence did they exert?

The Emotional-Volitional Tone in Our Actions

Above, then, I have suggested that the primary influences we come to incorporate within ourselves in the course of our development into autonomous agents within our culture are aroused in us by the embodied, first-person expressions (mostly verbal) of others. But as we have seen, these expressions have only a once-off, transitory nature that gives them only a temporary place in our constitution. It is, I shall argue, in the *transitional understandings* and *action-guiding anticipations* that the expressions of the others around us (who at first are our teachers) arouse in us, in our dialogically-structured encounters with them—especially by their intonated voices, their often-exaggerated facial expressions, and gestured bodily postures—that we find what is crucial to our sociocultural development into autonomous members of our community.

Now it is not easy to take notice of these jointly created, transitional or passing phenomena that occur spontaneously between us simply as a consequence of our interlivingness, so to speak. For whenever one person acts spontaneously in response to another, not only can the first person's actions *not be accounted* as wholly their own—for what they do is, to an extent, partly shaped by influences originating in the other—but many other features of their behavior also *cannot be experienced* as desired or wanted by them. These aspects of our actions are neither yours nor mine; they are truly "ours"—indeed, as we saw above, we rely on such shared spontaneous responses in expecting others to respond to the ungovernable, effortless aspects of our utterances as we ourselves do, or else we could not speak our mother tongue with them. We can credit as *our own* behavior only what we ourselves intend; all else just *happens* to or within us—and this is where the strangeness of the dialogical becomes of crucial importance: for it exerts its effects in us in the unique, invisible, uncategorizable, time-contouring of the bodily efforts we have to make in expressing ourselves *and* in coming to an understanding of others' expressions. And it is with the goal of their coming to embody these effects, that, to repeat, our "children are brought up to perform *these* actions, to use *these* words as they do so, and to react in *this* way to the words of others" (Wittgenstein 1953: no. 6).

In other words, central to our understanding of the use of words, our own and other people's, is not our having an inner mental representation of what a person's talk is *about*, of what *caused* the person to utter particular words. It is the arousing of an expectation that is crucial, the expectation that something next must happen. I say my friend's name: "Arlene." She turns toward me, looks at me with a questioning expression, and in a tone of voice expressing interest says: "Yes?"

Rather than its representational function (which it sometimes clearly does have), it is an utterance's capacity to motivate, to "call for" a precise kind of response (that will itself "call" for further responses) from others that is crucial. Thus, central among the many other features of such responsive talk is its orientation toward the future: "The word in living conversation is directly, blatantly, oriented toward a future answer-word; it *provokes* an answer, *anticipates* it and structures itself in the answer's direction. Forming itself in an atmosphere of the already spoken, the word is at the same time determined by *that which has not yet been said but which is needed and in fact anticipated by the answering word*. Such is the situation of any living dialogue" (Bakhtin 1981:280, my emphases).

But our sensibility in such exchanges is even more subtle and shaded than this. Even if the sounds we hear are sounds of *agreement*, we can hear them distinctively as *sympathetic agreement*, as *patronizing agreement*, as *hurried agreement*, as *inconsequential agreement*, as *reluctant agreement*, as *unexpected* or *surprised agreement*, and so on. Similarly with all other heard responses.[7] They are all subtly shaded, nuanced, or intonated in such a way as to enable us, mostly, to "go on" with those to whom we must respond in reply, with at least decorum and courtesy, and sometimes, to "go on" in ways appropriate to more complex aims: "the word does not merely designate an object as a present-on-hand entity, but also expressed by its intonation my valuative attitude toward the object, toward what is desirable or undesirable in it, and, in so doing sets it in motion toward that which is yet-to-be-determined about it, turns it into a constituent moment of the living, ongoing event. Everything that is actually experienced," says Bakhtin, "is experienced as something given and as something-yet-to-be-determined, is intonated, has *emotional-volitional tone,* and enters into an effective relationship to me within the unity of the ongoing event encompassing us" (1993:32–33, my emphasis).

Even if we are unmoving in space, as I intimated above, we can be sensed by others as making—indeed, as *intentionally* or *effortfully* making—expressive movements over time, expressive movements that reach in an anticipatory fashion toward the future. Thus, here, in his use of the expression "emotional-volitional tone," Bakhtin is suggesting that at every moment, as we voice an unfolding utterance, there is an element of personal choice as to the turns we take: "The word in language is half someone else's. It becomes 'one's own' *only when the speaker populates it with his own intentions,* his own accent, when he appropriates the word, adapting it to his own semantic and expressive intention. Prior to this moment of appropriation, the word does not exist in a neutral and impersonal language (it is not, after all, out of a dictionary that the speaker gets his words!), but rather it exists in other people's mouths, in other people's contexts, serving other people's intentions: it is from there that one must take the word, *and make it one's own*" (Bakhtin 1981:293–294, my emphases).

Indeed, what makes a person's words *their own words* are the efforts (the intentions) they exert—and that we can sense them as exerting in their speech—to make their talk conform to a "something" they are *trying* to express. We can hear these *efforts* "in" their utterances, in the time-contour of the emotional-volitional tone of their expressions. And, as we intentionally shape at least some aspects of the unfolding time-contour of our utterances, so can listeners, in being continuously "moved" or "touched" in this way and that, sense the turns we take, the choices at each choice point we make. Thus what we lose when we take patterns of words outside the actual living contexts of their use is not what the words mean, but what a person meant in saying them, their "point."

It is this loss that we can characterize as a person's loss of voice, and ultimately as the repression of the living voice by the methodological requirements of social scientific research. In other words, to study only the forms or patterns in what is already given (as in transcripts and codings of interactions, etc.) as already completed objects at hand is to "lose the phenomena" (Garfinkel 2002:264–267), i.e., we lose the unique transitional understandings and action-guiding anticipations of the yet-to-be-determined, present in both speakers and listeners alike, that are only generated, i.e., jointly created, in the dialogical dynamics at work in all our dialogically structured exchanges.

Wittgenstein brings such an issue to our attention with the following example: "When I read a poem or a narrative with feeling, surely something goes on in me which does not go on when I merely skim the lines for information," he suggests. "The sentences have a different ring. I pay careful attention to my intonation. Sometimes a word has the wrong intonation, I emphasize it too much or too little. I notice this and show it in my face" (1953:214). Indeed, our orientation or relation to the utterance of the words of the poem is quite different in the two cases: when it is read quickly, with a neutral tone for information, we can expect a response such as: "OK, I get the picture, so what? Why are you telling me this (information)?" But when such words are read slowly, in measured tones, we might expect a response such as: "Yes, how moving . . . I'm deeply touched!" As we have already emphasized, such "touchings" and "movings" can be of crucial importance in orienting us in the conduct of our relations with those around us.

Wittgenstein thus brings to our attention the matter of our tones of voice in a way similar to Bakhtin, but by use of a different vocabulary. He talks of the "essential references" occurring in an utterance thus: "In saying 'When I heard this word, it meant . . . to me' one refers to a *point of time* and to a *way of using the word*. (Of course, it is this combination that we fail to grasp.) And the expression 'I was then going to say . . . ' refers to a *point of time* and to an *action*. I speak of the essential *references* of the utterance in order to distinguish them from other peculiarities of the expression we use. The references that are essential to an utterance are the ones which would make us translate some otherwise alien form of expression into this, our customary form" (1953:175).

In other words, because we are brought up to react spontaneously in *this* way to the words of others, and to use *these* words as others do, it is important to us that we share with the others around us certain silent, invisible, and individually unobservable linkings[8] between words—Whorf speaks of this as a "rapport between words" (1956:67)—that enables them to work together in our construction of a meaning. These linkings do not already exist and are not already laid down in embodied patterns. They exist in the emotional-volitional tones, the essential references of our expressions, in the efforts[9] that go into our expressing of them, and into our understandings of the expressions of others. Hence our need, if a form of words doesn't spontaneously arouse in us the activation of these linkages, to translate it into our customary forms, our customary ways of speaking, thus to get the "feel," the "sense" of it. It is this rapport between words—the "glue" that links our utterance of a sequence of separate words in general into a unique, only once occurrent (Bakhtin 1993), meaningful whole—lying unnoticed in the background to our thought and talk that Wittgenstein has sought in his grammatical investigations to bring to the forefront of our attention.

Examples in the Teaching of a Practice

I hope at this point that we can see the importance of a number of major (interlinked) themes in Wittgenstein's later philosophy: The first is the crucially important role of people's previously unnoticed spontaneous living reactions to events in their surroundings. Once these reactions are noticed, and we realize with Wittgenstein that "nothing is hidden" (1953: no. 435), then there is no need to search for radically hidden "mechanisms" to understand how we can understand each other. From this insight come his explorations of some of the pitfalls of our not quite realizing the nature of our own needs in our inquiries— we think we need explanations and general theories, whereas in fact our real need is for concrete examples described in such a way that they "strike" us, i.e., call out characteristic responses from us spontaneously: "Not only rules, but also examples are needed for establishing a practice. Our rules leave loop-holes open, and the practice has to speak for itself" (1969: no. 139).

With this last comment in mind, and aware that we still have a long way to go before an understanding of what sociocultural investigations of a Wittgensteinian kind might actually look like, let me add here that in fact there is no shortage at all of striking examples relevant to the teaching of such a practice. What follows is an almost-random list of what seem to me to be relevant examples, and very many more could easily be added.

We might start with Campos and Stenberg's (1980) claims about "social referencing," i.e., the fact that young infants often turn toward a caregiver's facial expression to evaluate or gain orientation toward otherwise indeterminate events (see also Emde and Sorce 1983). More recently, Brooks and Meltzoff (2002) have shown how twelve-month-olds, once eye contact is gained with them, will spontaneously look to where an adult looks—as long as the adult's eyes were open, but not if they were closed. Indeed, we might go further here to suggest, as Wittgenstein does above, that in their spontaneous responses to their caregiver's expressions, infants are not just merely disambiguating novel events, but literally discovering from their caregiver's expressions, the unique way in which they *should* relate to their surroundings on this occasion. Shotter and Gregory (1976) outlined such an occasion with Samantha at eleven months, when a mother's expectation of social referencing *failed to occur*: Samantha had successfully placed a shape in a form-board, but then had straightaway gone on to grab the next piece, even when her mother had said, "There's a clever girl." Her mother tapped her arm, stopping the next grab in its tracks, thrust her face in Samantha's, and repeated her praise slowly, with emphasis, allowing Samantha to proceed only after a moment of smiling eye-contact—that is, only after a moment of common reference had been established.

Dunn (1988) notes that even at eighteen months, infants "show" or "display" in their everyday ways of acting that they anticipate adults' responses to previously forbidden actions—they act into the situation in a teasing way, for example, or recognize a situation to be deliberately evaded. Kidwell (2005) confirms this. She shows not only that young infants (one to two years of age) have a keen sense of how their "naughty" actions will be viewed by others, but that their actions are "social" in the sense that they are subtly angled to occasion specific kinds of responses from the adults around them—for instance, actions are often "managed" in ways that will mislead caregivers from inferring wrongdoing. Reddy (1991), describing a whole collection of incidents in which an offer-withdrawal teasing game was played by quite young infants (approx. nine months old), points out that teasing as such is impossible unless one has a knowledgeable expectation of how others will react to the withdrawal of an offered object. Here, Spitz's (1957) early comments on infants approaching forbidden objects eagerly, while uttering the word "no"—undoubtedly heard from the others around them previously—is perhaps relevant.

Kagan (1981) too has studied similar such moments when infants (around fifteen months) express distress at failing to imitate an action modeled to them by an adult, implying an awareness of what a competent performance *ought* to have been like. Similarly, he found what he called "mastery smiles" following successful task completion (or when adults complied with requests). In each case, the infants' actions "show" that they react to sequences of actions just performed, and anticipate responses yet to come, doing both in a socially evaluative way.

What is brought out in all the studies mentioned—by Campos and Stenberg, Brooks and Meltzoff, Dunn, Shotter and Gregory, Kidwell, Reddy, Spitz, and Kagan—is how an infant's actions are interrelated with, or interwoven into, the actions of others, both those preceding as well as those following them, and how their developing understanding is displayed in the expectations and anticipations they exhibit in interrelating their actions with those of others. In addition, we, in making sense of their actions—instead of needing to refer to the supposedly radically hidden mental states inside their individual heads—can refer to the observable behavior occurring between them and those around them, to the detailed, sequential interplay of interrelated responses as they unfold in the achievement of specifically meaningful exchanges. There is thus no need to search for intellectualist-representational interpretations of this behavior—the child's behavior can be seen as a refinement or elaboration of her initial spontaneous reactions to the circumstances in question.

Given all the exemplary possibilities listed above, our task in a Wittgensteinian sociocultural psychology would not be to analyze them (along with all the others that could be added to them) in regard to the question of which suggested possibility could empirically (i.e., scientifically) be shown to be the correct explanation of children's capacities to read the minds of others. For in fact, in a Wittgensteinian approach almost all would be crucial examples of real developmental possibilities of one kind or another. Our task would be of quite a different kind: once they are arrayed before us, our next task would be that of arranging all these possibilities into some kind of order—sequencing them according to the particular, practical aim of our inquiry at the time.[10] But the dream of welding them all into a single, logical system, if the multidimensionality of human life and the necessity for human judgment is to be sustained, would (thankfully) be impossible.

"There is," suggests Wittgenstein, "a kind of general disease of thinking which always looks for (and finds) what would be called a mental state from which all our acts spring as from a reservoir" (1965:143). And, as he sees it, "a main cause of philosophical disease [is] a one-sided diet: one nourishes one's thinking with only one kind of example" (1953: no. 593). False-belief research, for instance, seems to be driven by a single, particular "grammatical picture" of not only what it is for a child to have *an understanding* of another's mind, but also of what it is for us to have *an understanding* of the child's understanding—that picture is, of course, the "picture-theory" of mind, the idea that we understand events in our surroundings only indirectly, in terms of a representation made up of separate elements that can be reconfigured in a rule-governed way, ahead of time, to give us a new representation, a "prediction," of future outcomes.[11] As cognitivists have said, such a theory must be seen as "the only game in town." But, rather than being indicative of what in fact is actually involved in children developing an understanding of what is "in the mind" of another, such research seems to be much more indicative of the degree to which children subjected to such research have developed the ideology of those testing them.

Missing in this whole approach, to repeat, are people's spontaneous, embodied, expressive reactions to events occurring around them—and it is in terms of these expressive reactions that we make evaluative judgments on each other's actions. Without such *situated* reactions, everything comes to hinge on arguments about *interpretations*[12]—in an unending search for "the truth." This is the import of Wittgenstein's insistence that the "the meaning of a word is its use in the language" (1953: no. 43). For, as he saw it: "When philosophers use a word—'knowledge,' 'being,' 'object,' 'I,' 'proposition,' 'name'—and try to grasp the essence of the thing, one must ask oneself: is the word ever actually used in this way in the language-game which is its original home?—What we do is to bring words back from their metaphysical to their everyday use" (no. 116). In other words, once certain crucial words—such as "mind," "belief," "social," "theory," "referencing," etc.—are all removed from their everyday usage in practical contexts and said in the neutral emotional-volitional tone appropriate to theoretical talk in a seminar room or conference hall, they can arouse only quite special expectations and can direct our attention only in quite special directions in accord with the special disciplinary forms of talk that those in seminar rooms or conference halls have been trained into (see above). The countless uses to which such terms can be put in everyday contexts have been excluded.

Central, then, in the Wittgensteinian approach to sociocultural studies I have outlined above are the spontaneously occurring expectations and anticipations according to which we all "go on" with each other in our everyday practical affairs, and which are usually left unnoticed in the background to all our daily interactions.

As I see it, Wittgenstein's great achievement is to have opened up for us a whole new, previously unnoticed realm of inquiry: into the *expressive* aspects of our behavior, the ways in which a person's facial and bodily expressions, and tones of voice—partly spontaneous and partly intentionally controlled—can create in the others around him or her not only a sense of that person's attitudes and values in relation to the things around, but also very different action-guiding anticipations as to how that person is next going to act. But more than this, unlike the methods in traditional scientific research, which are oriented toward the task of finding patterns and regularities in our conduct, his methods are oriented toward grasping what is novel and unique in our conduct, toward understanding events in our daily affairs for, as Garfinkel so nicely puts it, yet "another first time" (1967:9). In other words, as I see it, Wittgenstein's methods help us to resolve what seems to me to be *a*, if not *the*, central cultural dilemma of our times: the struggle we all of us wage daily, to gain control over our own lives.

But if human freedom and unique individuality are to make any sense, if our living of our lives is to remain open to our own choices, and if we are free to create new ways of relating ourselves to the others and othernesses around us, but still act in ways shared with others, then there can be no single, fixed, and finished order in our lives together. For any finalized explanatory scheme of a properly logical, systematic, and scientific kind would inevitably close the essential openness of our human lives. The great achievement in Wittgenstein's investigations is the extent to which he has succeeded in putting all "this indefiniteness, correctly, and unfalsified, into words" (1953:227). The theoretical understandings of academic experts and other professionals, which seek to close the openness of our everyday lives together (in the interest of a particular set of orderly rules or principles of their own devising), need to be treated for what each is—a (perhaps hopeful) suggestion for a previously unnoticed possibility for a current next step forward, rather than as a (quite often dangerous) dogmatic truth for all time. Thus, instead of neo-Darwinian arguments seeking to eliminate other suggestions as unfit, an album of such previously unnoticed possibilities for shared ways of going on—an album of new beginnings and beginnings— might be of practical usefulness in the same way as the *Philosophical Investigations* is useful.

In practice, then, Wittgensteinian investigations into sociocultural issues would not involve researchers in continually arguing for theories, either in terms of evidence derived from attempts to test them empirically or in terms of whether they adequately encompass conceptually all the relevant phenomena, as they seem continually to do at present. Instead, they would face a different kind of task: that of coming to know our "way about" inside the vast realm of activities involving ourselves and our children—coming to an understanding of all the different others and othernesses around us. For, to repeat, what Wittgenstein wants in his investigations is merely a *description* of the facts that matter in relation to the issue concerned—a description that, if one was initially intellectually disoriented, *justifies* saying to those around one (at least for the immediate practical purposes in hand): "Now I know how to go on" (1953: no. 154). He is concerned, as we have seen, not with difficulties of the intellect (with problems that can be solved by the application of reasoning) but by difficulties of the will, i.e., orientational or relational difficulties—difficulties of a kind very different from those we currently try to resolve by our methods of scientific research. Many, especially in the field of social constructionism, have taken Wittgenstein's philosophical remarks piecemeal; they need to be taken as a whole.

Notes

1.   For that would involve him in documenting such unique events, paradoxically, in general terms, thus losing their crucial uniqueness.

2.   This is apparent in Kripke's (1982) infamous, "skeptical" misinterpretation of Wittgenstein's supposedly "paradoxical" remark that "no course of action could be determined by a rule, because every course of action can be made out to accord with the rule" (1953: no. 201). If this were so, this would mean that all rules are up for interpretation, and that, for instance, there can be no such thing as a *correct response* to a question, all we could do would be to appeal to the brute, but contingent fact, that in our community there happen to be widespread ways of

doing things—social conventions rule, OK! This is a flagrant misinterpretation of Wittgenstein. His point is that skeptical problems (and their solutions) are signs that we have misconstrued our own needs in our philosophical discussions: we think we need to appeal to *theories* and *explanations*, when in fact we don't. We merely need careful descriptions of the facts; and one crucial fact is that in every-day life, there are correct answers to questions. We cannot just talk as we please. "It can be seen that there is a misunderstanding here. . . . What this shows is that there is a way of grasping a rule that is *not* an *interpretation*, but which is exhibited in what we call 'obeying the rule' and 'going against it' in actual cases" (no. 201). "When I obey a rule, I do not choose. I obey the rule *blindly*" (no. 219). It is the ignoring of our spontaneous, embodied reactions and responses, and the turning of everything to do with our understanding each other's actions into a cognitive problem, that is one of the major inadequacies in current psychological, philo-sophical, and social inquiries.

3.   As Wittgenstein points out, usually we are not at all puzzled and bewil-dered by people's talk about their inner states, their inner feelings, etc. "The feel-ing of an unbridgeable gulf between consciousness and brain processes: how does it come about that this does not come into the considerations of our ordinary life? . . . It is when I turn my attention in a particular way toward my own conscious-ness, and, say to myself: THIS is supposed to be produced by a process in the brain! . . . But I did not utter the sentence in the surroundings in which it would have had an everyday and unparadoxical sense" (1953: no. 412).

4.   In this connection, perhaps it is a pity that Vygotsky didn't draw more on James' chapter on "stream of thought," in which he would have found James suggesting that "large tracts of human speech are nothing but *signs of direc-tion* in thought, of which direction we nevertheless have an acutely discrimina-tive sense, though no definite sensorial image plays any part in it whatsoever" (1890:252–253). And later, in discussing the "tendencies" (anticipations, expecta-tions) we feel before the occurrence of a word or thought, he also claims "that 'tendencies' are not only descriptions from without, but are among the *objects* of the stream, which is thus aware of them from within, and must be described as in very large measure constituted of *feelings of tendency*, often so vague that we are unable to name them at all" (p. 254). Vygotsky would have found here, I think, many congenial thoughts as to how, by our own "instructive" use of words, we might "master" our own more spontaneous reactions to events occur-ring around us.

5.   By the use of the word "chiasmic," Merleau-Ponty (1968) wants to draw our attention to the complexly intertwined and dynamic character of the living unities to which our living activities give rise, both between us and the others and othernesses around us, and within ourselves. By their very living nature, they cannot be wholly captured in subjective or in objective terms; neither are they wholly orderly or wholly disorderly; nor need they in fact be constituted wholly from living components but rather may incorporate dead and inert parts in certain regions too. Central to their nature is their *reversibility*, by which he means that in adjusting our efforts to see something, for instance, we must let what we are

trying to see guide our looking. In other words, that something else makes itself seen within us.

6.   Polanyi introduces this term by way of discussing how we carry out a skilled act, such as hammering in a nail, and find within the unfolding activity itself the sensory directions we need to guide it toward a successful outcome: "When we bring down the hammer, we are certainly alert to the feelings in our palm and the fingers that hold the hammer. They guide us in handling it effectively, and the degree of attention that we give to the nail is given to the same extent but in a different way to these feelings. The difference may be stated by saying that the latter are not, like the nail, objects of our attention, but instruments of it. They are not watched in themselves: we watch something else while keeping intensely aware of them. I have a *subsidiary awareness* of the feeling in the palm of my hand which is merged into my *focal awareness* of my driving in the nail" (1958:55).

7.   "One cannot . . . understand dialogic relations simplistically or unilaterally, reducing them to contradiction, conflict, polemics, or disagreement. *Agreement* is very rich in varieties and shadings. Two utterances that are identical in all respects ('Beautiful weather!'—'Beautiful weather!'), if they are really *two* utterances belonging to *different* voices and not one, are linked by dialogic *relations of agreement*. This is a definite dialogic event, in the interrelations of the two, and not an echo. For after all, agreement could also be lacking ('No, not very nice weather,' and so forth)" (Bakhtin 1986:125).

8.   All linkages and relations occurring dynamically in joint action are individually unobservable.

9.   "Physiologists long ago established," says Polanyi, "that the way we see an object is determined by our awareness of certain efforts inside our body, efforts which we cannot feel in themselves. We are aware of these things going on inside our body in terms of the position, size, shape, and motion of an object, to which we are attending. In other words we are attending *from* these internal processes *to* the qualities of things outside. These qualities are what those internal processes *mean* to us. The transposition of bodily experiences into the perception of things outside may now appear, therefore, as an instance of the transposition of knowledge away from us, which we have found to be present to some extent in all tacit knowing" (1963:13–14).

10.   While, Wittgenstein says, "we want to establish an order in our knowledge of the use of language," he adds that the order he seeks is not a single, general order, but "an order with a particular end in view; one out of many possible orders; not *the* order" (1953: no. 132).

11.   This implies, of course, that the world "out there" also has the character of a picture, configured in terms of separate, self-contained elements, that one can only regard from afar, but not up close and personal.

12.   See note 2, and Wittgenstein's comments there about ways of acting that do *not* involve interpretation. As Wittgenstein notes, "it is not a kind of *seeing* on our part; it is our *acting*, which lies at the bottom of the language-game" (1969: no. 204)—our *spontaneous* ways of acting.

References

Bakhtin, M. M. 1981. *The Dialogical Imagination.* Ed. M. Holquist. Trans. C. Emerson and M. Holquist. Austin: University of Texas Press.

——. 1984. *Problems of Dostoevsky's Poetics.* Ed. and trans. Caryl Emerson. Minneapolis: University of Minnesota Press.

——. 1986. *Speech Genres and Other Late Essays.* Trans. V. W. McGee. Austin: University of Texas Press.

——. 1993. *Toward a Philosophy of the Act.* Ed. M. Holquist. Trans. V. Lianpov. Austin: University of Texas Press.

Brooks, R., and A. N. Meltzoff. 2002. The importance of eyes: How infants interpret adult looking behavior. *Developmental Psychology* 38:958–966.

Campos, J. J., and C. R. Stenberg. 1980. Perception, appraisal and emotion. In M. Lamb and L. Sherrod, eds., *Infant Social Cognition.* Hillsdale, NJ: Erlbaum.

Dunn, J. 1988. *The Beginnings of Social Understanding.* Cambridge, MA: Harvard University Press.

Emde, R. N., and J. E. Sorce. 1983. The rewards of infancy: Emotional availability and social referencing. In E. J. Call, E. Galenson, and R. Tyson, eds., *Frontiers of Infant Psychiatry,* vol. 2. New York: Basic Books.

Garfinkel, H. 1967. *Studies in Ethnomethodology.* Englewood Cliffs, NJ: Prentice-Hall.

——. 2002. *Ethnomethodology's Program: Working out Durkheim's Aphorism.* Ed. Anne Warefield Rawls. New York: Rowman and Littlefield.

James, W. 1890. *Principles of Psychology.* 2 vols. London: Macmillan.

Johnston, P. 1993. *Wittgenstein: Rethinking the Inner.* New York: Routledge.

Kagan, J. 1981. *The Second Year: The Emergence of Self-Awareness.* Cambridge, MA: Harvard University Press.

Kidwell, M. 2005. Gaze as social control: How very young children differentiate "the look" from a "mere look" by their adult caregivers. *Research on Language and Social Interaction* 384:417–449.

Kripke, S. A. 1982. *Wittgenstein on Rules and Private Language.* Cambridge, MA: Harvard University Press.

Merleau-Ponty, M. 1968. *The Visible and the Invisible.* Ed. Claude Lefort. Trans. Alphonso Lingis. Evanston, IL: Northwestern University Press.

Mulhall, S. 1990. *On Being in the World: Wittgenstein and Heidegger on Seeing Aspects.* London: Routledge.

Polanyi, M. 1958. *Personal Knowledge: Towards a Post-Critical Philosophy.* London: Routledge and Kegan Paul.

——. 1967. *The Tacit Dimension.* London: Routledge and Kegan Paul.

Reddy, V. 1991. Playing with others' expectations: Teasing and mucking about in the first year. In A. Whiten, ed., *Natural Theories of Mind: Evolution, Development, and Simulation of Everyday Mindreading.* Blackwell: Oxford.

Shotter, J. 1980. Action, joint action, and intentionality. In M. Brenner, ed., *The Structure of Action,* 28–65. Oxford: Blackwell.

———. 1984. *Social Accountability and Selfhood*. Oxford: Blackwell.

———. 1993a. *Cultural Politics of Everyday Life: Social Constructionism, Rhetoric, and Knowing of the Third Kind*. Milton Keynes: Open University Press.

———. 1993b. *Conversational Realities: Constructing Life Through Language*. London: Sage.

———. 2003. Cartesian change, chiasmic change: The power of living expression. *Janus Head: Journal of Interdisciplinary Studies in Literature, Continental Philosophy, Phenomenological Psychology, and the Arts* 61:6–29.

———. 2004. Wittgensteinian developmental investigations. *Brain and Behavioral Sciences* 271:121–122.

Shotter, J., and S. Gregory. 1976. On first gaining the idea of oneself as a person. In R. Harré, ed., *Life Sentences*. Chichester: Wiley.

Shotter, J., and J. W. Lannamann. 2002. The situation of social constructionism: Its "imprisonment" within the ritual of theory-criticism-and-debate. *Theory & Psychology* 125:577–609.

Spitz, R. 1957. *No and Yes: On the Genesis of Human Communication*. New York: International Universities Press.

Von Uexkull, J. 1957. A stroll through the world of animals and men. In C. H. Schiller, ed., *Instinctive Behaviour*. London: Methuen.

Vygotsky, L. S. 1966. Development of higher mental functions. In A. N. Leontyev, A. R. Luria, and A. Smirnov, eds., *Psychological Research in the USSR*. Moscow: Progress Publishers.

Wittgenstein, L. 1953. *Philosophical Investigations*. Trans. G. E. M. Anscombe. Oxford: Blackwell.

———. 1969. *On Certainty*. Oxford: Blackwell.

———. 1980. *Culture and Value*. Trans. P. Winch. Oxford: Blackwell.

3   Beyond the Enlightenment

Relational Being

Kenneth J. Gergen

We look back today to the Enlightenment of the seventeenth and eighteenth centuries as a period during which the Western world shifted from faith to reason as its core value. Interestingly enough, both faith and reason are quintessentially psychological concepts. In this sense, the transformation from the medieval to the "modern" world was dependent upon a radical reconstruction of the concept of the person. In the place of spirit or soul, the capacity for rational thought became the focal ingredient of the self. This shift from a sacred to a secular conception has been accompanied by enormous changes in the character of cultural life. At the outset, the governing powers of church and crown were substantially curtailed, making way for the establishment of the democratic state. With the displacement of the soul with reason as the central ingredient of self, neither church nor crown could sustain its position as chief agent of condemnation and approbation. As many see it, the authority for evaluation has been increasingly vested in the modernist institution of science. The creation of the modern State also owes its power to the accumulated agreement of the individual citizens. And at least in the United States, the centrality of the individual mind is accompanied by a constitutional guarantee of rights, however inadequately they are honored in the breach.

Yet, as many believe, the zenith of modernist culture has now passed; its fruits have been absorbed and its adequacy to contemporary world conditions is increasingly questioned. In certain respects the extension of modernist conceptions and practices seems inimical to the future well-being of the planet. Although there is much to be said on this account, the problematics of modernist culture can be traced in significant measure to the dominant conception of the person. When we make a fundamental distinction between self and other, we create a world of distances: me here and you there. We come to understand ourselves as basically alone and alienated. We come to prize autonomy—becoming a "self-made man," who "does it my way." To be interdependent is a sign of weakness and incapacity. To understand the world as constituted by separate individuals is also to court distrust, as one never has access to the private thoughts of others. And when alienated and distrustful, what is more appropriate than "taking care of number one"? Self-gain becomes an unmitigated virtue—for the economist, a rational calculus that necessarily governs individual choice. It is in this context that ethical injunctions to "love the other as the self" become intelligible. Self-love is presumed. Loyalty, commitment, and community are all thrown into question, as they potentially interfere with "self-realization." Such views now circulate widely through the scholarly culture.[1]

In my view many of the attempts within the social sciences—and indeed within the pages of the present volume—to move beyond the logo-centered conception of the person represent steps toward what may be viewed as a major historical transformation. It is a transformation that would lay to rest the Enlightenment conception of the person and its attendant travails, and locate an alternative that links the individual more fully to the social and cultural context. In effect, these attempts signal an openness, a curiosity, and a concerted investment in fostering a conception of the person in which separation, alienation, and contention are replaced with a sense of profound connection.

These have been central concerns for me over recent years, as I have grappled first with the conceptual problems inherent in dualist epistemology: the impasse of a hermeneutics of intersubjectivity, and the presumption of psychological or self-knowledge.[2] Such critical work has also formed the basis for a nondualist alternative to the Enlightenment conception of the person, one centered not in rational but in relational activity. In what follows I offer a brief sketch of the directions that I have found most promising. This account will be divided into three parts. First, it is important to illuminate more fully the background of my endeavors, namely their roots within the social constructionist turn in scholarship more generally. Following this account I will briefly develop the concept of what I term "relational being." From this perspective, relationships are not constituted by individual persons, but rather it is out of relational process that the very concept of the individual emerges. Finally, I wish to illuminate means for reconstructing conceptions of mental process in relational terms.

The Constructionist Turn

For me, the initial opening to the development of a relational account of human action emerged with the social constructionist turn in the scholarly world more generally. There are many stories to be told about the emergence of social constructionism, and I offer here but one, although one that is congenial with much common understanding. To be sure, one may trace the intellectual roots of social constructionism to Vico, Nietzsche, Dewey, and Wittgenstein, among others. More recently, Berger and Luckmann's *The Social Construction of Reality* (1966) was a landmark volume with strong reverberations across disciplines. However, the social movements and intellectual ferment taking shape in the late 1960s in the United States and Western Europe were also significantly influential. In the United States, resistance to the Vietnam War and to the country's political leadership was intense, and within this protest movement profound skepticism of the established order emerged. The academic community was deeply engaged in such resistance. The times were optimal for critically reassessing the established rationale and practices within the sciences and other scholarly traditions.

In brief, one can locate at least three major forms of broadly shared critique. The amalgamation of these forms of critique largely serve as the basis for most contemporary scholarship identified with social constructionism.[3] Perhaps the strongest and most impassioned form of critique of the dominant orders has been ideological. In this case, critics call into question taken-for-granted matters of fact and logic, and reveal the political ends that they serve. In effect, such analysis discloses the constructed character of "the real," in the service of liberating the reader from its subtle grasp. Within the scholarly world more generally, such "unmasking" has played a major role, from Marxist and feminist contributions to the work of Foucault (1979, 1980), and then onward to include critical voices in cultural studies, queer studies, and virtually every other group marginalized by mainstream, modernist traditions. The second major form of critique may be viewed as literary/rhetorical. With developments in semiotic theory in general and literary deconstruction in particular (Derrida 1976), attention was variously drawn to the ways in which linguistic convention serves as the forestructure for all claims to knowledge. Whatever reality may be, its representation is always dominated by such conventions. The third significant critique targeted foundational science (the supposed apex of the modernist tradition), and was stimulated largely by the 1970 publication of Thomas Kuhn's *The Structure of Scientific Revolutions*. Kuhn portrayed normal science as guided by paradigms of thought and practice shared by particular communities. In effect, the outcomes of science have not been demanded by the world as it is, but are the result of communal negotiation. This social account of science was further buttressed by a welter of research in the sociology of knowledge and the history of science (see, for example, Feyeraband 1978; Latour and Woolgar 1986; Woolgar 1988).

These three movements are all interwoven in contemporary constructionist inquiry. Together they also yield three major orienting assumptions forming the groundwork for my particular orientation to a relational account of human action: the social origins of knowledge, language as social action, and theory as political action. I discuss each of these assumptions below.

The Social Origins of Knowledge

At the outset, constructionist writings serve an enormous liberating function. They remove the rhetorical power of any person or any group claiming truth, wisdom, or ethics of universal scope—necessary for all. In this way they underscore the culturally and historically situated character of the Western self. They call into question all forms of psychological essentialism, including the concepts of cognition, emotion, motivation, intention, creativity, and so on.[4] Moreover, they serve as a vital stimulus to innovation. They enable us to bracket traditions of discourse, and to launch inquiry into new and more serviceable intelligibilities. Constructionist writings also point to promising directions for this kind of reconstructionist inquiry. Perhaps the most generative idea is that what we take to be knowledge of the world and self finds its origins in human relationships. What we take to be true as opposed to false, objective as opposed to subjective, scientific as opposed to mythological, rational as opposed to irrational, moral as opposed to immoral is brought into being by communal activity. This view stands in obvious contrast to the Enlightenment valorization of the individual knower, the rational, self-directing, morally centered, and knowledgeable agent of action. In effect, constructionist writings invite an appreciation of relationship as central to human understanding and action. It is not in the individual mind where knowledge, reason, emotion, and morality reside, but in relationships.

Language as Social Action

By placing the origin of knowledge in the communal sphere, constructionist writings also invite a major shift in the conception of language. On the modernist account, language was primarily a vehicle for the public expression of private mental states. It gained its significance primarily as a means of conveying the results of personal experience and reason. With observation and reason working in concert, the individual could become an arbiter of the real, a teller of truth. And because language could be shared, others were invited to judge the legitimacy of such declarations. Objectivity and truth became synonymous with a language that accurately pictures or mirrors the world as it is. Yet in the light of the social and linguistic critiques outlined above, this vision of language is thrown into question. There is no privileged route from observation to language. Rather, the language and practices of a community furnish the forestructure essential for processes of observation and thought to take place. It is here that Wittgenstein's (1953) proposal for a use-based conception of language becomes pivotal. Language gains its meaning not through its reflective capacities, but through game-like processes of relationship. And these game-like practices are lodged within broader "forms of life," or traditions of practice. Thus, as people coordinate their actions a major outcome is a system of signals or words. The words may serve to name the world for the participants. This is "a reward," you are "depressed," that is "a mammal," and so on. Such words are enormously important to sustaining these relationships. Not only do they represent the agreements regarding what exists for the participants, but they essentially constitute the glue by which their very forms of life—or traditions—are held together. There is no tradition of a jury trial without a language of guilt and innocence; no profession of psychology without a language of the mind; and little religion if the discourse of divinity has been abandoned.

Theory as Political Action

Social constructionism shares much with a pragmatic view of knowledge claims. That is, traditional issues of truth and objectivity are replaced with concerns about practical outcomes. It is not whether an account is true from a god's-eye view that matters; rather, we ask about the results for our lives that follow from taking any truth claim seriously. There can be many truths, depending on community tradition, but, as the constructionist asks, what happens to us—for good or ill—as we honor one as opposed to another account? There are no meaningful words without consequence.

Such a conclusion has had enormous repercussions in the academic community and beyond. This is especially so for scholars and practitioners concerned with social injustice, oppression, and the marginalization of minority groups in society. If communities create realities (facts and good reasons) congenial to their own traditions, and these realities are established as true and good for all, then alternative traditions may be obliterated. Regardless of whether we are speaking of scientific fact, canons of logic, foundations of law, or spiritual truths, as we formulate the world we implicitly favor certain ways of life over others. Thus, for example, the scientist may use the most rigorous methods of testing intelligence, and amass tomes of data that indicate racial differences in intelligence. However, to presume that there is something called "human intelligence," that people differ in their possession of this capacity, and that a series of question-and-answer games reveal this capacity is all specific to a given tradition or paradigm. Such concepts and measures are not required by "the way the world is." Most importantly, merely entering the paradigm and moving within the tradition is deeply injurious to those people classified as inferior by its standards. Or to put it another way, the long-standing distinction between facts and values—objective reflections of the world, and subjective desires or feelings of "ought"— cannot be sustained.

The implications for a sociocultural reconstruction of the concept of the person are clear enough. The primary question to consider in such efforts is one of political consequence. One need not be constrained by empirical evidence in such attempts, as such evidence is already constrained by the assumptive base on which the research was premised. Rather, the question is one of political poetics: how can we hammer together a "mobile army of metaphors" in such a way that they contribute to new and more promising forms of social practice? Nor should one be constrained by the styles of writing that we inherit within the scholarly tradition. To write in the favored styles of the academy may be productive only within these communities. Outside, such writing is scarcely intelligible. Or, in the terms of many critics, such accounts are "elitist." If cultural transformation is a chief goal of theoretical work, then alternative forms of communication are required. This may include writing in more popular vernaculars, but it may also include expanding the arena of communication to include art, photography, film, multimedia, and more.

Toward Relational Being

Developments in constructionist scholarship open a significant space for the sociocultural reconstruction of the person.[5] They demonstrate the constructed character of the modernist self, and replace the individual with social process as the origin of knowledge. They further suggest that we view language as a representation neither of the world nor of the mind, but as an action within social space. And finally, they invite the development of theory as a vehicle for social transformation. Yet, while the mental world is essentially deontologized, the question of how to proceed remains open; how could a theory of the person be constituted that did not rest on the presumption of an inner world of mind? Indeed, for Mead and Vygotsky—both progenitors of contemporary excursions into sociocultural conceptions of the person—the individual mind remained the focal point. For Mead, persons are related via a subjective or symbolic interdependence; for Vygotsky, cultural action formed the basis of what he viewed as "higher mental processes." There is virtually no sociocultural theorist writing today who parts with the subjective world, who embraces a conceptual space in which the self is emptied of content.[6]

While I fully appreciate the resistance to abandoning the psychological being, I believe that such resistance is itself a victim of the modernist dualism, an "in here" that registers or constructs an "out there." In my view, we proceed more fruitfully by abandoning the dualist tradition altogether. Rather, we may view human action as whole cloth, not driven, motivated, planned, intended, or otherwise fashioned by an inner world, but acquiring its very intelligibility as action only in relation to other actions. With this conception in place, we may fruitfully return to the potentials of psychological discourse. To appreciate the possibility of a fully relational account, it is first essential to explore the sociocultural constitution of intelligibility.

The Relational Origins of Meaning

If we cut discursive action away from a mental origin, we remove the locus of meaning from within the head, and place it in the social sphere. If we can render intelligible a means of understanding relational process as the origin of meaning, then it is compelling to view social process as the font of all that we take to be real, true, objective, rational, and good. And by implication, social process becomes the originating point for the very conception of a mental world. It is in this context that I find rich implications in the following propositions.

An individual's utterances in themselves possess no meaning. We pass each other on the street. I smile and say, "Hello, Anna." She walks past without hearing. Under such conditions, what have I said? To be sure, I have uttered two words. However, for all the difference it makes I might have chosen two nonsense syllables. You pass and I say, "Umlot nigen . . ." You hear nothing. When you fail to acknowledge me in any way, all words become equivalent. In an important sense, nothing has been said at all. I cannot possess meaning alone. One may object that even if not acknowledged, what I say might mean something to me personally. That may be, but the question then becomes, how did your utterances come to have personal meaning? We take up this issue shortly.

The potential for meaning is realized through supplementary action. Lone utterances begin to acquire meaning when another (or others) coordinate themselves to the utterance, that is, when they add some form of supplementary action (whether linguistic or otherwise). Effectively, I have greeted Anna only by virtue of her response: "Oh, hi, good morning" brings me to life as one who has greeted. Supplements may be very simple, as simple as a nod of affirmation that indeed you have said something meaningful. It may take the form of an action, e.g., shifting the line of gaze upon hearing the word, "Look!" Or it may extend the utterance in some way, as in "Yes, but I also think that . . ." We thus find that to communicate at all is to be granted by others a privilege of meaning. If others do not treat one's utterances as communication, if they fail to coordinate themselves around the offering, one is reduced to nonsense.

Combining these first two proposals, we see that meaning resides within neither individual, but only in a process of coordinated action, or co-action.[7] Both act and supplement must be coordinated in order for meaning to occur. Like a handshake, a kiss, or a tango, the actions of the individual alone are empty. Communication is inherently collaborative. In this way we see that none of the words that comprise our vocabulary have meaning in themselves. They are granted the capacity to mean by virtue of the way they are coordinated with other words and actions. Indeed, our entire vocabulary of the individual—who thinks, feels, wants, hopes, and so on—is granted meaning only by virtue of coordinated activities among people. The birth of "myself" lies within relationship.

Supplementary action is itself a candidate for meaning. Any supplement functions twice, first in granting significance to what has preceded, and second as an action that also requires supplementation. In effect, the meaning it grants remains suspended until it too is supplemented. Consider a therapy client who speaks of her deep depression; she finds herself unable to cope with an aggressive husband and an intolerable job situation. The therapist can grant this report meaning as an expression of depression, by responding, "Yes, I can see why you are depressed; tell me a little more about your relationship with your husband." However, this supplement too stands idle of meaning until the client provides the supplement. If the client ignored the statement—for example, by going on to talk about her success as a mother—the therapist's words would be denied significance. More broadly, we may say that in daily life there are no acts in themselves—that is, actions that are not simultaneously supplements to what has preceded. Whatever we do or say takes place within a temporal flow that gives meaning to what has preceded, while simultaneously forming an invitation to further supplementation.

Acts create the possibility for meaning but simultaneously constrain its potential. If I give a lecture on psychoanalytic theory, this lecture is meaningless without an audience that listens, deliberates, affirms, or questions what I have said. In this sense, every speaker owes to his or her audience a debt of gratitude; without their engagement the speaker ceases to exist. At the same time, my lecture creates the very possibility for the audience to grant meaning. While the audience creates me as a meaningful agent, I simultaneously grant to them the capacity to create. They are without existence until there is an action that invites them into being. Yet my actions also set constraints upon supplementation. If I speak on Freud, as an audience member you are not able to supplement in any way you wish. You may ask me a question about object relations theory, but not astrophysics; comment on the concept of repression but not on the taste of radishes. Such constraints exist because my lecture is already embedded within a tradition of act and supplement. It has been granted meaning as a "lecture on Freud," by virtue of previous generations of meaning givers. In this sense, actions embedded within relationships have prefigurative potential. The history of usage enables them to invite or suggest certain supplements as opposed to others—because only these supplements are sensible or meaningful within a tradition. Thus, as we speak with each other, we also set limits on each other's being; to remain in the conversation is not only to respect a tradition, but to accede to being one kind of person as opposed to another.

Supplements function both to create and to constrain meaning. As we have seen, supplements "act backward" in a way that creates the meaning of what has preceded. In this sense, the speaker's meaning—his or her identity, character, intention, and the like—are not free to "be what they are," but are constrained by the act of supplementation. Supplementation thus operates postfiguratively, to create the speaker as meaning this as opposed to that. From the enormous array of possibilities, the supplement gives direction and temporarily narrows the possibilities of being. Thus, for example, the therapist who inquires into a client's depression establishes a form of constraint. If the client is to remain sensible, he or she may readily accede to being depressed. A therapeutic question can harbor implications for an entire life trajectory.

While act/supplements are constraining, they do not determine. As proposed, our words and actions function so as to constrain the words and actions of others, and vice versa. If we are to remain intelligible within a tradition, we must necessarily act within these constraints. Such constraints have their origins in a history of co-action. As people coordinate actions and supplements, and come to rely on them in everyday life, they are essentially generating a way of life. If enough people join in these coordinated activities over a long period, we may speak of a cultural tradition.

Yet it is important to underscore that our words and actions function only as constraints, and not as determinants. This is so for two important reasons. First, the conditions under which we attempt to coordinate our actions are seldom constant. We are continuously faced with the challenge of importing old words and actions into new situations. As we do so, such words and actions acquire new possibilities for meaning. For example, you are visiting a farm and you point out to your child, "Look . . . that is a chicken." The word "chicken" thus gains its meaning from the way it is embedded in this configuration of events. Later that day, the farmer's wife comes to the dinner table bearing a large platter, and announces, "We are having chicken for dinner tonight." Now the word used in referring to the live and clucking animal refers to the individual pieces of cooked meat. As new situations develop, so will the same word acquire other potentials for meaning. More formally, all words are "polysemic": they may be used in many different ways.

A second important reason for our relative freedom of action lies in the fact that meaning making is always local. That is, coordination is always located in the here-and-now, in momentary and fleeting conditions—in the kitchen, the boardroom, the mine, the prison, and so on. These local efforts to coordinate give rise to local patterns of speaking and action—street slang, academic jargon, baby talk, jive talk, signing, and so on. And, because those who enter into such coordinations may come from different cultural traditions, new combinations are always under production. In effect, we inherit an enormous potpourri of potentially intelligible actions—each arising from a different form of life—and the repository is under continuous motion. Our actions may be invited by history, but they are not required. In this sense, we can indeed "step over our shadows"—and in order for us to function adequately in continuously changing circumstances, creative combinations will always be necessary.

Meanings are subject to continuous reconstitution via the expanding process of co-action. As has been shown above, we find that what an utterance means is inherently undecidable. No amount of discussion, discourse analysis, conversation analysis, or other attempt to determine what has been said can be determinative. Indeed, all such attempts to fix meaning are themselves entries into the relational process, and their own meaning is now in question. The meaning of any utterance is a temporary achievement, born of the collaborative moment. Further, as relations continue over time, what is meant stands subject to continuous alteration through an expanding arena of action/supplements. Such expansion may be far removed from the interchange itself (e.g., consider a divorcing pair who retrospectively redefine their entire marital trajectory), and is subject to continuous change through interaction with and among others (e.g. friends, relatives, the media, etc.).

In summary, I find the exclusive focus on the face-to-face relationship for determining meaning far too narrow. For whether "I make sense" is not under my control; nor is it solely determined by you, or by the dyadic process in which meaning struggles toward realization. Even at the outset, we largely derive our potential for coordination from our previous immersion in a range of other relationships. Actions within these relationships typically derive their intelligibility from traditions of long standing. We arrive in the present relationship as extensions of the distant past. And as the current relationship unfolds, it serves to reform the meaning of the past. These interchanges may be supplemented and transformed by still others in the future. In effect, meaningful communication in any given relationship ultimately depends on an extended array of relationships, not only "right here, right now," but how it is that you and I are related to a variety of other persons, and they to still others—and ultimately, one may say, to the relational conditions of culture and history. We are all in this way interdependently interlinked—without the capacity to mean anything, to possess an "I"—except for the existence of an extended world of relationship.

The Relational Reconstruction of Mind

While the concept of co-action enables us to view the relational process as sui generis, and not as a byproduct of inter-acting minds, this move is not in itself sufficient. In particular, if theory is to enter into social life, a far richer discursive palette is required. It is tempting to embark on the development of a new vocabulary for describing and explaining human action. However, such a vocabulary would be alien and obscure. It would not figure in any significant way in daily or institutional practices. This has indeed been the problem faced by various philosophers who have attempted to break the boundary of subject and object, person and world. I have deep admiration for the work of Heidegger, Merleau Ponty, and G. H. Mead, for example, but their vocabularies of understanding are both obscure and lacking in practical consequence. Therefore, let us not abandon in this pursuit the enormously rich vocabulary of inner life; instead, let us attempt to transform its meaning. We may refigure our understanding of this vast vocabulary so that it no longer contributes to the presumption of all against all. Rather, it is possible to unfold the concept of relational being in such a way that the mental vocabulary is fully a vocabulary of relationship. To illuminate the way, it is useful to consider four major proposals. If these logics are clear and compelling, the way is open to understanding the entire mental vocabulary as relational in origins and functions. I discuss such reframed understandings below.

Mental discourse originates in the process of co-action. It follows from the preceding proposals that the origin of all words referring to mental process emerge from the process of co-action. Terms such as "thought," "emotion," "intention," and the like are not the result of an inner assay, but of participation within a tradition of relationship. Thus, children do not first recognize that they think, or feel, or intend, and then locate a label for these states. Rather, within relationships they acquire a vocabulary of the mental world that implies the existence of such states. It is only within these relationships that sadness, anger, and the like become realities for the child.

Mental discourse functions in the service of relationship. If mental language is not a reflection of inner states, why do we use it at all? We are guided to an answer by the preceding discussion on the use-based conception of language. On this account we abandon the search for the truth of mental discourse, and are sensitized to its function within the sphere of relationships. In effect, mental discourse comes to have constitutive value within a culture. When we say, "Please come for a visit," "Look at that sunset!" or "Is that the number 9 bus?" there are social consequences. The result of saying such things is that people board planes, cast their gaze into the distance, or give us information. Mental discourse functions in just these ways. When someone says, "You make me so angry" or "You give me such pleasure," certain actions are invited, and others discouraged. Bursts of anger may correct your behavior, and expressions of pleasure invite you to repeat what you have done.

Mental discourse is social performance. As proposed, mental discourse is action within relationship. In this sense it is a performance for others. When it is viewed it as performance, attention is drawn to the way in which such discourse is embedded in fully embodied expression. Expressions of love, for example, are typically accompanied by movements of the eyes, head, and hands, along with appropriate posture. The spoken language is but one component of a full social performance. We may speak, then, of psycho-performances, that is, actions with or for others (present or implied) that include the discourse of the mind.[8] With the utterance "I was thinking that . . .," the speaker is not likely to be screaming or writhing on the ground. Rather, the tone of voice will probably be measured and the gestures minimal. With the utterance "I am angry," one is not likely to be grinning or hopping on one foot. He or she is far more likely to speak with lips tightened and possibly with clenched fists. In effect, thought and anger are not inside, searching for release in expression. They are fully coordinated bodily performances in which the words "thinking" and "anger" often (but not necessarily) figure. In this sense, we perform thinking and anger in the same sense that we might kick a ball or drive a car. "Thinking," "feeling anger," "kicking," and "driving" are all intelligible actions; it is simply that the first two carry with them mental terminologies.

Discursive action is embedded in co-active process. It follows from the preceding logic that the meaning of a psycho-performance is not the possession of the actor alone. Its meaning is born in co-action. Thus, for example, a young man professes his attraction for a colleague in a beautifully coordinated way—words, gestures, tone of voice, gaze ... an incandescent expression of devotion. Yet, from the standpoint of co-action, her supplement will ratify it as meaning one thing as opposed to another. She may respond with a reciprocal expression of affection, thus affirming that his actions were expressions of love. However, consider some alternative possibilities: "Oh, you are such a hopeless romantic," "You haven't a clue what you're talking about," or "Yea ... but you said that last week to Sue."

With these four propositions in place we are positioned for a full reformulation of mental life. Replacing the view of the mind as a private reserve of the bounded being, we move to social process as the origin of all that we take to be mental. In this light, "having a given state of mind" is to perform felicitously within a tradition of relationship. One does not so much possess a mental state as act in such a way that the possession becomes a shared reality. To have a mental life is to participate in a relational life.

At this point the reconstitution of psychology as relational performance joins hands with much work in discursive psychology (Edwards and Potter 1992). Thus, for example, in their early work Potter and Wetherell (1987) demonstrate the utility of reconstructing the concept of "attitude," as employed in social psychological research, by removing it from its position as anterior to behavior and placing it within actions of social declaration. To declare "I like Smith for president" is not a public expression of a private feeling, but a social act, or effectively, the doing of an attitude. Similarly, others have explored the potentials of viewing reason not as a mental phenomenon, but as a particular way of talking, arguing, or writing within a particular tradition (Billig 1996). Scholars from a range of disciplines have contributed to a view of memory as a socially constituted phenomenon.[9] To "have an accurate memory" is to engage in a culturally intelligible action.

Research on communal memory has stimulated others to consider the social origins of what we take to be private experience.[10] If we view sensation not as a "receiving into the mental world," but an intelligible action in the social world, we gain purchase on the concept of experience as relational. What we mean by visual experience, on this account, is an act of attending, and attentional acts are not random but relationally born. Still others have challenged the view of creativity as an individual origination, and explored the way in which creative acts are generated within communal traditions or enclaves. There is a substantial literature, both anthropological and historical, demonstrating the culturally constructed character of emotional performance.[11] This literature also throws into question the common assumption of emotion as biologically given. Drawing from this scholarship, I have attempted to illuminate how emotional performances are constituted within relational scenarios (Gergen 1994). This work specifically focuses on the co-active dimension of psycho-performances.

While robust in their implications, these various efforts raise many significant questions. For one, many scholars in the sociocultural domain are loath to abandon the concept of intentional action. Further, they are supported by the common sense that people do understand their intentions. We know that when we enter a bank, for example, we intend to deposit a check and not commit a robbery. To be sure, there is abundant literature demonstrating how intentions are attributed and negotiated in social interchange. However, the question remains as to how we can quite privately and quite commonly be so certain about our intentions. Let us answer the question in terms of psycho-performance. Like parts in a play, psycho-performances are culturally recognizable. When I am standing before a class I am engaged in a performance we call teaching. The students recognize what I am doing no less than I. There are unwritten rules about what I might do under these circumstances, and if I break these rules in a flagrant way (e.g., by striking a student for making a mistake), I will lose my job. How, then, do I identify what I am trying (intending, attempting, endeavoring) to do in the classroom? It is evident to me not from looking inward but from participating in the performance. Without hesitation I can tell you that I am trying to teach or intending to teach because I am indeed engaged in a recognizable performance. I recognize my intentions in the same way an actor recognizes he is playing the part of Hamlet and not Othello. To name my intentions is to name the performance in which by common standards I am engaged.

A second significant question concerns the fact that people are often alone, and during these times they seem to engage in what we commonly call thought, emotion, and desire. Do these experiences not count as psychological in the traditional sense of being separated from or independent of the socius? It is here that current work in cultural psychology, especially the Vygotskian tradition, points the way. In Vygotsky's famous line, "There is nothing in mind that is not first in all society" (1978:142). Or, in present terms, whatever is taking place privately has its origins in the sphere of co-action. However, the relational view developed here abandons the mind/world dualism represented in this statement. Rather, it is more useful to view actions in private as relational actions performed on a minimal scale. In effect, they are partial performances. Instead of uttering rational words out loud to another, for example, one utters them without sound. In the same way, an actor may rehearse his lines privately, or one may "hum to oneself" without making a sound. In effect, what we do privately is not taking place in another world, called "mind"; rather, what we are doing is essentially to engage in social life without the audience present. Implicitly there is always an audience for our private reveries.

In my view the scholarly development of a more historically and culturally sensitive conception of the person is essential. This is so not only because of the globally inimical consequences of the modernist/individualist tradition, but also because Western culture is moving rapidly toward a materialistic reduction of the person. The rapid expansion of brain science and its accompaniment in cognitive/neuro and evolutionary psychology is startling. Further, this expansion is fueled by major funding from both governments and the psychopharmacological industry. At this juncture, mental health professionals are virtually captive to the idea that the origin of human suffering inheres in individual brains. At the same time, I am skeptical of the potential for scholarly work alone to make significant cultural inroads. Abstract theory has little impact outside academic enclaves. In my view it is important that scholars work together with societal practitioners to translate into practical action the implications of their deliberations. Sociocultural accounts should move hand in hand with innovations in pedagogical and therapeutic practices. They should enter into efforts to transform both communities and organizations, to replace conflict with peace, and to bring about more viable forms of global life. It is within the context of action that the full meaning of such theoretical work will be realized.

Notes

1. See, for example, Bellah et al. 1985 and Lasch 1979.
2. See, for example, Gergen 1988, 1994.
3. For a more detailed account of these critiques within psychology, see Gergen 1994.
4. For further discussion of the historicizing of the modernist self see esp. Taylor 1989 and Seigel 2005.
5. An extended account of relational being is contained in Gergen 2009.
6. See, for example, Bruner 1990 and Wertsch 1985.
7. The concept of co-action owes a debt to both Herbert Blumer's *Symbolic Interactionism* (1969) and to John Shotter's writings (1980, 1993); each employs the concept of joint action, but with different conceptual implications.
8. I am indebted here to James Averill's account of emotions as cultural performances; see Averill 1982, Averill and Sundararajan 2004.
9. See, for example, Connorton 1987 and Misztal 2003.
10. See especially Middleton and Brown 2005.
11. See, for example, Rosaldo 1980, Heider 1991, Lynch 1992, and Wulff 2007.

References

Averill, J. R. 1982. *Anger and Aggression: An Essay on Emotion*. New York: Springer.

Averill, J. R., and L. Sundararajan. 2004. Hope as rhetoric: Cultural narratives of wishing and coping. In J. Eliott, ed., *Interdisciplinary Perspectives on Hope*, 127–159. New York: Nova Science.

Bellah, R. N., R. Madsen, W. M. Sullivan, A. Swidler, and S. I. Tipton. 1985. *Habits of the Heart: Individualism and Commitment in American Life*. Berkeley: University of California Press.

Berger, P., and T. Luckmann. 1966. *The Social Construction of Reality: A Treatise on the Sociology of Knowledge*. New York: Anchor.

Billig, M. 1996. Remembering the particular background of social identity theory. In W. P. Robinson, ed., *Social Groups and Identities: Developing the Legacy of Henri Tajfel*, 337–358. Oxford: Butterworth Heinemann.

Blumer, H. 1969. *Symbolic Interactionism: Perspective and Method*. New York: Prentice Hall.

Bruner, J. 1990. *Acts of Meaning*. Cambridge, MA: Harvard University Press.

Connorton, P. 1987. *How Societies Remember*. Cambridge: Cambridge University Press.

Derrida, J. 1976. *Of Grammatology.* Trans. G. C. Spivak. Baltimore: John Hopkins University Press.

Edwards, D., and J. Potter. 1992. *Discursive Psychology.* London: Sage.

Feyerabend, P. 1978. *Science in a Free Society.* London: Sage.

Foucault, M. 1979. *Discipline and Punish: The Birth of the Prison.* Trans. A. Sheridan. New York: Vintage.

——. 1980. *The History of Sexuality.* Trans. R. Hurley. New York: Vintage.

Gergen, K. J. 1988. If persons are texts. In S. B. Messer, L. A. Sass, and R. L. Woolfolk, eds., *Hermeneutics and Psychological Theory,* 28–51. New Brunswick, NJ: Rutgers University Press.

——. 1994. *Realities and Relationships.* Cambridge, MA: Harvard University Press.

——. 2009. *Relational Being: Beyond the Individual and the Community.* New York: Oxford University Press.

Heider, K. G. 1991. *Landscapes of Emotion: Mapping Three Cultures of Emotion in Indonesia.* Cambridge: Cambridge University Press.

Kuhn, T. 1970. *The Structure of Scientific Revolutions.* Chicago: University of Chicago Press.

Lasch, C. 1979. *The Culture of Narcissism.* New York: Warner.

Latour, B., and S. Woolgar. 1986. *Laboratory Life: The Construction of Scientific Facts.* Princeton: Princeton University Press.

Lynch, O. M. 1992. *Divine Passions: The Social Construction of Emotion in India.* Berkeley: University of California Press.

Middleton, D., and S. D. Brown. 2005. *The Social Psychology of Experience.* London: Sage.

Misztal, B. A. 2003. *Theories of Social Remembering.* Buckingham: Open University Press.

Potter, J. 1992. *Representing Reality.* London: Sage.

Potter, J., and M. Wetherell. 1987. *Discourse and Social Psychology: Beyond Attitudes and Behavior.* London: Sage.

Rosaldo, M. Z. 1980. *Knowledge and Passion: Ilongot Notions of Self and Social Life.* Cambridge: Cambridge University Press.

Seigel, J. 2005. *The Idea of the Self.* Cambridge: Cambridge University Press.

Shotter, J. 1980. Action, joint action, and intentionality. In M. Brenner, ed., *The Structure of Action,* 28–65. Oxford: Oxford University Press.

——. 1993. *Conversational Realities.* London: Sage.

——. 2007. *Conversational Realities Revisited.* Chagrin Falls, OH: Taos Institute Publications.

Taylor, C. 1989. *Sources of the Self: The Making of the Modern Identity.* Cambridge, MA: Harvard University Press.

Vygotsky, L. S. 1978. *Mind in Society.* Trans. M. Cole. Cambridge, MA: Harvard University Press.

Wertsch, J. V. 1985. *Vygotsky and the Social Formation of Mind.* Cambridge, MA: Harvard University Press.

Wittgenstein, L. 1953. *Philosophical Investigations.* Trans. G. E. M. Anscombe. Oxford: Blackwell.

Woolgar, S., ed. 1988. *Knowledge and Reflexivity: New Frontiers in the Sociology of Knowledge*. Beverly Hills: Sage.

Wulff, H. 2007. *The Emotions: A Cultural Reader*. New York: Oxford University Press.

4   Sociocultural Means to Feminist Ends

Discursive and Constructionist Psychologies of Gender

EVA MAGNUSSON AND JEANNE MARECEK

Feminist psychologists in many nations—the United Kingdom, the Nordic countries, Australia, New Zealand, Canada, and the United States—have been in the forefront of developing a number of the approaches presented in this book. As feminist psychologists explored the complexities of "identity," "gender identity," "masculinity," "femininity," and gender relations in everyday life, they confronted the inadequacy of the simplified and determinist models typical of mainstream psychology, whether the determining agents were seen to be biological or sociocultural. Everything to do with gender, they came to see, defied simple determinism, monocausality, universalism, linear cause-effect models, and static categorizations. Theorizing gender required the emergentist ontologies that underlie the psychologies presented in this book.

Feminist psychologists who espouse these approaches often call what they do "feminist discursive psychology," and we shall use that term in the rest of this essay. The term "discursive" has a dual meaning, reflecting the two meanings of its root, "discourse," in contemporary theory. First, "discourse" refers to language practices and talk as the medium of meaning-making and of social relations. The term also carries a second, broader meaning—as articulated by social theorists such as Michel Foucault, Pierre Bourdieu, and Judith Butler—of institutionalized practices and ways of thinking that set boundaries on what can be said about a specific topic. Discourses in this latter sense are heterogeneous assemblages of scientific, religious, legal, political, and moral statements, arrangements of physical space, language, and other social practices, all of which serve to define reality.

Feminist discursive psychology is not a single unified approach to psychological theory and method. It is possible to give examples of feminist discursive research that embody each of the approaches presented in this book. The family of feminist approaches do, however, share a common base. "Adding gender" and "adding feminist theory" necessarily transform certain important aspects of theory and research in psychology, be it conventional or sociocultural psychology. Furthermore, feminist psychologists—because they study gender and because their work is informed by cross-disciplinary feminist theories—have encountered challenges and possibilities that have prompted novel theoretical and methodological developments.

In this chapter, we describe work that has integrated feminist theories and critical gender studies with various strongly relational approaches to psychology. First, we describe some major theoretical and metatheoretical assumptions of feminist discursive psychologists. Next, we describe the variety of projects and topics that they have pursued. Because gender figures so prominently as an organizing feature of social life in most societies, the topics of research span the range of human activity. Feminist psychologists have also given priority to reflexive critical practice. That is, they have cultivated self-awareness of their own practices as researchers and those of the discipline at large. In this regard, they have examined how historic and contemporary psychological knowledge and practice have served to reaffirm certain meanings of gender, especially those that perpetuate the status quo. We subsequently discuss in some detail two illustrative examples of feminist discursive research, one on boys' masculinities and the other on women's experiences of coercive heterosexual relations. In the final part of the essay, we step back to assess the powers and limits of feminist discursive psychology. What questions, theoretical insights, and methodological developments have feminists brought to psychology? What do discursive approaches uniquely contribute to understanding gender? What new questions, avenues of investigation, and practical applications have these approaches opened? What obstacles have researchers who use these approaches encountered?

Major Theoretical and Metatheoretical Assumptions

Feminist discursive psychologists draw upon a variety of theoretical sources, including cross-disciplinary feminist theories, discursive psychology, social constructionism, and postmodern thought. Here we briefly present some of the central assumptions of feminist discursive psychology, many of which are shared by other approaches discussed in this book.

Situated Knowledges, Partial Truths, and Strong Objectivity

Feminist theorists and philosophers have rejected simple notions of objectivity and truth (see Haraway 1988; Harding 1986; Morawski 1994). They instead affirm that knowledge is always perspectival, always situated in some way. Knowers necessarily see from a particular angle of vision. They are always located in social and cultural forcefields. For example, we see history from our standpoint in the present and we necessarily bring present concerns and meanings to our analyses of the past. Moreover, knowledge is "interested": that is, there is a reason why a particular question is of interest. It follows then that "objective knowledge"—that is, knowledge that is not influenced by the knower's situation—is impossible. In assessing the credibility and trustworthiness of research, therefore, such criteria as validity, reliability, and logical inference are not sufficient. We must also assess the researcher's standpoint and its influence on the research process. Harding (1991) calls this expanded assessment of research "strong objectivity."

Assumptions About Gender

Gender is a central aspect of human experience and social life. Gender is not an essence, however, but a socially constructed identity. For feminists, gender means more than the designations male and female. In most societies, gender is a significant dimension of personal identity; it further serves as a primary means for distributing power, privilege, and status in various social groupings, such as families and workplaces. Yet although feminist discursive psychologists assert the importance of gender in social life, they reject the idea that gender is a biological or psychological essence. That is, they reject the assumption (sometimes called gender essentialism) that there are fundamental traits or characteristics that inhere in all males (and only in males) and others that inhere in all females (and only in females). For example, they are skeptical of claims that women are by nature nurturant, emotional, or relational and that men have an innate propensity for sexual aggression. In the view of feminist discursive psychologists, essentialist explanations of male and female behavior tend to be circular, if not tautological: they presume that which they endeavor to explain (Bohan 1993; Hare-Mustin and Marecek 1990).

Because feminist discursive psychologists reject gender essentialism, they eschew the project of cataloguing the presumed differences (or similarities) between women and men, a project that has long occupied a central place in psychologists' efforts to understand gender. Claims of gender difference, in their view, homogenize members of each gender, imposing a false uniformity on them. Further, such claims often polarize males and females, concealing the similarities between them. Also, the project of cataloguing male-female differences (or similarities) assumes that all humans fit into these two categories and that gender is just a reflection of anatomical difference. These assumptions have recently been called into question by cultural anthropologists, queer theorists, and transgender activists (Fausto-Sterling 2000; Herdt 1998; Parlee 1996).

Gender is socially constructed. Feminist discursive psychologists dispute the commonsense assumption that distinctions related to gender follow from intrinsic differences between women and men. They claim instead that the category system of gender and its meaning of gender as male-female difference is sustained through ongoing social negotiation (West and Zimmerman 1987). The cultural maintenance of this category system creates ideas of fundamental differences between women and men and also sometimes produces differences. A central project of feminist discursive psychology is to uncover the social processes by which categories, meanings, and hierarchies related to gender are produced and given force. These processes occur at many levels, including social institutions, cultural practices (such as language usage), and interactions between individuals. At all levels they serve to regulate individual behavior and social relations. They also establish hierarchies of worth and prestige regarding certain groups of people and certain kinds of behavior. Of particular interest is the question of how people come to feel that living up to the requirements of their gender category is a matter of free choice and an authentic expression of their inner desires.

Doing gender: Gender is both a social product and a social process. A third key assumption about gender is that it is produced in ongoing social interactions. A feminist discursive psychologist would say that people come to experience themselves as psychologically gendered because social gendering permeates daily experience. This is quite different from claiming that subjective gender is the result of adhering to a role or script imposed by the culture. Rather, gender meanings are continually (and collectively) negotiated, strengthened, revised, or undermined in the course of daily life. Discursive researchers focus on the processes by which gender is produced, as well as on the specific gendered meanings that result. They examine practices that sustain certain meanings of maleness and femaleness and practices that discredit others. Of course, individuals identify themselves (and are identified by others) in terms of many social categories besides gender. Depending on the specific social context, certain categories are more salient, and others less so. Thus, gender is rarely, if ever, only gender; it is always intertwined with other relevant social identities (Stewart and McDermott 2004). These include race or ethnicity, age group, social class, sexual identity, nationality, and immigration status.

Gender relations are invested with power. In all known societies, gender is a fundamental category for distinguishing among individuals, for distributing power, and for assigning status. Feminist researchers in several academic disciplines have examined historic and contemporary power relations between individual women and men and between women and men as social categories. Relationships between women and men can be seen as at least two kinds of relationships existing in parallel and sometimes at cross purposes: a relation between two individuals and a relation between two social categories. The second relation inevitably has an impact on the first. Gender is also implicated in distributing power and status among groups of women and among groups of men. As an example of this kind of power relation, consider the verbal and physical assaults that boys sometimes mete out on other boys who are perceived as effeminate or gay (e.g., Franklin 2004). Consider also the discourses that circulated among Europeans of the colonial era proclaiming the sexual immorality and lasciviousness of African and Asian women; these discourses served to prop up the image of the chaste and morally upstanding white woman (Hammonds 1997; Jayawardena 2007).

Gender and the power of the ordinary. An important question for feminist discursive psychologists is how power differences come to be seen as natural and inevitable, and sometimes even become invisible. For example, Nicola Gavey (whose work we describe below) has examined the social practices that normalize verbal and even physical coercion by men interested in obtaining sex, effectively making women "unrapeable." One explanation focuses on that which is seen as ordinary (and thus normal) in daily life. The ordinary has the power to function as a template that people voluntarily conform to; thus, it does not appear as "power." Indeed, what is ordinary is invisible, akin to the air we breathe. This kind of invisible power comes into being as people, through living and talking about their lives, create notions and stories about what is ordinary and expected. Such normality-defining stories both build up and sustain ideas about specific ways of being a person as the proper ones in a certain cultural context. In the case of gender, it is specific ways of being a woman, man, girl, or boy that come to be taken as proper and normal. In this manner the ordinary, with its implied definitions of normality, invisibly contributes to the production of certain kinds of gendered people. It is, quite simply, difficult to think differently about oneself as a gendered being in that particular context.

Social knowledge about gender is the basis for one's knowledge of oneself as a gendered person. Normality-defining discourses make available for people certain kinds of knowledge about themselves, while at the same time making other kinds of self-knowledge less likely. Such knowledge contributes to producing certain types of gendered persons, in a process that has been termed "subjectification" (Gavey 2005; Wetherell and Potter 1992). Subjectification involves two closely related steps. First, the discourses encountered in everyday life—what we might call common sense—build up a picture of what a certain kind of person is like. For instance, certain ways of being a woman in relation to a man come to seem "natural." Second, common sense also defines what are the normal, proper, and good ways of being and behaving in a particular time and place, leading people to desire to form themselves in accord with these definitions. This process contributes to producing certain types of gendered persons. For example, cultural discourses depict a white Swedish working-class woman in a heterosexual marriage in certain characteristic ways. These depictions make those ways of being and behaving accessible and "natural," as well as entailing "good" or proper femininity. These ways of being a Swedish working-class wife will then seem to be a particularly fitting and desirable expression of the kind of person such a woman is.

The concept "subject position" is often used by discursive psychologists as an analytical bridge between the social and the personal. The term denotes a way of enacting oneself that is made available in a particular social situation (Davies and Harré 1990). Social interactions bring forward an array of different subject positions. Feminist discursive psychologists are, as you might expect, particularly interested in those subject positions related to gender. For example, when a man says, "I know a nice girl like you wouldn't carry a condom," he makes available to his female partner the desirable subject position "nice girl" and, by implication, its undesirable antithesis. By taking up the desirable position, however, a "nice girl" risks unsafe sex. But what are the risks she assumes if she takes up the undesirable position of "bad girl"?

Gendered identity and gendered behavior are not wholly determined by social forces. Subjectification and gendered subject positioning do not wholly determine who a person is, what he or she can do, or what he or she wants to do or be. In social life (indeed, even in the course of a single interaction), many subject positions are made available. Herein lie possibilities for some degree of personal agency, as well as for the emergence of novel meanings.

People may take up a subject position or refuse it; they might take it up but enact it ironically. Moreover, new subject positions emerge in response to changes in material conditions. The Internet, for example, has enabled virtual communications involving new gendered identities. For better or for worse, the Internet has opened possibilities for gender display, concealment, and deception that were not previously possible. Another example is the widespread availability of new surgical and hormonal technologies, which have enabled people to modify primary and secondary sex characteristics, opening the way to a surge of experimentation with gender categories and sexual identities.

Now that we have reviewed some of the main orienting assumptions of feminist discursive psychologists, we shift the focus to consider how feminist discursive psychologists work and the kinds of projects they have pursued.

Feminist Discursive Psychology: Tools and Projects

Feminist discursive psychologists study the ways that mundane interactions and routine experiences produce gendered identities, subjectivities, and gender relations. Like many other culturally oriented psychologists, they locate their research projects in everyday settings and they listen to ordinary talk. They have often criticized conventional psychological research methods such as laboratory experiments and standardized scales as "context-stripping" (Marecek 2001; Parlee 1979). As Michelle Crossley has put it, "We are no longer satisfied sitting behind our computers feeding dummy data into SPSS. . . . We need, and want, to find out more, . . . to boldly open ourselves to questions and issues that have been artificially closed off by a discipline that has trained us to think and act in severely limited and circumscribed ways" (Crossley 2000:180).

Social life is permeated by gender orders—categories and hierarchies related to gender. Moreover, except in extraordinary circumstances, everyone presents some kind of "genderedness" (whether a traditional gendered category or a transgressive one). Therefore, questions of gender span the range of human activity. To give just a few examples: researchers have studied such diverse groups as schoolchildren, fraternity brothers, body builders, phone sex workers, and convicted rapists in order to observe how people in these groups jointly construct the meaning of maleness and femaleness and "do gender" in the course of their social interactions. Other researchers have studied gendered power relations in contexts including dating relationships, heterosexual marriages, workplaces, and academic settings. Intimate violence—an extreme of power—has been a topic of special concern to feminists, with many studies of the experiences of victims (and, less commonly, perpetrators) of rape, childhood sexual abuse, and physical violence. Other researchers have investigated sexual identities, work that has challenged conventional notions of an orderly progression of "stages" of identity development and of unitary and stable "sexual orientations." Yet other researchers have studied heterosexist, heteronormative, and homophobic discourses and practices, showing how they are deployed in everyday contexts to shore up a speaker's heterosexual identity, patrol the boundaries of masculinity, and otherwise ensure the hegemony of heterosexuality.

Recognizing the power invested in the mental health professions (and the ever-expanding self-help culture that is its populist counterpart), feminists have paid special attention to gendered meanings in the knowledge base of psychiatry and clinical psychology. They have paid special attention to the official codification of disorders and the disputes over certain categories of disorder. Researchers have investigated how some behaviors categorized as psychiatric symptoms paradoxically enact or symbolize qualities that are valued ways of being male or female. Others have investigated gendered meanings and gender-based power hierarchies in psychotherapy and in other aspects of mental health treatment. Yet other feminist discursive workers have examined linguistic practices that therapists can use to disrupt gendered power hierarchies and to open possibilities of more progressive and equitable gender enactments.

We now turn to two concrete examples of feminist discursive projects. First, we describe the research program of Nigel Edley and Margaret Wetherell on the conversational production of masculinities. With their focus on boys' conversations, Edley and Wetherell offer a close analysis of male gender enactment at the most local level. In contrast, Nicola Gavey's research, our second example, focuses on cultural discourses about masculinity, femininity, and male-female relations and their connection to individual women's experiences of unwanted sex.

The Conversational Details of Modern Masculinities

Margaret Wetherell and Nigel Edley, two psychologists based in the United Kingdom, have looked closely at interaction patterns in conversations, while also training an eye on the culture-specific interpretative resources available to speakers. Their research focuses on the local production and negotiation of masculinity in interactions and they consequently stress agency in their analyses. Wetherell and Edley conceptualize masculinity as those activities—behaviors, forms of talk, stories, and so on—that are seen as masculine in a particular cultural context. In a typical British context, those activities might include watching soccer games, drinking beer at the pub, being the first off when a traffic light changes to green, doing some carpentry and household repairs, and tending to the lawn.

Performing such activities causes a man to be perceived as having masculine inner traits (that is, as being a manly person), not simply as being a person who happens to be performing activities coded as male in his culture. This is so because prevailing commonsense notions conceptualize masculinity as a set of inner traits. In contrast, Wetherell and Edley do not view such activities as symptoms of masculinity. Instead, they see the practices themselves as producing masculinity. For them, masculinity is not a set of inner mental precursors such as "masculine traits." Instead, masculinity is something men and boys achieve in daily interaction with other people; it is a *consequence* of masculine-coded behaviors, not their cause. When men and boys behave in accord with their culture's norms of masculinity, they are seen by themselves and others as masculine. Moreover, many of these activities become mundane routines. As a result, they come to be perceived as "natural" and then perhaps attributed to biology or evolution. At the same time, individuals who stray from prevailing ideals and norms incur harsh social sanctions. In this way, social forces define not only the "good" or proper ways of being a man or boy but also what is not proper or good in a specific context. Masculinity is thus both socially constructed and socially restricted. Edley and Wetherell illuminate in close detail how the construction and restriction take place in young men's talk.

Wetherell and Edley focused on conversations among small groups of boys or young adult men, facilitated by a male researcher. Their work was guided by the orienting assumptions we have described above, but with their own twist, derived partly from feminist theory and partly from a desire to make use of the range of contributions offered by discursive psychologists (Edley 2006; Wetherell 1998). They pay close attention to conversational patterns in talk about gendered topics. They are attuned both to how speakers navigate the demands and expectations in their local social settings and to the larger sociopolitical backdrop. Four analytic concepts are key in their studies: interpretative repertoires, subject positions, the rhetorical character of talking and thinking, and ideological dilemmas.

Gendered interpretative repertoires. When the young men in Wetherell and Edley's studies told stories and gave accounts of their experiences, they frequently appealed to the shared views, knowledge, and opinions that united them as a group. Discursive psychologists call such collective views interpretative repertoires. An interpretative repertoire is, to quote Wetherell, "a culturally familiar and habitual line of argument comprised of recognizable themes, commonplaces and tropes (doxa)" (1998:400). The term "interpretative repertoire" is closely related to the term "discourse"; both refer to distinctive ways of talking about things. However, researchers who speak of "interpretative repertoires" tend to be interested in local meanings and in individuals' efforts to navigate among those meanings. Those who use the term "discourse" tend to focus on the broader culture and to be more concerned with the ways that cultural discourses form or influence subjective experience and knowledge (Edley 2001). The use of the term "interpretative repertoire," then, usually signals a researcher's emphasis on agency.

To exemplify: Wetherell and Edley analyzed how a group of teenage boys discussed the sexual exploits one of them had had during the previous weekend (Edley 2001; Wetherell 1998; Wetherell and Edley 1998). In the conversation, these young men accessed such interpretative repertoires as the following: male sexuality as performance and achievement; sexuality as a basic instinct easily released by being drunk; sex as something that a man should feel lucky to get; sexual relations as rightfully restricted to long-term committed relationships, not one-night stands; and sex as fun, healthy, and enjoyed equally by men and women. These different repertoires, as one might guess, positioned the speakers in dramatically different ways. As we shall see below, identifying gendered positionings is part of these researchers' strategies.

Gendered subject positions. Subject positions can be thought of as "places to stand" in a particular conversation. Wetherell and Edley stress that because subject positions are activated in relation to interaction partners, they are relative and transitory localizations. Of course, different standing places are not equal in prestige and power. The relative power and status associated with a subject position are often connected to gender. As long as power is not equally distributed to men and women, we can expect that subject positions that are gendered will differ in power.

Subject positions do not differ only in power; they also differ in the degree to which they are troubled or untroubled. In the boys' conversation about sexual exploits, the researchers noted that speakers referred to different interpretative repertoires. Those references gave the speakers access to a variety of more or less comfortable subject positions as the conversation unfolded. Examples included being a sexual predator; being on the moral low ground because of irresponsible sex; being drunk and thus not accountable for one's actions; and being a responsible and loving committed partner. As the conversation proceeded, a boy would take up one position for a brief time and then abandon it in favor of another, possibly more comfortable, position. This illustrates an aspect of subject positions that Edley and Wetherell emphasize: such positions are not permanent. On the contrary, in ongoing conversation, people often change positions in an effort to accomplish certain conversational goals, such as placing themselves in a good light. Discursive psychologists call this striving "accountability management" (Horton-Salway 2001).

Thus, for Wetherell and Edley, people are active agents who—although invited into certain subject positions by societal forces and conversational interventions—constantly navigate and negotiate these positions in order to relocate themselves in positions they find comfortable. In any interaction, some positions are more comfortable (untroubled) than other positions, which will be felt as "troubled" (Wetherell 1998). Also, some positions may be troubled in one conversational setting but not in another.

For instance, for the young men in this study, the position of sexual predator seemed to be untroubled at some points in the conversation, but quite troubled at others.

Rhetorical thinking and ideological dilemmas. Wetherell and Edley stress that both speech and thinking are always rhetorical. That is, when people speak, they always relate to other people's points of view: they argue against them, agree with them, and so forth. Wetherell and Edley argue that thinking is best seen as conversation that has turned inward, a view inspired by Lev Vygotsky (Wertsch 1990) and Michael Billig and his coworkers (Billig, Condor et al. 1988). In this view, there is no clear-cut dividing line between the social and the psychological or between what is inside and what is outside an individual's mind. Thinking retains a great deal of the dialogical character of speech. A person's mind can be seen as a kind of meeting place for a multitude of voices that emanate from and are traces of the countless conversations that he or she has taken part in. Subjectivity is, therefore, fundamentally social and rhetorical, rather than individual and idiosyncratic.

Any culture contains many forceful and often divergent "voices," that is, opinions, contradictions, and oppositions. Therefore, individuals will always face an abundance of ideological dilemmas. In this usage, "ideology" refers to the practical ideas, rules, and ideals for handling daily life—what is often called "common sense." These ideas and rules are far from a coherent set; rather, they reflect the multiple conflicting voices in that culture. Any culture's common sense will provide voices and ideologies enough to enable one to account for all kinds of social and subjective activities (Billig 2006).

Edley and Wetherell (1999) listened to a group of young men in their late teens talk about their thoughts about their future lives. All the boys pictured themselves as living with a woman and having children, but the way they talked about combining parenthood and paid work showed the ideological dilemmas swirling around them. They talked about wanting children and wanting to be very involved with their children, but at the same time wanting to invest their energies in a career. They also talked about wanting an egalitarian relationship with the female partner, yet found it appropriate that she work only part-time or stay home with the children. Time and time again, the boys endorsed ideals of equality between themselves and their future partners, but then juxtaposed these ideals with practical considerations that would prevent equal sharing. Thus, they claimed to be free of sexism, while in the same breath defending gender inequality. To borrow Edley and Wetherell's words, such inconsistencies show how "these young men are the battleground upon which the war between cultural ideals is raging" (1999:186).

Wetherell and Edley's research shows how feminist discursive psychology can help bring to light at least some of the mundane processes by which subjectivity is continually being gendered in culturally predictable ways. Next we turn to a different but complementary approach to discursive psychology, one that highlights broad cultural meanings associated with gender and the ways in which those meanings shape individual women's subjective experience in sexual encounters and the range of interaction possibilities open to them.

The Psychology and Technologies of Heterosexual Coercion

Nicola Gavey, a New Zealand–based researcher, has studied women's experiences of unwanted sex and rape. She analyzed women's choices in sexual encounters, which are often limited. Her findings suggest that today's cultural exhortations to "just say no" to unwanted sex are at best simplistic and at worst an invitation to victim-blaming. Gavey's work draws on feminist theories, poststructural theory, and discursive psychology, although with a different focus from that of Wetherell and Edley. Gavey gives priority to examining how the wider historical and political context bears on women's experiences and actions. She therefore focuses on the cultural discourses that impinge on and form women's subjectivity. Her argument is that discourses on gender and sexuality typically serve as a cultural scaffolding for male-centered heterosexuality and often obliterate the experiences of female partners. When these discourses about sexuality dominate, women often find that saying "no" to a male partner who wants sex feels virtually impossible. Often this leads women to accept actions that might otherwise be called rape. How does this come about? What are the specific discourses and how are they deployed in sexual encounters? How do these discourses inflect women's narratives of their sexual experiences? Gavey's work seeks to answer questions like these.

Gavey takes as her starting point the assertion that sexual desires, practices, and identities are not natural but are constituted through various normative discourses and practices that position women and men differently in relation to sexuality (Gavey 2005). For Gavey, the power relations between women and men are implicated in the construction of men's and women's sexuality. She builds much of her theoretical argument on Michel Foucault's study of the history of sexuality (1980; 1981). However, she finds it necessary to add lessons from feminist theory (Bordo 1997). To quote Gavey, "It has to be said that attention to the specificities of gender is lamentably absent in Foucault's analysis of power and sexuality" (2005:91). She also reminds readers of feminists' analyses of the body as a site for the exercise of power, noting that these contributions have often been omitted from the history of discourse theory (cf. Bordo 1993). Below we describe some important practices and assumptions of her approach.

Discourse analysis of women's narratives of heterosexual experiences. Gavey's work is based on in-depth, semistructured interviews in which women relate accounts of sexual encounters with male partners, particularly those encounters that were not consensual. When analyzing the accounts, Gavey assumes that people's ways of talking about their experiences and living their lives are grounded in cultural discourses. Following from this assumption, she focuses on the relationship between talk and actions. She reads interview texts for what they reveal about cultural discourses regarding sexuality, actual sexual practice, and how these two are related (Gavey 2005). She thus combines a discursive reading of women's stories with a reading that takes them as realistic descriptions of events. Although this might seem contradictory, Gavey argues that it is necessary in order to "generat[e] a materially grounded understanding of how the discursive characteristics (meanings and practices) of gender and heterosexual sex can limit possibilities for women's agency in heterosexual encounters" (2005:98).

Gavey draws on the seminal work of Wendy Hollway (1984) to identify dominant discourses of heterosexuality in contemporary culture. Contemporary male sexuality is to a great extent shaped by what Hollway called the "male sexual drive discourse." This discourse holds that sexual desire is a strong and often overwhelming drive that all men experience, and one that men are compelled to satisfy. Gavey argues that this discourse often puts women in a position where they have little agency or choice in heterosexual encounters. Gavey's analysis draws upon Michel Foucault's (1981) concept "power/knowledge."

Gendered power/knowledge and subjectivity. "Power" for Foucault and Gavey means both power in its ordinary sense and also being able to do something. Knowledge means understanding in a wide sense. Coupling power and knowledge highlights how one is able to do something only in relation to how one is able to make sense of it (Gavey 2005). This means that a dominant discourse—the culturally accepted way of making sense of things—inevitably enables and constrains what people are able to do.

Gavey claims that the cultural sense-making of heterosexuality and its practice have distributed benefits and burdens unevenly between women and men. This unevenness has led to a culturally approved gendered complementarity: the male sex drive discourse is usually complemented by what Hollway (1984) termed "the have/hold discourse." In this discourse, sex for women is understood as a means to an end (preferably achieving a monogamous relationship with a man) rather than an end in itself. Gavey argues that these and other traditional male-related and female-related discourses work in concert to prescribe heterosexual desire and other aspects of heterosexual relationships. In doing this, the discourses specify the range of possible subjectivities for women and for men (Gavey 2005). Subjectivity is not wholly determined by these discourses, however; people can actively select among them.

Disciplinary power, gender, and sex. "Disciplinary power" is Foucault's term for denoting how, in contemporary society, human life is regulated through "the power of the Norm" (Foucault 1979:184). Throughout modern history such regulation has become increasingly more internalized and voluntary, involving self-surveillance and voluntary conformity (Foucault 1979). Social institutions (for example, schools, universities, hospitals, workplaces, the law, heterosexual marriage, and psychology) are sites for different kinds of disciplining. Disciplinary power is nearly invisible, appearing simply as standards for how people are expected to live, to which people willingly comply. Disciplinary power is thus not merely constraining, it is also productive. It produces meanings, practices, and desires that people wish to embrace. The meanings, practices, and desires that compose gender are produced through such disciplinary processes.

Gavey's research explores the disciplinary power involved in producing gendered meanings, desires, and practices of hetero-sex (Gavey's term for heterosexual intercourse). In her analyses of women's accounts of their experiences of coercion, Gavey highlights the subject positions that the dominant discourses of heterosexuality make available for women. Examples include "good lover," "frigid bitch," "paying your dues for flirting," and "sex as part of the job" of a wife. Gavey points out that hetero-sexual encounters can be narrated in culturally acceptable ways without any reference to a woman's desire or pleasure. In fact, she concludes, "the absence of a woman's desire and pleasure is not only permissible, but almost unremarkable" (Gavey 2005:142). To understand how this can be, Gavey examines the implicit knowledge that dominant discourses of sexuality pro-vide about "normal" and expected ways of being sexual.

Normalizing processes and gendered invisible knowledge. As mentioned above, what is taken as "normal" sexuality is shaped by domi-nant discourses such as the male sexual drive discourse and the have/hold discourse. Gavey argues that habitual "normal" rou-tines may also shape people's sexual desire. In the stories told by the women she interviewed, dominant discourses of sexuality produced certain kinds of invisible and unreflected knowledge. This knowledge limited the women's choices in heterosexual encounters. For the women to whom she spoke, simply "saying no" to a sexual overture was not all that simple, and often not a viable option at all.

Norms of femininity: The social production of compliant subjects. Domi-nant discourses of femininity may make it particularly difficult for women to resist the discourse of a strong male sex drive. Traditionally, good femininity has involved being nurturant and caring, worrying about others before oneself, being gentle and sometimes acquiescent, and not asserting one's own needs and wants. An assertive and forceful "no" to unwanted sex may ill fit a woman's image of herself (and her partner's image of her as well) (Gavey 2005). Yet according to the women Gavey interviewed, a quiet "no" often is not enough. In nonconsent situations, a woman must either force herself to step out of traditional femininity to assert her "no" forcefully or remain within the bounds of femininity and acquiesce. For Gavey's interviewees, the first option went against a number of taken-for-granted notions about femininity and masculinity. The second option, which acquiesces to the male sex drive discourse, served to "save the face" of the situation. For a large number of the women, the second course of action was preferred, at least partly because it resonated with their image of what kind of woman they were. In Gavey's words, "some women may experience it as 'easier' to 'let sex happen' than to keep resisting when they don't want it" (2005:152).

Cultural scaffolding of "consent": What if she had said "no"? Decisions and choices are always made within a context, or what Gavey refers to as cultural scaffolding. "Free choice" must always be understood within the limits of the cultural scaffolding that surrounds it. This cultural scaffolding limits what options are available and also sets the costs and benefits connected to each option. A woman's "free choice" to say no to sex must be understood within the limits of the cultural scaffolding of heterosexuality. It is this context that sets the consequences if a woman makes a choice other than the culturally preferred one. Gavey argues that because of the cultural scaffolding of heterosexuality as male-centered sexuality, women often consent to sex for reasons unrelated to their own sexual desire. These include wanting to protect a man's ego, wanting to avoid being seen as a "frigid bitch," wishing to avoid violent coercion, and putting an end to relentless nagging (Gavey 1992).

Gavey's work is an example of a type of feminist discursive psychology that emphasizes the role of the broader cultural context in forming women's subjective experiences, including their experiences of choice and consent. This analytic approach focuses less on the details of interactions, and more on women's accounts of their experiences. Also, the approach takes a "both/and" position by analyzing interviewees' accounts for traces of cultural discourses while holding them to be realist accounts of events that happened.

Taking Stock: The Possibilities and Problems of Feminist Discursive Psychology

We hope that our descriptions of the research programs of Wetherell, Edley, and Gavey have convinced you that feminist discursive approaches are a useful way to gain insight into the workings of gender in everyday life. In what follows, we stand back to consider briefly what the melding of discursive approaches and feminist thought has yielded thus far. Then we consider some tensions that feminist discursive psychologists face.

Most important, feminist discursive psychology has opened areas of study to psychologists that were previously unimaginable. Discursive psychologists look beyond the "small s" social of small groups (often no more than random groups of college students temporarily assembled in the laboratory) to ask questions about the capital S Social, society. Feminist discursive researchers have also brought cultural gender politics into the study of psychic life and social behavior. Not only have they insisted that personal experience cannot be divorced from culture and society, they have also begun to develop conceptual and methodological tools to study their interrelation.

Feminist discursive psychologists have also emphasized critical reflection on the discipline of psychology. For them, any discipline—no matter how scientific it claims to be—is inevitably embedded in its cultural surround. They have studied how dominant discourses shape psychological knowledge and practice, cycling from the larger culture into scientific knowledge and back again, now stamped with the imprimatur of science (e.g., Crawford 1995). They have also identified the traces of cultural discourses in the diagnoses, treatment practices, and research findings of the mental health professions (e.g., Gremillion 2002).

Feminist discursive psychologists have pressed gender researchers to reformulate (or even jettison) some old questions. For example, they questioned the merits of studying sex differences (cf. the collection of essays edited by Celia Kitzinger [1994]). Taking a strong constructionist position, one of us has suggested that the voluminous literature on psychological sex differences should be read as an archive of shifting cultural narratives about the sexes rather than as a record of progressively more accurate and refined answers to the "difference question" (Marecek 1995).

Lastly, feminist discursive research projects often yield novel ways of thinking about social problems that can lead to novel solutions. The studies by Edley, Wetherell, and others on masculinities, and by Gavey and others on gendered sexuality and heterosexual coercion, for example, suggest new ways to address heterosexual coercion, gay-bashing, bullying, sexual harassment, and wife-beating. The studies typically shift the focus away from the search for a few "bad apples" (deviant, criminal, or mentally disturbed individuals) to the larger cultural meanings and discourses that exonerate bad behavior not only in the perpetrators' minds but also in the minds of bystanders, police, juries, and perhaps even victims.

Across the disciplines, discursive and interpretive approaches have raised political concerns of a substantive sort for some feminists. They have been concerned that the rejection of gender essentialism and acceptance of postmodern ideas may undermine the category "women" as a valid basis for politics. This, they say, is particularly worrying because it comes at a time when women have been successfully mobilizing politically around that identity. Feminist scholars have further worried that an emphasis on the socially negotiated nature of reality can slide into a relativism that obviates any moral or ethical stance against injustice. This is an issue that has been vigorously debated not only by feminist philosophers but also by postmodern thinkers. A related critical issue for feminist and other discursive workers is how to theorize the relation of subjectivity to the social surround without losing sight entirely of the self and relinquishing the possibility of agency. As we saw, both Wetherell and Edley and Gavey were attentive to this need in their work. The issue of social determinism is an area of ongoing discussion in all discursive approaches, and it is mentioned in several other essays in this book.

Another critical consideration for feminist discursive psychologists is the reception of their work by other psychologists. This is a concern shared by many of the approaches discussed in this book. Many conventionally trained psychologists and students find discursive work alien and confusing. One stumbling block is that its language is different from the language to which they are accustomed. Another is that discursive studies do not yield the universalized "if-then" assertions or cut-and-dried "sound bites" that conventional psychology often serves up. Such intelligibility problems have made it difficult for discursive approaches to gain ground in psychology, even as discursive studies have become part of the standard repertoire of approaches in other social science disciplines. Often, psychologists who reject feminist discursive studies are unaware that such work is founded on different metatheoretical and epistemological assumptions from their own. It is crucial for feminist discursive researchers to clarify such fundamental differences. At the same time, it is important to explicate the points of similarity between conventional research and feminist discursive research (cf. Burman 1997; Camic, Rhodes, and Yardley 2003).

Feminist discursive psychology is not a finished project. Many of the intellectual puzzles that feminist discursive psychologists have faced continue to demand attention and effort. Perhaps especially, there is more work to be done to understand the complicated intersections of gender and other markers of social identity and hierarchy, such as race/ethnicity, age, class, sexual identity, and disability.

We have argued that feminist discursive psychology offers both a powerful theoretical framework for understanding gender and a useful set of research tools. "The personal is political" has been a touchstone of the feminist movement since the 1960s. Discursive psychology provides a means to make that slogan into a practical mandate for feminist research. As can be seen above, it enables the study of mundane conversational power relations—what we might call the micropolitics of gender. It also brings the study of cultural gender politics into the purview of psychology. Further, it offers some tools to study what Foucault has called "power from below," that is, the process by which dominant discourses come to shape individual subjectivity.

Nearly thirty years ago, Mary Brown Parlee (1979), in a review essay titled "Psychology and women," urged feminist psychologists to incorporate key texts of feminist theory—work "too rich for the blood" of conventional psychologists—in their work. She further challenged feminists in psychology to invent ways to interrogate the conditions of women's everyday reality. Feminist discursive psychologists have taken up the challenges that Parlee posed.

References

Billig, M. 2006. A psychoanalytic discursive psychology: From consciousness to unconsciousness. *Discourse Studies* 8:17–24.

Billig, M., S. Condor, D. Edwards, M. Gane, D. Middleton, and A. Radley. 1988. *Ideological Dilemmas: A Social Psychology of Everyday Thinking.* London: Sage.

Bohan, J. 1993. Regarding gender: Essentialism, constructionism, and feminist psychology. *Psychology of Women Quarterly* 17:5–21.

Bordo, S. 1993. Feminism, Foucault, and the politics of the body. In C. Ramaza-noglu, ed., *Up Against Foucault: Explorations of Some Tensions Between Foucault and Feminism*, 179–202. New York: Routledge.

——. 1997. *Twilight Zones: The Hidden Life of Cultural Images from Plato to O.J.* Berkeley: University of California Press.

Burman, E. 1997. Minding the gap: Positivism, psychology, and the politics of qualitative methods. *Journal of Social Issues* 53:785–802.

Camic, P. M., J. E. Rhodes, and L. Yardley, eds. 2003. *Qualitative Research in Psychology: Expanding Perspectives in Methodology and Design*. Washington, DC: American Psychological Association.

Crawford, M. E. 1995. *Talking Difference: On Gender and Language*. London: Sage.

Crossley, M. L. 2000. *Introducing Narrative Psychology: Self, Trauma, and the Construction of Meaning*. London: Open University Press.

Davies, B., and R. Harré. 1990. Positioning: The discursive production of selves. *Journal for the Theory of Social Behaviour* 20:43–65.

Edley, N. 2001. Analysing masculinity: Interpretative repertoires, ideological dilemmas, and subject positions. In M. Wetherell, S. Taylor, and S. J. Yates, eds., *Discourse as Data: A Guide for Analysis*, 189–229. London: Sage.

——. 2006. Never the twain shall meet: A critical appraisal of the combination of discourse and psychoanalytic theory in studies of men and masculinity. *Sex Roles* 55:601–608.

Edley, N., and M. Wetherell. 1999. Imagined futures: Young men's talk about fatherhood and domestic life. *British Journal of Social Psychology* 38:181–194.

Fausto-Sterling, A. 2000. *Sexing the Body*. New York: Basic Books.

Foucault, M. 1979. *Discipline and Punish: The Birth of the Prison*. London: Penguin.

——. 1980. Truth and power. In C. Gordon, ed., *Power/Knowledge: Selected Interviews and Other Writings, 1972–1977*, 109–133. New York: Pantheon.

——. 1981. *The History of Sexuality* 1: *An Introduction*. Harmondsworth: Penguin.

Franklin, K. 2004. Enacting masculinity: Antigay violence and group rape as participatory theater. *Sexuality Research and Social Policy* 1:25–40.

Gavey, N. 1992. Technologies and effects of heterosexual coercion. *Feminism & Psychology* 2:325–351.

——. 2005. *Just Sex? The Cultural Scaffolding of Rape*. London: Routledge.

Gremillion, H. 2002. In fitness and in health: Crafting bodies in the treatment of anorexia nervosa. *Signs* 27:381–414.

Hammonds, E. 1997. Toward a genealogy of black female sexuality: The problematic of silence. In M. J. Alexander and C. T. Mohanty, eds., *Feminist Genealogies, Colonial Legacies, Democratic Futures*, 170–182. New York: Routledge.

Haraway, D. 1988. Situated knowledges: The science question in feminism and the privilege of partial perspective. *Feminist Studies* 14:575–599.

Harding, S. 1986. *The Science Question in Feminism*. Ithaca, NY: Cornell University Press.

——. 1991. *Whose Science? Whose Knowledge? Thinking from Women's Lives*. Buckingham: Open University Press.

Hare-Mustin, R.T., and J. Marecek. 1990. *Making a Difference: Psychology and the Construction of Gender*. New Haven: Yale University Press.

Herdt, G. H. 1998. *Same Sex, Different Cultures*. New York: HarperCollins.

Hollway, W. 1984. Gender difference and the production of subjectivity. In J. Henriques, W. Hollway, C. Urwin, C. Venn, and V. Walkerdine, *Changing the Subject: Psychology, Social Regulation, and Subjectivity*, 227–263. London: Methuen.

Horton-Salway, M. 2001. The construction of M.E.: The discursive action model. In M. Wetherell, S. Taylor, and S. J. Yates, eds., *Discourse as Data: A Guide for Analysis*, 147–188. London: Sage.

Jayawardena, K. 2007. *Erasure of the Euro-Asian: Recovering Early Radicalism and Feminism in South Asia*. Colombo, Sri Lanka: Social Scientists' Association.

Kitzinger, C., ed. 1994. Should psychologists study sex differences? Special feature. *Feminism & Psychology* 4:501–546.

Marecek, J. 1995. Gender, politics, and psychology's ways of knowing. *American Psychologist* 50:162–163.

——. 2001. After the facts: Psychology and the study of gender. *Canadian Psychology* 42:254–267.

Morawski, J. G. 1994. *Practicing Feminisms, Reconstructing Psychology: Notes on a Liminal Science*. Ann Arbor: University of Michigan Press.

Parlee, M. B. 1979. Psychology and women. *Signs* 5:121–133.

——. 1996. Situated knowledges of personal embodiment: Transgender activists' and psychological theorists' perspectives on "sex" and "gender." *Theory & Psychology* 6:625–645.

Rose, N. 1996. *Inventing Ourselves: Psychology, Power, and Personhood*. New York: Cambridge University Press.

Stewart, A., and C. McDermott. 2004. Gender in psychology. *Annual Review of Psychology* 55:519–544.

Wertsch, J. 1990. *Voices of the Mind: A Sociocultural Approach to Mediated Action*. London: Harvester Wheatsheaf.

West, C., and D. H. Zimmerman. 1987. Doing gender. *Gender & Society* 1:125–151.

Wetherell, M. 1998. Positioning and interpretative repertoires: Conversation analysis and post-structuralism in dialogue. *Discourse & Society* 9:387–412.

Wetherell, M., and N. Edley. 1998. Gender practices: Steps in the analysis of men and masculinities. In K. Henwood, C. Griffin, and A. Phoenix, eds., *Standpoints and Differences: Essays in the Practice of Feminist Psychology*, 156–173. London: Sage.

——. 1999. Negotiating hegemonic masculinity: Imaginary positions and psycho-discursive practices. *Feminism & Psychology* 9:335–356.

Wetherell, M., and J. Potter. 1992. *Mapping the Language of Racism: Discourse and the Legitimation of Exploitation*. New York: Harvester Wheatsheaf.

Part II

Hermeneutic Approaches

Hermeneutics and Sociocultural
Perspectives in Psychology

FRANK C. RICHARDSON AND BLAINE J. FOWERS

The chapters in this book wrestle with the question of what it
means to view psychological processes and human action as not just facilitated by culture and society but actually constituted by them. In our view,
raising and trying to answer this question takes social inquiry to a new
and long overdue level of seriousness and maturity. We will address this
question from the point of view of philosophical hermeneutics (Gadamer
1989; Guignon 1991; Heidegger 1962; Taylor 1989) and interpretive social
science (Bishop 2007; Richardson, Fowers, and Guignon 1999; Slife
and Williams 1995). In the hermeneutic view, there are subtleties in the
matter of sociocultural perspectives on psychological phenomena that
require careful attention. One is that since humans are involved in some
sense as active, responsible agents in social and cultural life, it would
appear that there is a profound and intimate kind of mutual influence, or
co-constitution, between the "forces" of history, culture, and society, on the
one hand, and psychological processes, on the other. Another issue, easy
to overlook, is that the human activities of social theory, research, and the
interpretation of research findings themselves have to be counted among
the psychological processes that are thoroughly embedded in and constituted by culture and society. Thus, social theory and research are "a form
of practice" (Richardson and Christopher 1993; Taylor 1985b). They do not

stand apart from the human fray with some sort of pristine objectivity. Rather, they are entirely among the practical, moral, or spiritual things that human beings do in working out the meaning of their lives.

The Hermeneutic Tradition

The term "hermeneutics" comes from the Greek word for interpretation, and the field is sometimes called the theory of interpretation. Early in its development in the sixteenth century, the aim of hermeneutics was seen as providing methods for interpreting texts, especially scripture and ancient texts, works whose meaning or application no longer seemed entirely clear in a new age. Friedrich Schleiermacher (1768–1834) clarified the famous "hermeneutic circle," according to which our understanding of any part of a text, work, or individual life is shaped by our initial understanding of the *whole* of it. At the same time, however, our understanding of that whole is continually revised by our encounter with and modified understanding of its *parts*.[1]

Wilhelm Dilthey (1833–1911) expanded Schleiermacher's ideas into a general theory of interpretation for the human sciences.[2] Dilthey argued that we do not come to understand our objects in the human sciences by subsuming them under general laws. Rather, we understand a work of art or historical event when we immediately grasp its meaning in terms of categories of significance, purpose, or value, categories generally absent from the constructions (laws and theories) of the natural sciences. According to Dilthey, this kind of understanding is not a narrowly rational process but involves all of our mental powers of intellect, empathy, and will.

In the end, Dilthey's philosophy of the human sciences never resolved a deep tension or contradiction in his thought, some version of which we still struggle with today. On the one hand, he saw all of our efforts to understand as part of a historical flux in which we are inextricably embedded—and thus can never fully objectify. Our understanding of the wider context of a work or event significantly influences our understanding of it, at the same time that the way we come to interpret the meaning of that work or event shapes, in turn, our understanding of its wider context.[3] On the other hand, Dilthey was troubled by relativism. He was very much a modern thinker, influenced by the Enlightenment, who still held out hope of finding some way or method to objectively ground our interpretations of meaningful human phenomena. When the dilemma is framed in this way, however, it is hard to see any way out of it.[4] By the end of the nineteenth century, it had become clear that hermeneutics could not remain focused on developing techniques for interpretation because the attempt to develop a method of interpretation evoked all of the contradictions and dilemmas of the subject-object dichotomy. For this reason, hermeneutics embarked on a more thoroughgoing ontological inquiry into the being of those entities that understand and interpret, that is, human beings. It was felt that only by deeply rethinking the very nature of the human realm and human being would it be possible both to capture the fullness of lived experience, as Dilthey wished to do, and yet clarify how we might reasonably conclude that some interpretations (and moral judgments) are better than others.

That is a tall order, indeed! To move toward this goal, contemporary hermeneutics tries to work out a conception of humans as self-interpreting beings whose existence is shaped by a shared background of meanings. We will outline this view below. First, however, it may be useful to sketch the hermeneutic analysis of some of the dominant views of what social science is or should be that have crystallized over the last century or so. In the effort to understand, as hermeneutics sees it, we are always going "back to the future" through reinterpretation of the inherited views and values that shape our outlook on the world. Often, the challenge involves questioning some of our key presuppositions, rather than just making needed adjustments while still perpetuating unawares the assumptions of the viewpoint we are trying to reform or revise.

Mainstream Social Science

The bulk of twentieth- and twenty-first-century social science has been guided by an ideal of explanatory or empirical theory. That ideal means going beyond finding raw correlations among interesting variables and achieving law-like correlations that are *both* theoretically derived *and* empirically confirmed. Only theory that permits precise predictions extending beyond what has already been observed is thought to constitute genuine knowledge or to benefit practice by allowing us to instrumentally influence the course of events in a reliable manner. Moreover, as Moon points out, "even radical post-Kuhnian views of social science continue to accept at least tacitly the naturalist view of scientific explanation in terms of the subsumption of individual events under general laws," or a "nomological account of explanation" (1983:172).

Serious doubts have been voiced for decades, both within and without the social sciences, about whether genuine empirical theory of this sort ever has been or could be achieved in connection with human action in its real-life social and historical settings (Flyvbjerg 2001; Gergen 1982; Taylor 1985b). Correlational and experimental findings may illumine patterns and relationships among events in the social world. But the *reason* they do so cannot be that they reflect universally applicable causal laws or models of the sort regularly uncovered in the natural sciences. Well-developed theory to ground them is simply lacking. Without necessarily adopting all of his social constructionist viewpoint, one might agree with Kenneth Gergen's astute observation that a "fundamental difference exists between the bulk of the phenomena of concern to the natural as opposed to the sociobehavioral scientist." Thus, "there appears to be little justification for the immense effort devoted to the empirical substantiation of fundamental laws of human conduct. There would seem to be few patterns of human action, regardless of their durability to date, that are not subject to significant alteration" (1982:12).

This failure to achieve the kind of explanatory power so evident in the natural sciences leads many to doubt that it is either possible or desirable for mainstream social scientists to attempt to detach themselves from influencing and being influenced by cultural and moral values to the extent they would like. The ideal of value-freedom or value-neutrality in the field of psychology has probably fostered much in the way of honesty, fairness, and careful thinking. But surely it has caused much confusion and done real harm as well (Richardson 2005; Slife, Smith, and Burchfield 2003). A little reflection suggests that dedication to this ideal embroils researchers in the paradox of firmly believing that they *ought* to be strictly neutral or objective. This is not just a conceptual contradiction but a concrete, existential one. The kind of wholehearted dedication to this ideal demanded of theorists (and psychotherapists) is exactly the same kind of heartfelt allegiance to particular cultural and moral values they are morally charged to spurn at all costs! In the absence of genuine empirical theory and actual value-neutrality, we are left with a most unsettling question: On what *basis*, then, do working social scientists interpret their findings and correlations? The philosopher David Hoy observes that

> theory choice in the social sciences is . . . more relativistic than in the natural sciences, since the principles used to select social theories would be guided by a variety of values. Unlike a natural scien-

tist's explanation, which relies on the pragmatic criterion of predictive success, a social scientist's evaluation of the data in terms of a commitment to a social theory would be more like taking a political stand.   (1986:124)

"Descriptivisms"

In the absence of the achievement of incontestable "science," mainstream social science has long been haunted by a sense of self-doubt, even if covered over with bravado. Over the course of the twentieth century, this worry, along with doubts about the meaningfulness of its findings and, to many, concern about its acutely depersonalizing accounts of human phenomena, has led to diverse efforts to rethink the field. Increasingly refined arguments have been mounted to the effect that difficulties in achieving explanatory theories of social reality may be due to a profound epistemological inappropriateness of the explanatory ideal to its subject matter. D'Andrade captures the essence of many of these critiques with his suggestion that conventional models of scientific explanation seem inadequate to describe the "semiotic sciences," inquiry that studies "'imposed' order based on 'meaning' rather than on natural or physical order." This kind of imposed order "creates meaning and is created by the attempt to convey meaning." It is an "arbitrary order, which can change rapidly and varies from place to place and time to time" (1986:22). In other words, human actions and emotions, indeed our very selves, unlike events in the natural world, are symbolically structured aspects of social reality. They are constituted by their location within the practices and norms of "language games," traditions, or forms of life. Thus, they would be different if these practices and norms were different. A radical implication of this view is, as Taylor puts it, that "personal interpretation enters into the very definition of the phenomenon under study" (1985a:121).

Ideas of this sort concerning meaningful human action have been incorporated into social inquiry via phenomenological approaches, ethnomethodology, and many kinds of "qualitative" research. Bernstein (1976) suggests the helpful label "descriptivist" for these approaches. But Bernstein also argues convincingly that descriptivist approaches typically adhere to some degree to the ideal of the purely disinterested or morally neutral theorist. Descriptivists fail to gauge the extent to which we ourselves are historically and practically or morally embedded in the realities into which we inquire, making disinterested neutrality quite impossible and aspirations to it possibly inauthentic and harmful.

The Achilles heel of descriptivist approaches has always been a fatal ambiguity about the extent to which the descriptions are more than the investigators' constructions. They speak as if we were giving some kind of objective account of the patterns of action or meaning studied, without which it would appear that "anything goes." But there is good reason to think that all such accounts are creative, value-influenced interpretations of the reality portrayed. Indeed, there appears to be an ongoing relationship of mutual influence or, more precisely, co-constitution between interpreter and object. The descriptivist metatheory leaves us with the uncomfortable dilemma of having to choose between an unattainable "objectivism" or a distressing "relativism" (Bernstein 1983), with no good alternative in sight.

Moreover, there is the problem of ideology (Bernstein 1976; Habermas 1991). If the self-understandings of social actors contain systematic distortions that reflect the sorts of repressions and rationalizations Freudians and Marxists analyze (which surely they sometimes do), descriptivist accounts will be poor at detecting them. They will tend to portray oppressed workers as happy campers and grim workaholics as proud citizens because of the accepted ideology of their society (accepted by the workers and workaholics, too), and thus uncritically support the status quo.

Social Constructionism

In view of these difficulties, it is perhaps no wonder that a variety of postmodern and social constructionist theorists bite the bullet and fully accept, or even try to make a virtue of, what they take to be the inescapable value-ladenness and hence (they feel) ultimate arbitrariness of social research and theory. This approach is richly exemplified by leading American social constructionist thinkers like Gergen (1982; 1985), Rorty (1982), and Sampson (1985), who weave some of the critiques of mainstream social science and insights discussed above into a somewhat coherent and compelling new metatheoretical option for social inquiry.

The social constructionist orientation opposes the modern, decontextualized view of the self with what it takes to be a radically contextualized alternative. In this view, humanity is "a self-interpreting way of being whose practices have enabled it to act as if it had a whole series of different natures in the course of history" (Dreyfus 1987:65). Culture does not differently clothe the universal human; it infuses individuals, fundamentally shaping them. The patterns of human life are for the most part "social artifacts," not naturalistically lawful occurrences. In life and social theory, there is "no 'truth through method'" (Gergen 1985:272). Rather, in both, understanding results from an ongoing "negotiation of meanings." This frees us up to characterize the meanings, stories, and norms that imbue our practices and institutions in appropriate terms, as the rich cultural forms they are. Both social theory and the worlds it represents are products of the rules or conventions of a particular community. But such theory lacks any independent "factual warrant." Familiar modern gaps between theory and practice, subject and object, and fact and value are closed to a great degree in this approach. The "facts" of our life-world are really embodied meanings, to which we gain access mainly as participants. We interpret them, or negotiate interpretations of them, in the ongoing business of living.

In this view, our theories, narratives, and values lack any objective foundation beyond the swirl of negotiated meanings in our life-world. The only appropriate basis for evaluating our beliefs and practices is according to their "pragmatic implications" (Gergen 1985:275). This means that we evaluate theories or narratives in terms of our preferred ends or values, and that our success in getting others to pursue the ends we favor depends on our "capacity to invite, compel, stimulate, or delight the audience, and not on criteria of veracity" (Gergen 1985:272).

Social constructionism reinforces and clarifies our understanding of human action as embedded in webs of significance, and moves beyond "descriptivisms" by illuminating further how our theories are creative interpretations of social reality that shape it and are shaped by it in turn. It stresses that social theory is a historically embedded activity, profoundly conditioned by the cultural context in which it takes place; as Gergen puts it, it is the "result of an active, cooperative enterprise of persons in relationships" (1985:267).

Nevertheless, social constructionism seems to convey a somewhat confused and implausible view of human agency. Individuals in this view appear to be at once both (a) radically contextualized in and shaped by society and history and (b) radically free to reinterpret social reality and themselves however they wish. This view of human agency gives voice to the general idea of our being shaped by history and culture as we shape them in return. But it does so with an odd blend of harsh determinism

and untrammeled freedom. We might ask: if we are radically contextualized, how do we get the leverage needed to radically reinterpret and reinvent ourselves? And, if we are remarkably free to reinterpret and redirect
our course in this way, why have we not just reproduced a version of the
radical freedom of the modern independent, self-subsistent, masterful
self—indeed, an almost existentialist version (Richardson and Christopher 1993) of that kind of self?—a strong form of the very sort of decontextualized human agency social constructionist theory helps us to cut
down to size and relocate in culture and history.

Also, social constructionism seems to have a serious problem with
moral relativism. It suggests that eliminating metaphysical and moral
universals will free us by itself from modern pretensions, return us to
some sort of historical belongingness, and foster more humane and fulfilling kinds of living. But what would keep us from completely throwing
out the cherished modern values of freedom and universal respect—some
version of which most of us are deeply committed to even if we do not
feel they are a sufficient ethics—in exchange for some comforting new
tyranny? And why would the newly invented vocabularies and practices
constructionists encourage us to endlessly invent and negotiate mean
anything to us? How could they foster any sense of purpose or conviction that might counter the temptation to sell out to modern illusions of
power and absoluteness, or to the distractions of a consumer society, or
to the role of victim in a "culture of narcissism," which some postmodern
theorists help to document?

In addition, there seems to be some difficulty with the key constructionist notion of evaluating our beliefs and values strictly in terms of their
"pragmatic implications." After all, it is hard to see how we can evaluate different belief systems or ways of life in this manner when what we
mean by pragmatically beneficial or deleterious in any given case will be
determined by the belief system or way of life we currently inhabit! Also,
there is the issue that evaluating our obligations strictly in terms of their
"pragmatic implications" is just not what most of us *mean* by making
commitments or exercising responsibility. In the place of any notion of
truer beliefs or more authentic narratives, constructionists would put a
"creative participation in the unending and unfolding meaning of life"
(Gergen and Kaye 1992:183). But it is difficult to see how, within this perspective, we might make our way from one point of view to another except
by some sort of arbitrary, unthinking lurch in one direction or another
(Taylor 1985a).

Finally, a close examination of social constructionist writings suggests that these authors do not regard all of our beliefs and values as thoroughly relative and revisable. They seem to at least tacitly endorse a set of familiar modern liberal values concerning the dignity and worth of individuals, individual freedom, and opposition to arbitrary authority. In other words, these authors seem to try to have their cake and eat it, too (e.g., Rorty 1987a). On the one hand, they endorse the thoroughgoing relativism of constructionist theory; on the other hand, they roundly condemn most forms of domination and inequality! They even seem to view relativism as a means for advancing certain of their (perhaps in many ways worthy) moral commitments.

Ontological Hermeneutics

In line with much postmodern/social constructionist thought, hermeneutic thinkers criticize the "foundationalism" that infects conventional social science. Perhaps all the schools of thought represented in this volume would welcome the implication of so-called post-empiricist accounts of the history and philosophy of science (Bernstein 1983; Kuhn 1970; Richardson and Fowers 1998) that all human understanding is thoroughly creative and interpretive rather than simply obedient to an independent order of fact. Although some postmodern thinkers (e.g., Rorty 1987b) believe that there are no important differences between the natural and the human sciences, hermeneutic thinkers contend that even though both are indelibly interpretive, there still are critical distinctions to be made between natural science and much of social inquiry.

Perhaps the main point of contrast between them is the central place occupied in the natural sciences by the exercise of a special capacity for abstraction that we might call "objectification." To adopt an objectifying stance toward things is to ignore or abstract away from "subject-related qualities.". Such qualities include most of the meanings of and relationships among things that show up within our ordinary experience, concerned with our shifting desires, values, and aims. Thus, to take an objectifying stance means to attempt to "regard the world as it is independently of the meanings it might have for human subjects, or of how it figures in their experience" (Taylor 1980:31). Obviously this approach has proved its mettle in modern science and its applications. However, there is no good reason to deny the validity of other *kinds* of interpretations of our experience and events, reflecting different *ways* of being involved with the world. It no longer seems proper to many of us to insist that reality must be only that which is formulated through the approach of abstraction and objectification. We have learned to question the detached, somewhat depersonalizing, "spectator" view of knowing and relating to the world that this approach encourages.

As a result, hermeneutics largely rejects not just positivism or logical empiricism but the whole modern epistemological enterprise that maintains it can establish valid knowledge by certain methods, and by them alone. Taylor suggests that we take a "wider conception of the epistemological tradition" as incorporating a number of basic beliefs and values. For example, we would never entertain foundationalist ambitions in the first place if we did not conceive of knowledge as the "inner depiction of an outer reality" or the "correct representation of an independent reality" (1995:2). Then everything from truth to technology depends, we think, on anchoring our beliefs in that independent reality. Of course, this representational view leads to insoluble puzzles concerning, among other things, how we can gain indubitable access to realities *through* our mental representations that are at the same time *independent* of them. Given this view of knowledge, we tend to oscillate endlessly between realism and skepticism. We don't know whether to believe that science alone delivers truth or that we "create our own reality," and often settle for a dissonant and unstable mix of the two. But a credible alternative to the representational view is hard to come by, so it tends to remain our de facto modern stance toward the world.

Furthermore, Taylor (1995:7ff.) argues that the representational outlook fits hand in glove with the widespread modern picture of the self as disengaged, disembodied, and atomistic, or "punctual." This self is "distinguished . . . from [the] natural and social worlds, so that [its] identity is no longer to be defined in terms of what lies outside . . . in these worlds." The modern self is ideally ready to freely and rationally treat both itself and the outside world instrumentally, to alter both in ways that better secure individual and social well-being, however they are conceived. Thus, the representational outlook begins to look like a central strand of our way of life in modern culture, one that many feel purchases valuable freedoms at the price of a good deal of alienation. Indeed, Taylor suggests that the modern notion of a "punctual self" confronting a natural and social world to which it has no essential ties is as much a *moral* as a scientific ideal. It "connects with . . . central moral and spiritual ideas of the modern age," views "freedom as self-autonomy," and seeks "to be self-responsible, to rely on one's [own] judgment, to find one's purpose in oneself." Within this outlook, any overlap between self and world compromises the individual's integrity and dignity.

It would seem that many of our contemporary political and therapeutic ideals reflect and reinforce this profound aspiration to individuality and separateness. Also, this connection with modern ideals helps explain why the goal of mainstream social science for the most part has been strictly value-neutral explanations or descriptions of human dynamics, and why it is so comfortable treating cultural and moral values as purely subjective—something that social constructionism tends to do in its own way also. We seem impelled to maintain that such meanings and values are subjective choices. The only generally conceivable alternative is that meanings and values are imposed from the outside in a way that compromises our autonomy and integrity in a domineering manner. Perhaps our lengthy persistence in the face of such limited success in mainstream social science reflects not so much admirable diligence as a stubborn attachment to the one-sided individualism and horror of arbitrary authority that, in part, inspire the representational outlook.

Hermeneutic Ontology

Hermeneutic thinkers are committed to reconceptualizing this representational view of knowledge, including its associated moral ideals, in a fundamental way. They agree with critics of foundationalism and the subject-object ontology who insist that we have no direct or immediate access to a "real" world or transcendent norms independent of our interpretation of things. Claims that we do are really just additional interpretations that need to be grounded as well, producing an infinite regress from which there is no exit. However, according to hermeneutics, the typical postmodern attempt to get past modern representationalism is overly hasty and incomplete. Guignon (1991:96ff.) suggests that when it becomes clear that we can have no direct access to "Nature as it is in itself" distinct from our interpretations, we may experience a "feeling of loss" that would seem to dictate that we are merely "entangled in perspectives" or that "there is nothing outside the text." Paradoxically, though, this postmodern "picture of our predicament as cut off from reality makes sense only because of the way it contrasts with the binary opposition of self vs. world it is supposed to replace." For example, the view that "signs refer only to other signs" is parasitic on the very opposition between "sign" and "signified" it is trying to discard. Thus, this approach may confusedly perpetuate the very axioms of thought it is trying to replace!

Hermeneutic philosophy tries to include all these considerations and outline a more plausible account of human action and social life, namely, a hermeneutic ontology. This view is generally quite hospitable to the idea that psychological processes and human action are partly constituted by culture and society, not separate, greatly self-sustaining processes merely facilitated by them. To begin with, in this interpretation humans are "self-interpreting beings" (Taylor 1985a). The *meanings* we work out in the business of living make us to a great extent what we are, in sharp contrast to the viewpoint that our behavior is determined mainly by genetic and social influences to be described for us by a branch of natural science. Moreover, individual lives are "always 'thrown' into a familiar life-world from which they draw their possibilities of self-interpretation. Our own life-stories only make sense against the backdrop of possible story-lines opened by our historical culture" (Guignon 1989:109). Instead of thinking of the self as an object of any sort, hermeneutic thought follows Heidegger (1962:426) in conceiving of human existence as a "happening" or a "becoming." Individual lives have a temporal and narrative structure. They are a kind of unfolding "movement" that is "stretched along between birth and death." In Guignon's words, just as "events in a novel gain their meaning from what they seem to be pointing to in the long run . . . so our past lives and our present activities gain their meaning from a (perhaps tacit) sense of where our lives are going as a totality" (1993:14).

What does it mean to participate in this kind of temporal and storied existence? Social scientists generally seek answers through abstraction and objectification and by forging a knowledge of lawful or repeated patterns in events that occur regardless of the everyday meanings these events have for us or the evaluations we make of them. But there is a more fundamental, ultimately *practical* kind of understanding that humans always and everywhere thrash out together, one that does not primarily mean comprehending events mainly as "instances" of a general concept, rule, or law. In everyday life and in a more systematic way in the human sciences, people seek to understand the changeable *meanings* of events, texts, works of art, social reality, and the actions of others in order to appreciate them and relate to them appropriately, along the story-lines of their living.

According to a hermeneutic ontology, however, this understanding or interpretation of meaning has a distinctive character. Historical experience changes the meaning events can have for us, not because it alters our view of an independent object, but because history is a dialectical process in which both the object and our knowledge of it are continually transformed. Thus, for example, both the meaning of the American Revolution and my lived understanding of freedom continue to be modified in the dialogue between them. So we are immersed in and deeply connected to this process rather than essentially detached from it as scientistic, "descriptivist," and even postmodern approaches all tend to suppose.

In this view, a basic fact about humans, according to Heidegger (1962), is that we *care* about whether our lives make sense and what they are amounting to. Therefore, we have always taken some stand on our lives by seizing on certain roles, traits, and values. Indeed, humans "just are the stands they take in living out their lives" (Guignon and Pereboom 1995:189). Thus, we live within dense webs of concrete life-relations in a holistic life-world, one in which our shared meanings and values are just as much "out there" in our practices and institutions as "in here" in our thoughts and feelings about outer events. In this way, hermeneutics tries to begin to bridge the gap between the mental and the physical, and between self and world, that has bedeviled so much modern thought and life.

This hermeneutic ontology contrasts sharply with the portrayal of human being that underlies mainstream social science. Whereas traditional social science assumes that human behavior is the outcome of a nexus of natural causal forces that operate timelessly and universally on us, hermeneutics construes human action as self-interpreting within a rich life-world redolent with sociohistorical meaning and oriented toward ends and ideals about which we care deeply. The hermeneutic perspective raises profound questions about the defensibility of a social science that aims to produce a disengaged objective account of independent facts. Although it might be tempting to jettison social science as irredeemably misguided, hermeneutic thought does not counsel an outright rejection of empirical inquiry into human affairs.

Reformulating Social Inquiry

A hermeneutic reformulation of social inquiry would begin by recognizing that all of our efforts at self-understanding are interpretations that are partly shaped by our situatedness in an ongoing historical and cultural life-world. Far from attaining a detached perspective on human activity, social inquiry is a form of practice in pursuit of the good of knowledge, engaged in by inquirers who care deeply about that pursuit and about the life-world being studied.

If psychology and other social sciences were to follow the direction indicated by ontological hermeneutics, of what would we seek knowledge? If human action is self-interpreting—and, thereby, self-constituting—how can we fashion reliable knowledge of beings whose knowledge tends to alter their way of being? If, as inquirers, we are participants in, rather than detached observers of, the social world we study, how can we gain a purchase on a changing life-world in which we are embedded? If it is the case, as hermeneutic thinkers argue, that all human endeavors are shot through with inconsistencies, ideologies, and blindspots, how are we to sort through self-contradiction, ideology, and the inescapable finitude of our vision? These are daunting questions, but with appropriate modesty in our aims and proceedings, we can fashion an approach to social inquiry that will do greater justice to the human realm.

The place to start is where we find ourselves, as interested participants in a form of life who seek to better understand ourselves. The effort to better understand a given way of life amounts to a kind of cultural self-reflection in which patterns of action and intercourse are examined critically, characteristic problems and contradictions are explored, and guiding ideals are made explicit and scrutinized. Cultural self-reflection is an ongoing, critical evaluation of the goods, practices, and character ideals that comprise a cultural tradition. The purpose of this inquiry is to better understand and critique what is taken to be human flourishing in a way of life and to learn about and foster activities and practices that are conducive to living well.

In spite of its apparent drawbacks, studying a way of life from the perspective of a participant has two distinct advantages. First, it allows us to frankly admit our genuine interest in the outcome of our research rather than seeking refuge in third-person circumlocutions and bland verbiage. Second, as participants in a way of life, we have a great deal of knowledge and insight about how people interact and make their way. This insider knowledge frequently piques investigators' interest in a topic and informs our initial approaches and hypotheses. All of this is frequently disguised in universal theoretical terms and quasi-detached descriptions of populations and problems. If we truly were detached observers, it is entirely unclear why we would care to expend so much time, effort, and money on our investigations, or how we would actually gain access to such problems from a fully disengaged perspective.

Such an account raises important questions about objectivity, which is generally premised on detachment and procedure. There is no reason that participant observers cannot strive for a high degree of objectivity, as long as that does not require abstraction from and objectification of the life-world, and a thorough disengagement of the observer. Objectivity remains a key value of hermeneutic inquiry in attempting to be open to being instructed by what one observes, to recognize fallibility, to be willing to correct errors, and to recognize and reduce the sway of personal or perspectival biases. There are, no doubt, many procedures that can aid observers in practicing this objectivity, but there are no rules or measures that can guarantee it.

Granting that investigators are participants in the form of life they study, how can they gain an objective perspective on something of which they are a part, and, according to hermeneutics, something that helps to shape investigators' own outlooks and intentions? There are at least three important domains of access that enable participant-observers to analyze contemporary human action in-depth: through complexities internal to a given society; through historical contrast; and through engagement with other ways of life.

Although being a participant in a given way of life does both shape one's outlook and provide the background understandings necessary for action, this situatedness does not render one incapable of reflection on and critique of that way of life. There are many invitations to reflection as a participant in a life-world. The most common instance arises in everyday attempts to act in accordance with one's way of life because each action one undertakes is an interpretation of what the tradition indicates as appropriate. In each of these interpretative actions, questions can arise about exactly what the tradition calls for and how the individual can best respond to that call. For example, there are shared understandings of what teaching ought to look like in every form of life, but each teacher will enact those understandings differently, in response to the age and learning capacity of the students, the nature of the material to be taught, and the degree of mastery the students need to attain. The necessity of interpreting the role of the teacher is presented to the teacher as a question, which is answered in the enactment, but can also prompt reflection on and critique of what the tradition seems to call for. Such reflection can lead to novel interpretations, deeper understanding of the tradition, or critique. Inquiry into the enactment of teaching can be productive in similar ways.

Another kind of spur to reflection arises because forms of life tend to have a multivocal character, with substantial disagreement and tension among the various ways to understand how best to instantiate them. Indeed, one of the best ways to understand traditions is to see them as extended debates on what it is to carry on that particular tradition. Individuals and groups will often feel called upon to reflect on these disagreements to better understand their sources, potential harmonies, and essential differences. To return to the example of teaching, the contemporary debate over the role of high-stakes testing in public schools in the United States displays enormous differences in perspectives on what should be taught, how it should be taught, and how those questions get answered. As a result, a great deal of public and private soul searching has taken place regarding what it is to teach.

We will mention one other important inspiration to reflection within a form of life that arises through the inconsistencies and self-contradictions found in all traditions. Given human fallibility and vulnerability to self-deception, such inconsistencies are inevitable. As individuals and groups struggle with the tensions and confusions these inconsistencies produce, we are called upon to attempt to better understand and respond to the contradictory demands of our situation. One prominent contemporary example of this is the fragility of marriage, which is fueled by the demand for emotional fulfillment through marriages that are intended to be lifelong. Paradoxically, this model of marriage has put enormous pressure on marriages, leading to a recent easing of divorce strictures, an unprecedented divorce rate, a decreasing marriage rate, and an increasing prevalence of cohabitation (Fowers 2000). An examination of social science evidence has led some to characterize this as the decline of marriage (e.g., Popenoe 1993) and create a "marriage movement" designed to shore up this institution (e.g., Institute for American Values 2000). Others have declared that it is time to abandon the traditional concept of marriage in favor of seeing all marital statuses as equally valid lifestyle choices (e.g., Allan 2008). Cultural inconsistencies such as this create a great deal of tension and turmoil within societies and call for serious self-reflection and debate about what the tradition calls for.

At times, the questions and disagreements just discussed can lead those conducting social inquiry to turn to historical sources for a better understanding of contemporary dilemmas and debates. At other times, important questions about contemporary practices and beliefs are raised through direct contact with our history. As we contrast our contemporary understandings and actions with those of our forebears, we will inevitably be led to reflect on our current mode of life and the ways that it harmonizes with, and diverges from, our historical roots. This comparative examination can throw significant new light on our self-understanding. To continue with the example of marriage, one of the most fruitful ways to gain a better understanding of the current dilemma is to examine the historical roots of the emotionally fulfilling marriage. A survey of the history of marriage makes it clear that the joining of romantic love and individual fulfillment with marriage is a very large-scale social experiment that began in the eighteenth century that has placed unprecedented strains on marriage (Fowers 2000; see Stone 1979 and Phillips 1988 for rigorous historical analyses). Similarly, numerous authors have offered critiques of the excessive individualism and its negative consequences in contemporary psychology and American society (e.g., Richardson, Fowers, and Guignon 1999; Sandel 1996; Taylor 1989). Twenge (2000) conducted an empirical examination of historical shifts over four decades in anxiety and depression in the United States and concluded that as individuals have become more independent and isolated, normative levels of anxiety and depression have increased. These sources suggest that historical comparisons, whether conceptual or empirical, can help to shed light on dominant cultural patterns and create the necessary space to reflect on those patterns.

The third major opportunity for cultural self-reflection is made available through interchanges with other cultural perspectives. As we come into contact with other worldviews, the contrasts with our own way of life will be evident and plentiful if we are open to them. The ubiquity of cultural contrast opportunities makes it clear that the primary question is one of openness to encounter the other. Cultivating the willingness to allow cultural differences to raise questions about one's own worldview is a significant achievement, as it flies in the face of the natural ethnocentrism that arises from being embedded in a form of life (Fiske 1998; Hewstone, Rubin, and Willis 2002; Triandis 1995). Fowers and Davidov (2006) described the personal transformation that is necessary for the pursuit of multicultural competence as the virtue of "openness to the other." They argued that openness is a virtue because it is aimed at a particular good (cultural competence), is knowledge based, requires consistent action in line with that good and knowledge, involves a wholehearted pursuit of the good, and requires practical wisdom to carry it through (Fowers 2005).

In this essay, we are suggesting that a primary aim of hermeneutically informed social inquiry is cultural self-knowledge. In order to pursue the kind of cultural self-reflection necessary to improve our self-understanding, we must practice openness to the other as well. The ability to recognize and pursue the historical and cultural contrasts that are readily available to promote this good of self-knowledge requires awareness of how to recognize and conceptualize these contrasts, consistent attention to and follow-through on the contrasts, a commitment to pursuing them, and the practical wisdom to know when and how to make use of such comparisons. There are many ways that cultural self-reflection through cultural contrast can be pursued. One of the most prominent has been in the critique of individualism in North Atlantic societies through the contrast with collectivism (e.g., Triandis 1995). This critique has been pursued conceptually and empirically in hundreds of publications that have involved productive reflection on core cultural matters such as self-interest, identity, selfhood, social relations, and social hierarchy. The culturally based critique of individualism has highlighted the role of individualism in social science and society and paved the way to a widespread recognition of the one-sidedness and negative consequences of unquestioned individualism.

Dialogue

The virtue of openness to the other is practiced through ongoing dialogue with what is seen as other, whether that is the unspoken and unrecognized aspects of one's form of life or the historical or cultural other. Dialogue with the other is very difficult because the substance of our experience, beliefs, practices, and institutions, indeed our very identity, is always constituted through culture, self-understanding, and language, all of which can be called into question in dialogue. In addition, the outcomes of this process of mutual influence and dialogue are unpredictable and are capable of "potentially endless innovation" (Taylor 2002:129). As a result, we live in a certain quintessentially human, exquisite, sometimes unbearable tension. On the one hand, we harbor self-defining beliefs and values concerning things we care about greatly, in which we have a "deep identity investment" (p. 141). On the other hand, our identities are partly formed by how we understand our differences from others. Because both our ideals and our images of others are always partial or distorted in some way, it is not enough just to compromise and get along with others.

Rather, dialogue involves learning from the past, others, or other cultures. In this sense, we depend upon them greatly in understanding matters closest to our own hearts, an often uncomfortable and taxing situation. To gain such learning, we have to open ourselves to other perspectives, let them call us to account and question us and allow at least some degree of what Gadamer (1989) calls a "fusion of horizons" to take place, a melding of insights that incorporates old ones and new in a transformed outlook. This transformation exacts some degree of dislocation inasmuch as our self-understandings with our concomitant perceptions of others will shift as we carry out this kind of discourse. In doing so, we sometimes incur a deeply personal, sometimes painful "identity cost" (141).

Openness to the other permits new information and the viewpoints of others to confront one with challenges as well as divergent, possibly valid insights or perspectives. That validity can be tested only by overcoming temptations to defensiveness and deception, accepting the challenge, not distancing oneself, in the main, but commonly drawing closer to the realities and feelings involved in order to see things more clearly and weigh them more sensitively, and eventually allowing an altered or refined understanding to take shape—even though it may sometimes entail wrenching "identity cost."

It is a hard fact, and a most interesting one, that we can't return to abandoned perspectives for the reason that they no longer square with our current best convictions and/or interpretations. Also, we can't simply adopt the "truth" of a new or different perspective merely because it is useful or pleasing to do so. Thus, we can never reach the thoroughly disengaged position that would be required to assert a confident, thoroughgoing relativism or perspectivism. So it is an illusion to think *either* that we can stand apart from all convictions *or* that we can reach a final resting place of truth with a capital "T." Rather we have to struggle for new and possibly better insights through risky encounter and dialogue.

Following Gadamer (1989), we characterize such dialogue as an interplay of "openness" and "application" (Richardson, Rogers, and McCarroll 1998). In this view, it usually takes earnest convictions to have the personal strength (involving virtues like courage and humility) to practice genuine openness to the views and evaluations of others. Somewhat paradoxically, however, such openness entails actually granting provisional authority to another's standpoint to challenge our beliefs and prejudices. Of course, that kind of openness runs the danger of compromising our judgment and perhaps rationalizing an unjust status quo due to the influence of enticing or intimidating authorities. That danger mainly can be avoided (requiring such personal qualities or virtues as integrity and tenacity) through rigorous application, in which we strive to discern whether or not an insight or point of view makes better sense of the motives and circumstances with which we currently struggle. To be sure, this kind of application or interpretation runs the risk, in turn, of our cleverly interpreting events or principles in a conveniently self-serving manner. The only cure for that kind of arbitrariness or inauthenticity is further, sometimes annoying or painful openness to challenge from others. The main point is that, living as we do "between conviction and uncertainty" (Downing 2000), we can neither escape sincere moral ideals and convictions nor rely on any sure-fire methods for validating them, but must continually put them to the test in life and dialogue.

Sacks (2002) coined the phrase "the dignity of difference" to highlight the importance of honoring the differences we recognize in others. His view is that in order to improve upon our own best traditions and insights and to learn something new, we actually *depend* upon the perspectives of others to illumine realities that inevitably escape our limited angle of vision, even when it directs itself to the most sensitive and important ethical and spiritual questions. Honoring the dignity of difference, in his view, allows us to go beyond both a narrow "tribalism" and the kind of modern "universalism" that, even as it contributes to undoing many forms of arbitrary authority, also too hastily and presumptuously claims to define the way of the universe.

The philosopher Alasdair MacIntyre (1998) outlines the core process of the struggle for understanding in a way that parallels the hermeneutic conception of dialogic understanding. To begin with, every major moral culture or standpoint presupposes some view of human nature, activity, and morality that it claims or assumes is by and large true. This notion accords well with the view of hermeneutic philosophers to the effect that commitments and claims of this sort are "inescapable" (Taylor 1989). According to MacIntyre (1998), what follows from all this is that when we encounter others with whom we differ in some significant way, within one of our communities or traditions or from other communities or traditions, we implicitly and inevitably present our judgments and way of life as deserving assent by these others. As a result, at least tacitly, "we invite those others to radical self-criticism" (p. 5). But this invitation, if we are honest about it, presupposes "that truth is a good." MacIntyre has in mind not truth as an abstract ideal that swings free from particular moral standpoints, but truth as a "good that is already implicitly acknowledged" within the warp and woof of the actual practice of any standpoint that claims to be worthy of the allegiance of rational, reflective people. According to MacIntyre (p. 7), if some inescapable recognition of truth as a good is presupposed by nonfrivolous moral standpoints, then "the relativists, if they are to give good reason for taking the claim that relativism in true, must also recognize truth as a good, whatever one's standpoint, and to the extent they do so they abandon relativism."

Furthermore, in MacIntyre's view, recognition of truth as a good obligates us to "undertake the tasks of radical self-criticism to which [we] have invited others" (1998:5). It commits us to what he suggests we might term an "ethics of enquiry" that has as its main goal the "achievement of truth through a dialectical development of critical objections to our initial shared beliefs" (p. 6). We have to start from our own beliefs, but anyone is a potential partner in this inquiry. In the nature of the case, our interaction and conversation with others will have to be governed by "certain rules and exhibit certain virtues," including such principles as that each person should be "able to speak in turn and at appropriate length," and that attention should be directed to the "substance of the arguments and not to who utters them," both of which are forms of the virtue of "justice in conversation" (p. 7).

In the hermeneutic view, we do not control the direction of our cultural conversation so much as participate responsibly in it. Its many surprises do not undermine that responsibility or integrity so much as extend our understanding of what they are about in unpredictable ways. An interpretive social science that accepts that we are thoroughly embedded in and shaped by history and culture is reticent about trying to show people or communities how to live in any definitive way. Its practitioners would be happy to contribute to collective reflections and search for understanding by modestly helping to clarify some of the meanings we live by. Justice Learned Hand once put it this way: "The spirit of liberty is the spirit which is not too sure it is right."

Notes

1.   Think of the process involved in reading a novel or getting to know a person over time. They seem to proceed in this way.

2.   For a brief overview of the history of hermeneutic thought, see Richardson, Fowers, and Guignon 1999, chap. 9.

3.   The same thing happens in everyday life, as Dilthey saw. We make initial sense of the situations and challenges we face in terms of some wider story or set of purposes we bring to the event. But such encounters often include novel or unforeseen elements that may require us to work out a deeper or more refined understanding of the events or people involved. This altered sense of the meaning of the situation shapes, in turn, our understanding of the wider story of the life we are leading, which then initially frames the meaning of what we encounter at the next turn in the road. In this way, the wider story and meaning hammered out of particular events circle around one another endlessly.

4.   We might say that Dilthey's project was shaped by three hard-to-reconcile influences. In the sprit of the Romantic movement, he wished to recapture the fullness of lived experience. Also, he rejected any sort of speculative metaphysics, like Hegel's, that tried to go behind historical life to a realm of Ideas or discern an end, or *telos*, toward which history was headed. And finally, he was drawn to some of what J. S. Mill and nineteenth-century positivism had to say about the need for an empirical base for genuine knowledge, one that would provide some kind of objectivity.

References

Allan, G. 2008. Flexibility, friendship, and family. *Personal Relationships* 15:1–16.

Bernstein, R. 1976. *The Restructuring of Social and Political Theory*. Philadelphia: University of Pennsylvania Press.

———. 1983. *Beyond Objectivism and Relativism*. Philadelphia: University of Pennsylvania Press.

Bishop, R. 2007. *The Philosophy of the Social Sciences*. London: Continuum.

D'Andrade, R. 1986. Three scientific worldviews. In D. Fiske and R. Shweder, eds., *Metatheory in Social Science*, 19–41. Chicago: University of Chicago Press.

Downing, J. N. 2000. *Between Conviction and Uncertainty: Philosophical Guidelines for the Practicing Psychotherapist*. Albany: State University of New York Press.

Dreyfus, H. 1987. Foucault's therapy. *PsychCritique* 2.1:65–83.

Fiske, S. T. 1998. Stereotyping, prejudice, and discrimination. In D. T. Gilbert and S. T. Fiske, eds., *The Handbook of Social Psychology*, 4th ed., 2:357–411. New York: McGraw-Hill.

Flyvbjerg, B. 2001. *Making Social Science Matter: Why Social Inquiry Fails and How It Can Succeed Again*. Cambridge: Cambridge University Press.

Fowers, B. J. 2000. *Beyond the Myth of Marital Happiness*. San Francisco: Jossey-Bass.

———. 2005. *Virtue and Psychology: Pursuing Excellence in Ordinary Practices*. Washington, DC: American Psychological Association.

Fowers, B. J., and B. J. Davidov. 2006. The virtue of multiculturalism: Personal transformation, character, and openness to the other. *American Psychologist* 61:581–594.

Gadamer, H.-G. 1989. *Truth and Method*. 2nd rev. ed. Trans. J. Weinsheimer and D. Marshall. New York: Crossroad.

Gergen, K. 1982. *Toward Transformation in Social Knowledge*. New York: Springer.

——. 1985. The social constructionist movement in modern psychology. *American Psychologist* 4:266–275.

Gergen, K., and J. Kaye. 1992. Beyond narrative in the negotiation of therapeutic meaning. In S. McNamee and K. Gergen, eds., *Therapy as Social Construction*, 166–185. London: Sage.

Guignon, C. 1989. Truth as disclosure: Art, language, history. *Southern Journal of Philosophy* 28:105–121.

——. 1991. Pragmatism or hermeneutics? Epistemology after foundationalism. In J. Bohman, D. Hiley, and R. Schusterman, eds., *The Interpretive Turn*, 81–101. Ithaca, NY: Cornell University Press.

——. 1993. *Overcoming Dualism: A Hermeneutic Approach to Understanding Humans*. Unpublished manuscript, University of South Florida.

——. 2002. Hermeneutics, authenticity, and the aims of psychotherapy. *Journal of Theoretical and Philosophical Psychology* 22:83–102.

Guignon, C., and D. Pereboom. 1995. Introduction: The legacy of existentialism. In C. Guignon and D. Pereboom, eds., *Existentialism: Basic Writings*. Indianapolis: Hackett.

Habermas, J. 1991. *The Philosophical Discourse of Modernity*. Cambridge, MA: MIT Press.

Heidegger, M. 1962. *Being and Time*. New York: Harper and Row.

Hewstone, M., M. Rubin, and H. Willis. 2002. Intergroup bias. *Annual Review of Psychology* 53:575–604.

Hoy, D. 1986. Power, repression, progress. In D. Hoy, ed., *Foucault: A Critical Reader*, 123–147. New York: Blackwell.

Institute for American Values. 2000. *The Marriage Movement: A Statement of Principles*. New York: Institute for American Values.

Kuhn, T. 1970. *The Structure of Scientific Revolutions*. 2nd ed. Chicago: University of Chicago Press.

MacIntyre, A. 1998. Moral pluralism without moral relativism. Paper delivered at the Twentieth World Congress of Philosophy, Boston, MA, August 1998.

Moon, J. 1983. Political ethics and critical theory. In D. Sabia and J. Wallulis, eds., *Changing Social Science*, 171–188. Albany: State University of New York Press.

Phillips, R. 1988. *Putting Asunder: A History of Divorce in Western Society*. Cambridge: Cambridge University Press.

Popenoe, D. 1993. American family decline, 1960–1990: A review and appraisal. *Journal of Marriage and the Family* 55:527–555.

Richardson, F. 2005. Psychotherapy and modern dilemmas. In B. Slife, J. Reber, and F. Richardson, eds., *Critical Thinking About Psychology: Hidden Assumptions and Plausible Alternatives*, 147–170. Washington, DC: American Psychological Association.

Richardson, F., and J. Christopher. 1993. Social theory as practice: Metatheoretical frameworks for social inquiry. *Journal of Theoretical and Philosophical Psychology* 13:137–153.

Richardson, F., and B. Fowers. 1998. Interpretive social science: An overview. *American Behavioral Scientist* 41:465–495.

Richardson, F., B. Fowers, and C. Guignon. 1999. *Re-envisioning Psychology: Moral Dimensions of Theory and Practice*. San Francisco: Jossey-Bass.

Richardson, F., A. Rogers, and J. McCarroll. 1998. Toward a dialogical self. *American Behavioral Scientist* 41:496–515.

Richardson, F., and T. Zeddies. 2001. Individualism and modern psychotherapy. In B. Slife, R. Williams, and S. Barlow, eds., *Critical Issues in Psychotherapy: Translating New Ideas Into Practice*. Thousand Oaks, CA: Sage.

Rorty, R. 1982. *Consequences of Pragmatism*. Minneapolis: University of Minnesota Press.

——. 1987a. Solidarity or objectivity? In J. Rajchman and C. West, eds., *Post-analytic Philosophy*, 3–19. New York: Columbia University Press.

——. 1987b. Method, social science, and social hope. In M. Gibbons, ed., *Interpreting Politics*, 241–260. New York: New York University Press.

Sacks, J. 2002. *The Dignity of Difference: How to Avoid the Clash of Civilizations*. London: Continuum.

Sampson, E. 1985. The decentralization of identity: Toward a revised concept of personal and social order. *American Psychologist* 40:1203–1211.

Sandel, M. 1996. *Democracy's Discontent: America in Search of a Public Philosophy*. Cambridge, MA: Harvard University Press.

Slife, B., A. Smith, and C. Burchfield. 2003. Psychotherapists as crypto-missionaries: An exemplar on the crossroads of history, theory, and philosophy. In D. Hill and M. Krall, eds., *About Psychology: At the Crossroads of History, Theory, and Philosophy*. Albany: State University of New York Press.

Slife, B., and R. Williams. 1995. *What's Behind the Research? Discovering Hidden Assumptions in the Behavioral Sciences*. Thousand Oaks, CA: Sage.

Stone, L. 1979. *The Family, Sex, and Marriage in England, 1500–1800*. New York: Harper.

Taylor, C. 1980. Understanding in human science. *Review of Metaphysics* 34:3–23.

——. 1985a. *Human Agency and Language: Philosophical Papers* 1. Cambridge: Cambridge University Press.

——. 1985b. *Philosophy and the Human Sciences: Philosophical Papers* 2. Cambridge: Cambridge University Press.

——. 1989. *Sources of the Self*. Cambridge, MA: Harvard University Press.

——. 1995. *Philosophical Arguments*. Cambridge, MA: Harvard University Press.

——. 2002. Gadamer and the human sciences. In R. Dostal, ed., *The Cambridge Companion to Gadamer*, 126–142. Cambridge: Cambridge University Press.

Triandis, H. C. 1995. *Individualism and Collectivism*. Boulder, CO: Westview.

Twenge, J. M. 2000. The age of anxiety? Birth cohort change in anxiety and neuroticism, 1952–1993. *Journal of Personality and Social Psychology* 79:1007–1021.

Waite, L. J., and M. Gallagher. 2000. *The Case for Marriage: Why Married People Are Happier, Healthier, and Better Off Financially*. New York: Doubleday.

Warnke, G. 1987. *Gadamer: Hermeneutics, Tradition, and Reason*. Stanford: Stanford University Press.

6 The Space of Selfhood

Culture, Narrative, Identity

MARK FREEMAN

"My Story"

My primary interest in this chapter is to call attention to the myriad ways in which "my story"—the narrative one tells about one's life—is permeated by "secondhand" sources ranging from others' stories all the way to the vast array of cultural media that indeed *mediate* experience. This does not necessarily make my story any less "mine": whatever the sources of selfhood might be, there remains an irrevocable "my-ness" about the story I come to tell about the movement of my life. It does, however, suggest that what is "mine" is, at one and the same time, permeated by what is "other" and, in turn, that any and all attempts to separate selfhood from its sociocultural surround must fail. There is a further implication as well: "my story," insofar as it emerges from what has come before me—from the very *tradition* into which I was born and from which my life has acquired its very sense and shape (see especially Gadamer 1982)—extends well beyond the confines of the stretch of time between birth and death. As Ricoeur puts the matter:

There is nothing in real life that serves as a narrative beginning; memory is lost in the hazes of early childhood; my birth and, with greater reason, the act through which I was conceived belong more to the history of others—in this case, to my parents—than to me. As for my death, it will finally be recounted only in the stories of those who survive me. I am always moving toward my death, and this prevents me from ever grasping it as a narrative end.   (1992:160)

From the perspective being drawn here, the temporal boundaries of my story thus expand, to include both the "before" of my birth and the "after" of my death. So too does the *space* of selfhood: far from being bound to the confines of my own firsthand experience, it extends into the very fabric of culture and history.

Along these lines, Bruner offers: "It is probably a mistake to conceive of Self as solo, as locked up inside one person's subjectivity, as hermetically sealed off." It is better conceived as "intersubjective or 'distributed' in the same way that one's 'knowledge' is distributed beyond one's head to include the friends and colleagues to whom one has access, the notes one has filed, the books one has on one's shelves" (1991:76; see also Brockmeier 1997; Wang and Brockmeier 2002). By exploring what I am here calling the space of selfhood, therefore, it may be possible to shed new light on the interrelationship between culture, narrative, and identity.

The Narrative Unconscious

The ideas being considered in the present chapter may be traced back, in part, to an experience I had in the city of Berlin during which, after several days of exploring the various sights, I suddenly found myself undone, caught in an emotional vortex that was an admixture of horror, disbelief, and sorrow. It was my first time visiting the city; although I had certainly been prepared for some emotional challenges, given my own Jewish background, my knowledge of some of the terrible events that had taken place there, and so on, the initial days of my visit passed unexceptionally. But then came this strange and utterly unanticipated experience, tied somehow to the city itself. Rather than simply being a fascinating, disturbing site, it had become a kind of living being, suffused, paradoxically, with death. What I suggested at the time was that death seemed literally to be in the air, invisible and yet tangible, as if the horrific events that had taken place there had somehow left behind ghosts of times past. The city had become truly menacing, and it left me shaken.

The question I had to ask in the aftermath of the experience was: What exactly had happened? However much I felt that death was in the air, it presumably was not. Or, to put the matter somewhat differently, whatever I felt was in the air I had presumably brought there, via my own hermeneutical "prejudices"—my expectations, my knowledge, my background, and, not least, my imagination. I surmised at the time that, although I wasn't especially knowledgeable about Berlin, I must have carried with me enough of a storehouse of information, ideas, and images to "activate the undercurrents," as I had put it in an earlier piece, of the spectacles observed. Memory, I wrote, "becomes a curious amalgam of fact and fiction, experiences and texts, documentary footage, dramatizations, movies, plays, television shows, fantasies, and more" (Freeman 2002:199). It was also in the context of this experience that I began to entertain the notion of the "narrative unconscious," which, I suggested, "refers not so much to that which has been dynamically repressed as to that which has been lived but which remains unthought and untold, i.e., to those culturally-rooted aspects of one's history that have not yet become part of one's story" (p. 193). In any case, and to make a long story short, I became interested in thinking about those dimensions of memory—and of selfhood—that on some level may be said to go beyond the confines of an individual life.

One might argue in response to this conceptualization that, strictly speaking, the phenomenon I experienced in Berlin did not involve *memory* at all, that there is a conflation here of memory and tradition, of those aspects of culture and history that are "inherited" from the past, perhaps unknowingly. Consider in this context what Susan Sontag has to say about photographs in *Regarding the Pain of Others*:

> The familiarity of certain photographs builds our sense of the present and immediate past. Photographs lay down routes of reference, and serve as totems of causes: sentiment is more likely to crystallize around a photograph than around a verbal slogan. And photographs help construct—and revise—our sense of a more distant past, with the posthumous shocks engineered by the circulation of hitherto unknown photographs. Photographs that everyone recognizes are now part of what society chooses to think about, or declares that it has chosen to think about. It calls these ideas "memories," and that is, over the long run, a fiction. Strictly speaking, there is no such thing as collective memory. (2003:85)

"All memory," Sontag goes on to argue, "is individual, unreproducible—it dies with each person." What is often referred to as "collective memory," therefore,

> is not a remembering but a stipulating: that this is important, and this is the story about how it happened, with the pictures that lock the stories in our minds. Ideologies create substantiating archives of images, representative images, which encapsulate common ideas of significance and trigger predictable thoughts, feelings. Poster-ready photographs—the mushroom cloud of an A-bomb test, Martin Luther King, Jr., speaking at the Lincoln Memorial in Washington, D.C., the astronaut walking on the moon—are the visual equivalent of sound bites. They commemorate, in no less blunt fashion than postage stamps, Important Historical Moments; indeed, the triumphalist ones (the picture of the A-bomb excepted) become postage stamps. Fortunately, there is no signature picture of the Nazi death camps.   (p. 86)

It is true; there is no such "signature picture." But it is no less true that images of exactly those camps, with their skeleton bodies heaped atop one another, in deep pits, while those on the rim of the abyss do what is needed to erase them from the world, circulate widely in and through the modern mind. Images of just this sort, derived from multiple sources and supplemented, of course, by the imagination, had no doubt been operative in some way during that strange encounter in Berlin. And they are surely operative in the memories we have of events and experiences that take place during our own lifetime. This in turn suggests that "personal" memory is also, to a greater or lesser extent, a "stipulating," as Sontag puts it: "that this is important, and this is the story about how it happened, with the pictures that lock the stories in our minds." But here, of course, we enter (what some might consider) some uncomfortable terrain. "Do we really wish to fully blur the line between personal and cultural memories?" Raskin has asked. Raskin goes on to suggest that "there is a noteworthy difference between my personal firsthand memories of the September 11 terrorist attacks and my cultural, secondhand experience of the World War II attack on Pearl Harbor. In the sense that I lived through the former event and was not yet born during the latter, my 'memories' of each are qualitatively different." For this reason, "it may be misleading for me to claim 'memories' of Pearl Harbor—if what is meant by memories are first-hand recollections drawn from lived experience" (2002:226–227).

Raskin is of course quite right to distinguish the two events: one occurred during his lifetime and the other did not. He is also right to say that it would be very problematic to speak of his own "memories" of Pearl Harbor—just as it would be problematic (not to mention downright audacious and wrong) for me to speak of my own "memories" of the Holocaust—"if," as Raskin reminds us, "what is meant by memories are firsthand recollections drawn from lived experience." But it is precisely this meaning of memory that I want to interrogate here. Consider for a moment Raskin's own "firsthand memories" of the September 11 attack. Again, it is true that his relationship to the dreadful events of that day is qualitatively different from his relationship to Pearl Harbor; by virtue of the former being contemporaneous with his own life, there is a sense of directness, even immediacy, that Pearl Harbor cannot possibly have. But how "firsthand" are most of our memories of September 11? We saw newsreels and photos and read stories, and for many of us they came together with extraordinary power, even "presence." But the events of that day were mediated through and through by whomever had the video cameras, by newspeople, by witnesses, and more. It is possible, I realize, that Raskin was actually in New York City at the time and saw the planes hit. If so, the distinction he is making would surely be more compelling on some level. But of course many of those who were actually there at the time watched the same newsreels, saw the same photos, heard the same accounts. And undoubtedly, this secondhand information became folded into their own firsthand memories, such that, practically speaking, the two would become one: the memories of that day.

Along these lines, perhaps we can speak of different "registers" or "orders" of autobiographical memory: those that have a first-order reference to the actualities of lived experience and those that have a second-order reference, that is, that are "one step removed" from these actualities but that are still, in a distinct sense, part of "my past." "Memories," therefore, may consist not only of firsthand recollections drawn from lived experience but of those secondhand characteristics that are constitutive of "my past" and, in turn, "my story," and indeed "myself." Let me now try to flesh out the implications of these ideas by turning to several quite distinct cases in which what I earlier referred to as the "narrative unconscious" would appear to figure prominently.

Language, Culture, and the Challenge of Originality

Although Helen Keller was healthy at birth, she contracted a disease that left her deaf and blind at nineteen months of age. While she undoubtedly had retained some fragmentary memories from those first nineteen months, she had been left in a highly primitive psychological state—unable to think, to act purposefully, to relate meaningfully to the world. All of this changed with the arrival of her teacher, Annie Sullivan, who helped Keller understand the miracle of language. Wondrous though her early years with Sullivan were, there was, however, an incident, a very painful incident, that served to cast into question some of Keller's incredible gains. In a burst of inspiration, she had written a story. "My thoughts flowed easily," she recalls. "I felt a sense of joy on the composition. Words and images came tripping to my finger ends" (Keller 1988 [1902]:48). Unfortunately, most of the story had originally been written by someone else. "The stories were so much alike in thought and language," Keller was eventually to admit, "that it was evident that [the original] story had been read to me, and that mine was—a plagiarism" (p. 49). Keller's discovery was a startling one: "I cannot always distinguish my own thoughts from those I read, because what I read becomes the very substance and texture of my mind. Consequently, in nearly all that I write"—including, one can assume, the autobiographical narrative that contains these very sentences—"I produce something which very much resembles the crazy patchwork I used to make when I first learned to sew" (p. 53).

It might be noted that there were some who doubted the allegedly accidental nature of Keller's plagiarism. In fact, it was but the first of a prolonged series of suspicions and accusations that were made against Keller. Her experience was "vicarious" and, on some level, *fake*, some had said. And so too was Keller herself. "She talks bookishly," one of her many critics had complained. "To express her ideas, she falls back on the phrases she has learned from books, and uses words that sound stilted" (cited in Lash 1980:573). Another critic had dubbed her a "dupe of words," maintaining that her avowed enjoyment of the arts, among other things, was "a matter of auto-suggestion rather than perception. . . . Wordiness, unreal emotion and, in the worst sense of the term, literature occupy a disconcerting place in her writing" (cited in Herrmann 1998:136–137). The problem, again, was not only with her writing, however; for some, it was with Keller herself, her seeming inauthenticity. "If only she could realize that it is better to be one's self, however limited and afflicted, than the best imitation of somebody else that could be achieved!" This critic seemed downright angry with Keller: "One resents the pages of second-hand description of natural objects, when what one wants is a sincere account of the attitude, the natural attitude towards life one of whose eyes and ears are sealed" (cited in Herrmann 1998:137). He, like so many others, wanted the real thing so he could experience the world as she did. And the fact that she seemed to be experiencing the world, or at least describing it, as *he* did simply made no sense. "Helen Keller," as yet another critic had concluded, "is a living lie" (cited in Herrmann 1998:84).

Keller would eventually provide elaborate responses to the charges of her alleged inauthenticity as a writer and as an individual (see Keller 1908; also Freeman 1993, 2000). Without going into detail regarding these responses, suffice it to say that she became acutely aware of the challenge, indeed the impossibility, of ever fully separating out her own language, her own memories, her own *self*, from those of others. For those who wanted access to her putatively unique world, there would be disappointment at her clichéd conventionality. But there were also those who would be able to recognize that, ultimately, her case was not appreciably different from anyone else's. "Oh, dear me," Mark Twain wrote, "how unspeakably funny and owlishly idiotic and grotesque was that 'plagiarism' farce! As if there was much of anything in any human utterance, oral or written, except plagiarism! . . . For substantially all ideas are second-hand, consciously and unconsciously drawn from a million outside sources, and daily used by the garnerer with pride and satisfaction borne of the superstition that he originated them" (cited in Lash 1980:146–147).

Whether Twain is right about the nature of originality remains open to question. As I have suggested elsewhere (Freeman 1993), the fact of our working, inevitably, with the "hand-me-downs" of language and history says nothing whatsoever about the uses to which they may be put; while some will appropriate them largely as is, and thereby repeat the status quo of things, others will take them in entirely new directions. This was surely the case with Helen Keller: plagued though she may have been by the otherness within her, she still emerged as one-of-a-kind, manifestly able to give out—in her thinking, her writing, and her very being—more than she took in. In a related vein, I have also suggested that while the "tools" employed in the construction of selfhood are indeed eminently social in nature, the "configurational acts" through which it occurs involve *poiesis*, "imaginative labor seeking to give form and meaning to experience" (Freeman 1999:99). Twain, I would therefore suggest, may have gone a bit too far in his zealous argument on Keller's behalf concerning the ubiquity of plagiarism. There can be little doubt, nevertheless, that the "million outside sources" to which he refers often find their way into the innermost corridors of experience. Indeed, as we shall see presently, they can enter into the very poetic processes through which the self is fashioned.

Memory and Selfhood

Despite the fact that, by his own account, he was "not a poet or a writer," Binjamin Wilkomirski aspired to rise to the challenge of depicting experience afresh, shorn of the conventions and clichés that so often bedeviled the adult mind (see especially Schachtel 1959). He writes as follows in the beginning pages of his book *Fragments: Memories of a Wartime Childhood*, which sought to chronicle his childhood experience of the Holocaust:

> I have no mother tongue, nor a father tongue either. My language has its roots in the Yiddish of my eldest brother, Mordechai, overlaid with the Babel-babble of an assortment of children's barracks in the Nazis' death camps in Poland.
>
> It was a small vocabulary; it reduced itself to the bare essentials required to say and to understand whatever would ensure survival. At some point during this time, speech left me altogether and it was a long time before I found it again. So it was no great loss that I forgot this gibberish which lost its usefulness with the end of the war.
>
> But the languages I learned later on were never mine, at bottom. They were only imitations of other people's speech.
>
> My earliest childhood memories are planted, first and foremost, in exact snapshots of my photographic memory and in the feelings imprinted in them, and the physical sensations. Then comes memory of being able to hear, and things I heard, then things I thought, and last of all, memory of things I said.   (1996:4)

The dangers are clear enough. "My earliest memories," Wilkomirski tells us, "are a rubble field of isolated images and events. Shards of memory with hard knife-sharp edges, which still cut flesh if touched today. Mostly a chaotic jumble, with very little chronological fit; shards that keep surfacing against the orderly grain of grown-up life and escaping the laws of logic." Shades of Schachtel: "If I'm going to write about it, I have to give up on the ordering logic of grown-ups; it would only distort what happened." All he can do is "try to use words to draw as exactly as possible what happened, what I saw; exactly the way my child's memory has held on to it; with no benefit of perspective or vanishing point." This, of course, is easier said than done: insofar as the story of "what happened" can be told only from the vantage point of the present, there is no possibility of "returning," revisiting a lost world. Nevertheless, on commencing his memorial work, "The first pictures surface, like upbeats, flashes of light, with no discernible connection, but sharp and clear. Just pictures, almost no thoughts attached" (p. 5). Poet or not, Wilkomirski, it would have appeared, was to become the Proust of the Holocaust and thereby bring us closer to the real than ever before. We would virtually be *there* with him, peering out at his world, feeling his terror and his pain.

The reviews were glowing. On the back of the book, it was suggested that "*Fragments* will surely take its place with works by Elie Wiesel and Primo Levi as a classic firsthand account of the Holocaust" (*Los Angeles Times*). This was a "brief, harrowing, and strangely beautiful book" that "vindicated" all children. "These broken fragments slice into the soul and draw blood. More than justice, fine art is rendered in these unsmoothed-out memories" (Maurice Sendak). The book was nothing short of "a small masterpiece [that] conveys in sparse, rhythmic prose the shattering effects of the Holocaust upon one child's life, human relations, and capacity to use language" (Daniel Jonah Goldhagen). Even "whilst describing horrors an adult mind can barely fathom . . . the voice remains so innocent" (Mary Karr). As Jonathan Kozol wrote, for *The Nation*, "This stunningly and austerely written work is so profoundly moving, so morally important, and so free from literary artifice of any kind at all that I wonder if I even have the right to try to offer praise."

It was too good to be true: Wilkomirski's book turned out to be—how shall one put it?—a work of fiction. This, at least, was the conclusion drawn by Elena Lappin in a fascinating article for *Granta* called "The Man with Two Heads" (1999). But the plot thickens. Despite the fictional status of the book, Lappin was convinced that Wilkomirski was "genuine." Among other reasons, "anguish like his seemed impossible to fabricate" (p. 61). Eventually, a comprehensive report was written about the book (Maechler

2001) that determined that "the elements of Wilkomirski's story are full of contradictions both in their particulars and in regard to historical reality" and that, most important, "they are incompatible with his own biographical reality." The conclusion reached in the report: "There is not the least doubt that Binjamin Wilkomirski is identical with Bruno Grosjean"—the actual person who authored the book, who had lived a life quite different from the one depicted therein—"and that the story he wrote in *Fragments* and has told elsewhere took place solely within the world of his thoughts and emotions" (p. 268).

It remains possible that Wilkomirski had simply lied about his past, that he had concocted a story, consciously and purposefully, that he knew would move people and thereby sell. By all indications, however, Wilkomirski's story—despite its patent falsity—was not a function of his having lied. What seems to have happened, in brief, was that Wilkomirski gave himself a history, a childhood, a *past* that he believed to have been true. By Maechler's account,

> Wilkomirski did not one day decide to carefully construct a character and devise a story with which to deceive the world. His present-day identity arose, rather, over the course of four decades, unplanned and improvised, with new experiences and necessities constantly woven into it and contradictions arising from a lack of any plan smoothed over, though over time with less and less success.   (2001:269)

As Maechler explains,

> The genesis of [Wilkomirski's] stories is bound up with traumatic experiences which ... we may assume had scarcely found their way into his autobiographical knowledge. The experiences from his early years have the dimensions of a cumulative trauma that eludes all understanding and yet is all the more determinative since it occurred during the phase when the child was developing an ability to speak, to think symbolically, and, finally, to shape experiences into stories. *Fragments* is the attempt of the adult Bruno Grosjean to assemble elements taken from humanity's remembrance of the Shoah in order to find a means of expressing experiences that were not verbally retrievable either when they occurred or later, and which for that very reason cried out for a narrative that would give them meaning.   (p. 269)

We need not pursue the details of this case much further. Operating on the assumption that Wilkomirski told his story in good faith—however false it may have been—it would seem that he had created a kind of *myth* about his past. He was "one of those suffering children" whose story had to be told; he was one of the many " 'children without identity,' lacking any certain information about their origins, with all traces carefully erased, furnished with false names and often with false papers too" (1996:154). The process of reconstructing the past had been an arduous one: "Years of research, many journeys back to the places where I remember things happened, and countless conversations with specialists and historians have helped me clarify many previous inexplicable shreds of memory, to identify places and people, to find them again and to make a possible, more or less logical chronology out of it. I thank them all" (pp. 154–155). As it turned out, they deserved more thanks than he knew. Unbeknownst to him, they had been the very sources of his "memory," the co-historians of his putative past, indeed the co-authors of his very self.

There is one significant difference between Keller's case and Wilkomirski's: while he had supposedly been *remembering* but was actually *imagining*, she had supposedly been *imagining* but was actually *remembering*. This difference aside, both had become the unwitting victims of their own narrative confusion: it simply wasn't clear where others' stories ended and their own began. Both cases also demonstrate the existence of aspects of autobiographical memory that can be called "unconscious." In Keller's case, bits of her own actual experience were transformed into pseudo-fictions. In Wilkomirski's case, pieces of "humanity's remembrance," as Maechler put it, were ultimately transformed into pseudo-memories. Whether or not "collective memory" is a viable concept, it is clear that humanity's remembrance and individuals' remembrance may be virtually of a piece in the work of fashioning and refashioning the self.

Deep History

Let me turn now to another case, decidedly less controversial than Wilkomirski's, that might serve to bring these issues into sharper relief. The following is from the introductory pages of Eva Hoffman's *After Such Knowledge: Memory, History, and the Legacy of the Holocaust*:

I had grown up with a consciousness of the Shoah from the beginning. My parents had emerged from its crucible shortly before my birth. They had survived, in what was then the Polish part of the Ukraine, with the help of Polish and Ukrainian neighbors; but their entire families perished. Those were the inescapable facts—the inescapable knowledge—I had come into. But the knowledge had not always been equally active, nor did I always want to make the inheritance defining.

Indeed, it was not until I started writing about it in my first book . . . that I began discerning, amidst other threads, the Holocaust strand of my history. I had carried this part of my psychic past within me all my life; but it was only now, as I began pondering it from a longer distance and through the clarifying process of writing, that what had been an inchoate, obscure knowledge appeared to me as a powerful theme and influence in my life. Until then, it had not occurred to me that I was in effect a receptacle of a historical legacy, or that its burden had a significance and weight that needed to be acknowledged. Now, personal memory appeared to me clearly linked to larger history, and the heavy dimensions of this inheritance started becoming fully apparent.   (2004:x)

Hoffman had discovered what I earlier referred to as the narrative unconscious. For her, this discovery attained a particular intensity by virtue of her membership in "the second generation," which she describes as "the hinge generation in which received, transferred knowledge of events is transmuted into history, or into myth" (p. xv).

Hoffman immediately goes on to acknowledge that, "while it has become routine to speak of the 'memory' of the Holocaust, and to adduce to this faculty a moral, even a spiritual value, . . . we who came after do not have memories of the Holocaust. Even from my most intimate proximity," she writes, "I could not form 'memories' of the Shoah or take my parents' memories as my own. Rather, I took in that first information as a sort of fairy tale deriving not so much from another world as from the center of the cosmos: an enigmatic but real fable" (p. 6). And yet, she continues, there was a distinct sense in which her parents' memories *did* become her own, albeit of a different order. She speaks of her parents' first communications, and how their "fragmentary phrases lodged themselves in my mind like shards, like the deadly needles I remember from certain fairy tales, which pricked your flesh and could never be extracted again" (p. 11). Hoffman continues with this theme in a graphic depiction of the world that had come to occupy her:

> In my childish mind, the hypervivid moments summoned by my parents registered themselves as half awful reality, half wondrous fairy tale. A peasant's hut, holding the riddle of life or death; a snowy forest, which confounds the senses and sense of direction. A hayloft in which one sits, awaiting fate, while a stranger downstairs, who is really a good fairy in disguise, is fending off that fate by muttering invocations under her breath and bringing to the hiding place a bowl of soup. The sister, young, innocent, and loved, standing naked above a pit that is soon to become her own mass grave. . . . Brutal-faced Germans with large vicious dogs. Humiliating orders shouted in a harsh language. . . . The pursuit of powerless people, bent silhouettes running desperately through an exposed landscape, trying to make it into the bordering woods. . . . Fields, trenches, pits of death. For others, barbed wire, skeletal figures, smoke, intimations of mass death. Every survivor's child has such images available right behind the eyelids. Later, through literature and film, through memoirs and oral testimony, these components of horror become part of a whole generation's store of imagery and narration, the icons and sagas of the post-Holocaust world.   (pp. 11–12)

Images aside, Hoffman had "absorbed [her] parents' unhappiness through channels that seemed nearly physical. The pain of their psyches," she writes, "reverberated in my body almost as if it were mine" (p. 14).

Hoffman herself is unsure how far to take this line of thinking. As she explains, "It was not that the mythical vision of the world I had put together from scraps of story and imagery was untrue. The mythology, after all, derived from reality. It was just that I knew it *as* mythology and had no way of grasping it as actuality" (p. 16). Two points deserve emphasis here. The first is that the "mythology" of which Hoffman speaks is not wholly to be severed from memory: this world she has put together, which has become *her* world, *is* rooted in her own bodily and psychical experiences; they too are "events," albeit of a different sort from those experienced by her parents. The second point is that memory, whether first- or second-order, is not wholly to be severed from mythology, from those "scraps of story and imagery" that often find their way into the figuration of actuality.

Hoffman also goes on to speak of much larger events, having to do with Poland, the Warsaw uprising, and so on, events that were far more distant than those that came the way of her parents. These too, she writes, "would become my meaningful history, the history it is urgent to know because it belongs to one's life, because it shapes ancestral fate and one's own sensibility" (p. 18). Such are "the paradoxes of indirect knowledge," a knowledge that continues to "haunt" Hoffman and others who "came after":

> The formative events of the twentieth century have crucially informed our biographies and psyches, threatening sometimes to overshadow and overwhelm our own lives. But we did not see them, suffer through them, experience their impact directly. Our relationship to them has been defined by our very "post-ness," and by the powerful but mediated forms of knowledge that have followed from it.   (p. 25)

Hoffman recognizes the dangers of framing the issues in this way, particularly the danger of speaking of "the second generation." Indeed, she raises the possibility that this sort of label might just be "another American affectation, a group 'identity' conveniently invented at the very moment when everybody was beginning to insist on having one" (p. 26). In her own mind, then, it took a certain audacity for this second generation to single itself out as a subject worthy of reflection. "There are so many ways to conceive of our lives, our identities, our stories—to shape memory and biography. It did not occur to me to think of myself as a 'child of Holocaust survivors' for many of my adult years. Other threads of causality, influence, development seemed more important; or at least I gave them other names. . . . Identities are malleable and multidimensional," Hoffman continues, "and I am reluctant to fix my own through reifying labels. And yet, we do not only define ourselves; we are also defined by our circumstances, culture, the perceptions of others and—perhaps most of all—the force of an internalized past" (p. 27).

One could argue here that Hoffman is simply employing a new lens through which to view her past. That is to say, it could have nothing whatsoever to do with memory, much less the narrative unconscious; there may be little more at work than the importation of a new sociological category to the trajectory of her life. On my reading, however, Hoffman's new way of conceiving of her life has the force of a revelation, a discovery: she has come to see quite new "threads of causality, influence, development," ones that had been operative and yet unacknowledged, unseen. Her identity had been defined and constituted in ways that had been essentially unbeknownst to her; and with her discovery, she has radically enlarged the scope of her own history as well as the story she can now tell about it. The space of selfhood thus expands.

Reflecting further on the phenomenon at hand, Hoffman too uses the very apt language of "haunting": "Something emerges from the past that we thought had been dead"—or that one never knew was alive—"but that has lain dormant in the turrets and caverns of the soul till it returns in the form of specters and shadows" (p. 65). These phenomena, she continues, "belong to the world of ghost stories and the gothic—psychologically speaking, a world of fantasy and inner distortion. For in the second generation, the anxieties, the symptoms, no matter how genuine in themselves, no longer correspond to actual experience or external realities." Indeed, she maintains, "They do not even correspond to anything that can be called 'memory.'" The second generation "has inherited not experience, but its shadows." This is not at all to diminish the power of the inheritance: for "wrestling with shadows can be more frightening, or confusing, than struggling with solid realities" (p. 66). But is it true to claim that the anxieties and symptoms of the second generation "no longer correspond to actual experience"? Didn't Hoffman herself actually experience some of the emotional pain felt by her parents? And hadn't this turmoil somehow been inscribed in her own history?

As Hoffman suggests, Halbwachs' notion of "collective memory" (1980) is surely relevant to present concerns (see also Fentress and Wickham 1992). In line with what she said earlier regarding her reluctance to employ the term "memory" in this context, however, this notion of collective memory is problematic in its own right, "veering between a useful and a misleading fiction. For within such 'memory,'"—Hoffman continues to place the term "memory" in scare quotes here—"there is no subject who remembers, no process of remembering, no link between reflection and experience" (pp. 165–166). In this respect, Hoffman and Sontag are of a piece. More problematic still is the fact that such "impersonal memory, much more than embodied, personal remembering, is malleable in the extreme, and highly susceptible to deliberate shaping or exploitation—to propaganda and censorship, to tendentious selectivity and willful emphasis. It is, in other words, an instrument not so much of subjective reflection or understanding as of cultural agendas or ideological purposes" (p. 166).

Hoffman is surely right about this. My own experience in Berlin and the various experiences she relates—removed as they are from the actualities that are their ultimate referents—are the products of highly schematized, even conventionalized images of people and places and things. Put another way, they are the product of memorial *forms*, prototypical patterns or templates, inflected with whatever firsthand knowledge might have been acquired. With first-order autobiographical memory, there is at least an "anchor," so to speak, of actuality, however schematically and conventionally this actuality may be viewed. With second-order autobiographical memory—should we elect to retain the term—the anchor is gone; and in its place there is a kind of montage, a poetically figured heterogeneous image, rounded off at its edges, perhaps as much a function of Hollywood as of our own personal experience. The implication is strange, indeed. It could be that Hollywood is itself partially constitutive of that very dimension of identity I discovered on that unsettling first trip to Berlin.

For Hoffman, the notion of "mediation" looms large: "those who have not lived through the Shoah"—or through anything else—"received its knowledge, at this late date, through mediations—sometimes several layers of them" (p. 178). But of course this is also true, to a greater or lesser degree, for those who *have* lived through the Shoah—or anything else. For them too, memory is suffused with all kinds of "extraneous" matter. And, as noted earlier, it is thoroughly conditioned by one's ever-changing vantage point at the present moment of remembering and narrating. To reiterate: I do not wish to *equate* the two situations; for epistemological as well as ethical reasons, to do so would simply be wrong. Nevertheless, the fact remains that many of the defining characteristics of *second*-order autobiographical memory may also be found in *first*-order autobiographical memory. Ultimately, in fact, there is one dimension that differentiates the two: the aforementioned "anchor," which entails the existence of a referent to what had once been sensorily present to the remembering person him- or herself: an attic, for instance, that smelled of wood and smoke and not only fear and despair.

Culture, Narrative, Identity

The question remains: Are we talking here about *memory*? In the final pages of her book, Hoffman suggests that she and other members of the second generation need "to disentangle the spectral memories that have inhabited us from the realities we inhabit" (p. 278). From this perspective, there seems to be an advantage of sorts to these memories being "spectral" rather than being rooted in external realities. Because these spectral memories are without anchor, perhaps they can dissipate more easily or be separated out from the actual. This line of thinking is in keeping with Hoffman's uncertainty about whether to even call the phenomenon she has been exploring "memory." But this very project of disentanglement, and dissipation, itself presumes that it is somehow possible to extricate ourselves from history and, in essence, to reconstruct our identity anew and afresh, *without* spectral adornments.

Helen Keller unquestionably needed to engage in a project of disentangling; by her own admission, she eventually had to learn how to marshal her own thoughts and perhaps not rely quite so much on others' words. Binjamin Wilkomirski needed to do so as well; at some point, he needed to acknowledge to himself that his imagination had carried him too far. As for Hoffman, finally, she is perfectly right to try to determine the ways in which her own narrative unconscious has been shaped by propaganda, by ideological designs and agendas, all of which have led her to a too-stereotypical view of history and of her own past. In each of these accounts, however—Keller's, Wilkomirski's, and Hoffman's—what we see is that this project of "disentangling" (of others' memories from one's own, of the actual from the fantastic, and, not least, of the *cultural* from the *personal*) cannot be brought to completion. More optimistically, what we also see is that it may be possible to move beyond the split that is frequently posited between the "inner" and the "outer," toward a more unitary conception, one that views "secondhand" information not as something *imposed on* memory but as *part of* it—as evidenced especially by its impact on personal identity.

As Edward Shils writes in *Tradition*, "It was a great achievement of moral and political philosophy to postulate the existence of a self-contained human being as a self-determining moral entity free from original sin and from the toils of a dark inheritance. The ideal was to expunge from human beings all that came from the past and hindered their complete self-regulation and expression." The result is that "there are undoubtedly many persons who regard their pasts as beginning only with their own birth" and who "believe that it lies within their powers to order entirely their own existence by their 'own' decisions and those of their contemporaries" (1980:43–44). But, "The individual as he perceives himself includes things which are not bounded by his own experiences"

(p. 50). Indeed, "his knowledge of his past is furnished by the history of his family, of his neighborhood, of his city, of his religious community, of his ethnic group, of his nationality, of his country and of the wider culture into which he has been assimilated." Memory, therefore, "is furnished not only from the recollections of events which the individual has himself experienced but from the memories of others. . . . From their accounts of their own experiences, which frequently antedate his own, and from written works at various removes, his image of his 'larger self' is brought to include events which occurred both recently and earlier outside his own experiences" (p. 51). It is precisely this "larger self" that I wish to invoke when speaking of the *space* of selfhood.

As Gadamer has added in this context, "It is time to rescue the phenomenon of memory from being regarded merely as a psychological faculty and to see it as an essential element of the finite historical being of man" (1982:16). "Self-reflection and autobiography," he writes,

> are not primary and are not an adequate basis for the hermeneutical problem, because through them history is made private once more. In fact history does not belong to us, but we belong to it. Long before we understand ourselves through the process of self-examination, we understand ourselves in a self-evident way in the family, society and state in which we live. . . . That is why the prejudices of the individual, far more than his judgments, constitute the historical reality of his being.   (p. 245)

As Gadamer goes on to note, "Our historical consciousness is always filled with a variety of voices in which the echo of the past is heard. It is present only in the multifariousness of such voices" (pp. 252–253) and thus "always includes more than it acknowledges of itself" (p. 255). There is a *surplus*, therefore, within memory, within historical consciousness, within autobiographical narrative, and, again, within the very fabric of selfhood.

As MacIntyre has noted, this way of thinking about memory and selfhood runs counter to modern individualism: "From the standpoint of individualism I am what I myself choose to be. I can always, if I wish to, put in question what are taken to be the merely contingent social features of my existence." Just as memory may be seen a purely internal faculty, fundamentally detachable from the world beyond the skin, we are here considering an attitude "according to which the self is detachable from its social and historical roles and statuses" (p. 205). Along with Shils, Gadamer and MacIntyre consider this a mistake; for "the story of my life is always embedded in those communities from which I derive my identity. I am born with a past; and to try to cut myself off from that past, in the individualist mode, is to deform my present relationships." My very identity, therefore, is in large measure a function of what I inherit, "a specific past that is present to some degree in my present. I find myself part of a history and that is generally to say, whether I like it or not, whether I recognise it or not, one of the bearers of a tradition" (pp. 205–206).

The phrase "whether I recognise it or not" brings us all the way back to the idea of the narrative unconscious. Many aspects of my historical inheritance are available to consciousness. But some remain hidden, and refer to that sort of "deep history," as I put it earlier, of which I may be largely unaware. This "hiddenness," I have suggested (Freeman 2002), is itself one of the legacies of modernity; for the fashioning of the ostensibly sovereign self, free to craft his or her story anew, effectively occludes those very historical and cultural moorings that are the ground of identity. Along these lines, it might be said that the modern self, for all of its countless memoirs and autobiographies, is a self that is in large measure unconscious of its own historical and cultural formation.

In closing, let me raise three additional ideas. The first involves the possibility of moving from a discourse of representation in thinking about autobiographical memory (tied to its faithfulness, or lack thereof, to the actualities of the past) to what might be called a *pragmatics*. What I am suggesting here is that, pragmatically or functionally speaking, perhaps we can think of autobiographical memory as referring to those features of our relationship to the past—whether actual or presumed, first-order or second-, that are constitutive of identity. This does not eliminate the epistemological problem at hand. As the narrative confusions and conflations found in Keller's and Wilkomirski's cases demonstrate, there can be utterly *false* autobiographical memories and it is frequently important to know it. But these memories, even in their patent falsity, nonetheless remain pivotal players in the fashioning of life narratives and, in turn, selves (see Flanagan 1996; see also Ricoeur 1992). There is a distinct sense in which Wilkomirski *became* the self he imagined himself to be, false memories and all. In this respect, his case provides a most valuable inroad into understanding the dynamics of self-fashioning.

The second idea concerns this process of self-fashioning. To emphasize the sociocultural constitution of memory and selfhood alike might lead some to assume that these phenomena are ultimately *epi*phenomena, determinate products of this or that mode of historical or cultural discourse. But it should not be forgotten that in each of the cases considered herein there has been *poiesis*, meaning-making, a process wherein the given—what I earlier referred to as the "hand-me-downs" of language, history, culture—has been transformed into something new: a past, a story, a *self*. Along these lines, memory and selfhood alike may both be understood as cultural "works," imaginative spaces where inner and outer worlds meet and become one.

Some important questions nevertheless remain: How exactly does it come to be that a "smaller" self emerges out of the rather "larger" one that Shils had spoken of? Out of the myriad influences that come our way, some of which even antedate our birth, some become more influential than others. How does this happen? How does it come to be that, out of the "variety of voices in which the echo of the past is heard," as Gadamer had put it, we come to speak "our own"? MacIntyre, finally, suggested that one of the excesses of individualistic thinking is that it can lead us to imagine that "I am what I myself choose to be," that I can "put in question . . . the merely contingent social features of my existence." At the same time, however, he is quick to emphasize that the self, far from being a simple *product* of such social features, emerges in and through *narrative*—which is to say, through the imaginative, poetic labor that gives form and meaning to experience. Is it possible to reconcile MacIntyre's indictment of simple "self-choosing" with his defense of narrative self-knowing? If in fact "the story of my life is always embedded in those communities from which I derive my identity," how does this story ever become "mine"?

Here I want to return briefly to the idea, stated at the outset of this chapter, that what is "mine" is, at one and the same time, permeated by what is "other." Indeed, what I wish to suggest is that the former, far from excluding the latter, relies on the latter as its very condition of possibility. Even as "my story" is "embedded" in the communities—and, more broadly, the tradition—from which I derive my identity, I am faced with the challenge of *making* something of my life, of finding my place in this tradition: of determining, within the limits tradition imposes, how to live, who to be. That there is some measure of choice involved seems clear enough. But this very element of choice exists only against the backdrop of those demands and those "goods" that inhere in the tradition from which my story and my *self* emerge. Taylor's reflections on the ethics of authenticity may be useful in this context: "Even the sense that the significance of my life comes from its being chosen—the case where authenticity is actually grounded on self-determining freedom—depends on the understanding that *independent of my will* there is something noble, courageous, and hence significant in giving shape to my own life" (1991:39). Indeed, "To shut out demands emanating beyond the self is precisely to suppress the conditions of significance, and hence to court trivialization" (p. 40). "Authenticity," Taylor argues, "is not the enemy of demands that emanate beyond the self; it supposes such demands" (p. 41). Otherness thus turns out to be at the very heart of what is "mine." And what is beyond the self, in culture and its demands, is thus constitutive of the very choices I make.

This leads me to the third and final idea. Much of narrative psychology, particularly the segment of it that looks toward the study of individual lives, remains oriented toward what happens between birth and death and focuses on firsthand personal experience. This, of course, is sensible enough; there is just so much one can do in an interview or, for that matter, in a biography or autobiography. Strictly speaking, however, "my story" and indeed my *self* cannot be delimited in this way, for as we have seen here, both emerge out of the ground that precedes me and that thus extends well beyond the perimeter of my life. It follows that a portion of narrative psychology would do well to include within its scope the project of discerning the multiple sources, both near and far, firsthand and secondhand, that give rise to selfhood. This in no way eliminates the place of the "I" in telling the self's story; the task of poetically fashioning an identity through these sources remains (Freeman 1999, 2002). But this very task must take place in the vast sociocultural space within which language, culture, and history operate. By acknowledging that vastness, we can appreciate more fully the vastness of the space of selfhood itself.

References

Brockmeier, J. 1997. Autobiography, narrative, and the Freudian conception of life history. *Philosophy, Psychiatry, Psychology* 4:175–200.

Bruner, J. 1991. Self-making and world-making. *Journal of Aesthetic Education* 25:67–78.

Fentress, J., and C. Wickham. 1992. *Social Memory*. Oxford: Blackwell.

Flanagan, O. 1996. *Self Expressions: Mind, Morals, and the Meaning of Life*. Oxford: Oxford University Press.

Freeman, M. 1993. *Rewriting the Self: History, Memory, Narrative*. London: Routledge.

——. 1999. Culture, narrative, and the poetic construction of selfhood. *Journal of Constructivist Psychology* 12:99–116.

——. 2000. Worded images, imaged words: Helen Keller and the poetics of self-representation. *Interfaces* 18:135–146.

——. 2002. Charting the narrative unconscious: Cultural memory and the challenge of autobiography. *Narrative Inquiry* 12:193–211.

Gadamer, H. G. 1982. *Truth and Method*. New York: Crossroad.

Halbwachs, M. 1980. *The Collective Memory*. New York: Harper and Row.

Herrmann, D. 1998. *Helen Keller: A Life*. New York: Knopf.

Hoffman, E. 2004. *After Such Knowledge: Memory, History, and the Legacy of the Holocaust*. New York: Public Affairs.

Keller, H. 1908. *The World I Live In*. New York: The Century Co.

——. 1988 [1902]. *The Story of My Life*. New York: New American Library.

Lappin, E. 1999. The man with two heads. *Granta* 66:28–65.

Lash, J. P. 1980. *Helen and Teacher: The Story of Helen Keller and Anne Sullivan Macy*. Reading, MA: Addison-Wesley.

MacIntyre, A. 1981. *After Virtue: A Study in Moral Theory*. Notre Dame: University of Notre Dame Press.

Maechler, S. 2001. *The Wilkomirski Affair: A Study in Biographical Truth*. New York: Schocken.

Raskin, J. D. 2002. Constructing the narrative unconscious. *Narrative Inquiry* 12:225–231.

Ricoeur, P. 1992. *Oneself as Another*. Chicago: University of Chicago Press.

Schachtel, E. 1959. *Metamorphosis: On the Conflict of Human Development and the Psychology of Creativity*. New York: Basic Books.

Shils, E. 1980. *Tradition*. Chicago: University of Chicago Press.

Sontag, S. 2003. *Regarding the Pain of Others*. New York: Farrar, Straus, and Giroux.

Taylor, C. 1991. *The Ethics of Authenticity*. Cambridge, MA: Harvard University Press.

Wang, Q., and J. Brockmeier. 2002. Autobiographical remembering as cultural practice: Understanding the interplay between memory, self, and culture. *Culture & Psychology* 8:44–64.

Wilkomirski, B. 1996. *Fragments: Memories of a Wartime Childhood*. New York: Schocken.

7   Agentive Hermeneutics

JEFF SUGARMAN AND JACK MARTIN

This chapter summarizes a sustained program of work over the past decade that has attempted to draw the contours of a psychology of personal existence and to advance arguments for the ontological uniqueness of its form (Martin and Sugarman 1996, 1997, 1998, 1999a, 1999b, 2001a, 2002, 2003; Martin, Sugarman, and Thompson 2003). The importance of this project resides in the fact that unless features of human psychology can be shown to be ontologically exceptional (i.e., irreducible to material, organic, or sociocultural properties) then psychology has no subject matter genuinely of its own and must relinquish its status as a distinct discipline. At the center of this project is the thesis that persons are self-interpreting human agents who emerge developmentally from biophysical and sociocultural determinants, yet who also are deeply implicated in their own self-determination in ways that are not reducible to these determinants. We term our thesis *agentive hermeneutics* to emphasize that human persons, unlike other animate and inanimate entities, develop psychologically by virtue of a socially and culturally capable, self-interpreting agency that comes to possess an understanding of its own particular existence.

Our thesis has four principal components: (1) a *levels of reality* approach to conceptualizing the ontology of psychological phenomena, (2) an *underdetermination* argument for human agency, (3) a hermeneutically inspired notion of *self as a kind of understanding* that discloses and extends a person's particular being and activity in the world, and (4) an account of the *developmental emergence* of persons as psychologically capable human agents. In what follows, we begin by sketching these four perspectives. Subsequently, we extend our thesis with an overview of two strands of our more recent work. One details the way in which our constantly emergent psychological agency is constituted through *perspective-taking* in conjunction with forms of *self-reactivity* (Martin 2005a, 2005b, 2006). The other elaborates a relational dynamic of *mutual self-revelation* by which we become present to ourselves through the actions of others (Sugarman 2006, 2008). Finally, we discuss some critical considerations by which our work might inform psychological theorizing and inquiry.

Levels of Reality

Among traditional doctrines of philosophical realism, it is commonly held that phenomena are real if they exist independently of human perception and conception. When this criterion is applied, physical and biological phenomena are presumed real, the reality of psychological phenomena becomes highly debatable, and sociocultural practices fall somewhere in between. Concomitantly, it also is widely accepted that physical, biological, sociocultural, and psychological phenomena are arrayed along a metaphysical continuum of some sort that permits various reductions, especially the reduction of mental phenomena to the physical constituents and requirements from which they issue. In keeping with these assumptions, many contemporary programs of psychological research regard human thoughts, actions, and experiences as reducible to what are often considered more fundamental neurophysiological, biological, evolutionary, or computational processes. In a different vein, postmodern psychologists (e.g., Gergen 1994), while eschewing the essentialism and foundationalism associated with philosophical realism, seem equally reductionistic in their treatment of psychological phenomena as reducible to narrative conventions, rhetorical devices, and other sociocultural practices.

In Martin and Sugarman 1999b we argued that such reductions make the mistake of equating requirement with identity; that is, of erroneously identifying that which is to be explained (i.e., psychological phenomena) with that on which it depends (i.e., biophysical and sociocultural factors and conditions). Attempting to repair this problem, we asserted that psychological phenomena such as reasons and intentions are real, not by virtue of being mind-independent, but because they can be determining of individuals' actions that, in turn, may influence self and others. Further, in our model, physical, biological, sociocultural, and psychological phenomena are not seen as arrayed along a single continuum that privileges the physical (i.e., all phenomena can be reduced ultimately to their physical constituents), but rather, are assumed to be distinct levels of reality nested within and interactive with each other in accordance with a general historical unfolding. The physical universe evolves, biological species emerge and evolve, societies and cultures develop and change, and human individuals emerge as psychological persons within sociocultural and biophysical contexts. On this account, psychological phenomena are understood to be nested within sociocultural practices, from which the former are constituted, while both psychological and sociocultural phenomena are nested within biological and physical levels of reality.

While physical and biological levels of reality, including human bodies, are necessary requirements for psychological phenomena and constrain what is psychologically possible, psychological phenomena cannot be reduced entirely to these levels of reality. This is because psychological phenomena also require sociocultural practices for their more specific constitution within particular historical traditions and forms of life. The psychological reality of individual humans (e.g., intentions, memories, imaginings, experiences, and so forth) emerges as a consequence of their immersion and participation in the societies and cultures to which such individuals are born, and within which they grow and develop. In this sense the psychological reality of individuals is not only constrained but actually constituted in large part by socioculturally shared beliefs and practices. In addition, because sociocultural reality is not fixed or static, but pluralistic and continually changing both across and within different societies, individual psychological reality may vary considerably across societies, individuals, and time.

Unlike physical and biological levels of reality, sociocultural and psychological reality do not exist independently of human perception and activity. However, this does not mean that they are not real. They exert undeniable influence in individual and collective human life. Human understanding, belief, deliberation, purpose, and action have very real consequences not only for human sociocultural reality (e.g., the ways in which ideas and inventions change collective practices), but also for physical and biological levels of reality (e.g., depletion of natural resources and environmental degradation).

The Underdetermination of Human Agency

The analysis of reality as comprised of distinct and irreducible, but also dynamically interrelated, levels defends a unique ontological status for psychological phenomena and supports an argument for the existence of human agency. We define human agency as the deliberative, reflective activity of a human being in framing, choosing, and executing his or her actions in a way that is not fully determined by factors and conditions other than his or her own authentic understanding and reasoning. According to this definition, human agency is both determined and self-determining.

In the argument we set out (Martin and Sugarman 2002; Martin, Sugarman, and Thompson 2003), the only factors other than agency (i.e., self-determination) alleged to determine human choice and action are: (a) physical/biological states and processes; (b) sociocultural rules and practices; (c) unconscious processes over which an agent has no control; and (d) random (chance) events. Assuming that these factors exhaust the plausible determinants of human choice and action, eliminating each and all of these options as fully determining demonstrates the underdetermination of human agency by factors and conditions other than agency itself, understood as a modest self-determination interactive with other relevant determinants.

Our denial of full physical/biological determinism of human agency begins with the observation that human actions are meaningful. "Meaning" refers to the conventional, common, or standard sense of an expression, construction, or sentence in a given language, or of a nonlinguistic signal or symbol. Thus, the meaningfulness of human actions requires sociocultural practices and conventions, the most important of which are language related. It follows that the only way in which human choice and action could be fully determined by physical/biological states and processes is if sociocultural practices and conventions are reducible to such states and processes. A full reduction of societies and cultures to physical biology seems highly improbable, given that we currently do not possess—nor, we would argue, are we likely to possess—adequate physical descriptions of sociocultural, linguistic practices. However, even in the unlikely event that psychologists were to articulate an entirely biophysical explanation of human individual and collective activity, the resources from which such an account would draw meaning are the very linguistic and other sociocultural conventions and practices it was attempting to explain.

Full sociocultural determinism of human agency also cannot be the case. The meanings and forms of sociocultural practices are not fixed and static but change over historical time. The ongoing and persistent historical change in individual and collective human life would not be possible if sociocultural conventions and practices were fully determinate of meaning. In order for sociocultural practices and conventions to change, they must be at least partially open-ended in ways that permit individuals to develop new meanings and possibilities for action that can contribute to social and cultural transformation. While sociocultural conventions and practices may enable individuals to develop psychological capacities to transform these very conventions and practices, the provision for such possibility is not determination.

Although the meanings of sociocultural conventions and practices are continually changing, societies and cultures nonetheless manifest a great deal of consistency and order. Because randomness cannot account for order, the sociocultural meaning that is required for human action cannot be random. Both biophysical and sociocultural evolution and development may be radically contingent, depending on unpredictable patterns of activity that function more or less well in shifting circumstances. However, such radical, unpredictable contingency certainly is not random, and may be interpreted evidentially subsequent to its occurrence. Moreover, at this point in our evolutionary and developmental history, we adult humans are at least partially aware of many of our choices and actions in ways that match and coordinate with the observations, accounts, and activities of others. Unconscious processes alone cannot account for such awareness and coordination of human choice and action.

Having eliminated full physical/biological and sociocultural determination of human action, and argued against random chance and unconscious processes alone, we are left with the conclusion that human choice and action, at least in part and sometimes, result from the irreducible (once emergent in biophysical and sociocultural contexts) understanding and reasoning of human agents. The underdetermination of human agency by these other conditions and factors does not mean that human agency is undetermined, only that it figures in its own determination. Such self-determination means that human agency is not reducible to

physical, biological, sociocultural, and/or random/unconscious processes, even though all of these may be required for its constitution. Simply put, requirement is not identity. Just, for example, as it is a mistake
to equate musical performance with the architecture and properties of
musical instruments or the score to be played, it is a mistake to equate
human actions and experiences with those neurophysiological or sociocultural conditions they require.

The importance of the foregoing arguments for the irreducibility and
underdetermination of human agency is that they establish the deliberative, reflective activity of a human being in framing, choosing, and executing his or her actions in a way that is not fully determined by factors and
conditions other than his or her own understanding and reasoning.

Self as Understanding

The third component of our account of the ontologically exceptional form of personal psychology is self-understanding or, more specifically, our conception of self as the understanding of particular being
(Martin and Sugarman 2001a; Martin, Sugarman, and Thompson 2003).
Our account of self-understanding borrows largely from a tradition of
thought found in Continental philosophy known as hermeneutics (see
Martin 2002; Martin and Sugarman 2001b; and Sugarman and Martin
2005 for explanations of hermeneutics with attention to its application
to psychology and references to other relevant work in this area). Hermeneutics is concerned broadly with the art and theory of interpretation, but
particularly with the interpretation of what it is to be human and how
human understanding is possible.

A hermeneutic approach to the study of human existence holds that it
is only by virtue of participating in human life as self-interpreting beings
who come to understand themselves in terms of a shared background of
sociocultural conventions and practices that we develop psychologically.
Our personhood and selfhood are the products of interpretive activity that
takes place against a background of historical and sociocultural meanings
and significance that structures and orients us as psychological beings.
Thus, from a hermeneutic vantage, human psychology is interpretive,
historical, social, cultural, and saturated with human interests and values.
In sum, a psychology informed by hermeneutics assumes that psychological phenomena cannot be understood apart from the history of interpre-

tations and descriptions given them. The discipline of psychology itself belongs to the history of the means human beings have developed for interpreting themselves psychologically; moreover, it is precisely this history that has constituted the objects and methods of psychological study.

In our hermeneutically inspired account, the necessity and inevitability of some kind of interpretive, historically, and socioculturally informed self-understanding is a significant aspect of human psychological development and what is entailed in becoming a person. Central to this view is a notion of understanding as a process through which the physical, sociocultural, and eventually the psychological world is revealed both tacitly and explicitly. Human understanding is both tacit and explicit. Tacit understanding is the kind of "know-how" that comes from coordinated acting with others in general accord with, but without explicit recognition and articulation of, the conventions, norms, and shared assumptions and practices of the sociocultural context. Much of our everyday practical activity is understood tacitly and occurs without a great deal of self-conscious reflection or questioning. Explicit understanding is achieved through a more purposefully engaged interpretation of the background of sociocultural meanings in relation to our particular concerns. Tacit understanding may become explicit, especially when our concerns or purposes are impeded in some way that requires us to interpret the assumed background of sociocultural belief and practice that provides meaning and intelligibility to our actions. For example, when we reach to open a door, we do not first discern its handle, hinges, and lock, deduce that it is a door, and then open it. Rather, the door presents itself simply as something to be opened or closed depending on our purposes. It is only if we were to find the door locked, for example, that we would make it an object of explicit reflection, abstract its features, and consider alternative courses of action.

All understanding opens up possibilities for the extension of psychological existence. However, given that tacit understanding typically is sufficient for the execution of everyday routines, it is the opening of possibilities through explicit interpretive activity that enables a psychological person to develop beyond whatever set of tacit understandings currently constitutes that individual's way of being. As the opening of possibilities, interpretive understanding is always ongoing, mutable, and incomplete. It ebbs and flows, as our various concerns and purposes arise in the course of living and acting.

Our life experiences as particular embodied beings in specific contexts enable certain tacit and explicit understandings to emerge as central components of ourselves. Self-understanding (self) is that part of a person's understanding that reveals aspects of her or his particular being in the world. Self is an ever-changing, dynamic process of understanding particular being. This said, self, as a core, necessary aspect of personhood, is related to particular identity, embodied being, and deliberative, reflective agency in ways that give it an existential and experiential grounding. This grounding ensures some necessary degree of stability within an overall pattern of ongoing development and change. Self is recognizable to itself, even as it shifts and evolves. As such, self as an understanding of particular being is capable of making aspects of itself (e.g., beliefs, desires, reasons, values) objects of its own experience and reflection. When such second-order, self-reflective capability emerges within the contextualized, developmental trajectory of an individual life, full-fledged psychological personhood is attained. Psychological persons are biophysically embodied beings with first-person experience and understanding of their lives that enable the exercise of both rational and moral agency (self-determination). Selves are not substantive or mysterious entities within persons, but rather consist of social and psychological relations of activity and understanding that define individual human beings and their lives.

We now turn to the fourth principal component of our overall thesis. Our account of developmental emergence links the preceding three components and demonstrates their relevance and interrelations in comprehending the distinctively agentive and hermeneutic character of the psychology of personal existence. Our developmental theory also clarifies the extent to which our reflective, deliberative agency and self-understanding emerge from, and depend upon, our more primary and pervasive, enactive existence and preconceptual engagement, and coordination, with others within our biophysical and sociocultural world.

Developmental Emergence

Human infants enter the world equipped with evolved bodies and brains that are uniquely socially and culturally capable, but with only a small number of currently functioning, primitive, and biologically given capabilities of limited motion and sensation (e.g., nonreflective movements and sensations associated with feeding and physical discomfort), and the prereflective ability to remember, in a very limited physical manner, something of what is encountered and sensed. However, the world into which infants are born is not only a natural habitat, but also a human "life-world" comprised of existing societies and cultures with historically established traditions and practices. Within the historical and sociocultural life-world, nested within the ever-present physical and biological world, caregivers and others interact with the infant in ways that furnish various practices, forms, and means of personhood and identity sustained and promoted by the particular culture and society into which he or she has been born. Whenever the infant appears to be attempting some intentional act, adults or more capable children supplement her efforts by interpreting and reacting to the infant's actions in ways that initiate her into the relational and linguistic practices of the society.

In the manner described by Vygotsky (1978, 1986), psychological development proceeds through the appropriation and internalization of relational and linguistic aspects of interactions that subsequently are transformed into the various psychological forms for thinking and understanding. The gradual incorporation of sociocultural means as psychological tools provides for increasingly sophisticated forms of thought, some of which, like memory and imagination, eventually enable reflective activity that is liberated from the immediate physical and sociocultural context. Learning to direct our thoughts and experiences through the use of psychological tools shifts our engagement and understanding from an unmediated and prereflective to a mediated and reflective consciousness. It is in this way that the unordered mental activity with which infants are neurophysiologically endowed develops into the structured patterns of mature minds.

We develop an awareness of our agency and understanding of ourselves in our ongoing interactions with others, which are mediated by practices and conventions comprising the sociocultural world. Incorporating not only language, but also the roles of speaker and listener, thought takes the form of conversation. Developing psychological persons learn to talk and relate to themselves in much the same way as others have talked and related to them. The reflexivity thus made possible yields an intentional awareness of oneself as both subject and object, and an understanding of one's embodied being in the world as a center of experiencing, intending, and acting. Self emerges in this way, as a kind of interpreted reflexive understanding that discloses and extends particular, individual existence. Given the inevitably unique history of individual experience within a lifeworld, and the capacity for self as the reflexive understanding of experience in that world, psychological persons are underdetermined by their constitutive, sociocultural and biological origins. The "self"-understanding and deliberations of such persons may, and frequently do, enter into their determination. Even as psychological persons continue to be formed by the relational and discursive practices in which they are embedded, they also come to contribute to those practices in innovative ways that reflect a self-interpreting agency.

Perspective Taking and Self-Reactivity

Vygotsky's (1978) developmental account of the internalization of meaning begins with the caregiver's response to the child's attempts to grasp an object. It should be noted that Vygotsky's analysis of the child's grasping effort owes much to Wundt (1973). According to this account, by presenting the object to the child, the caregiver transforms the child's act of grasping into the gesture of pointing, the meaning of which subsequently is appropriated and internalized by the child. Importantly, Vygotsky situates psychological development in relational interactivity, rather than in isolated individual activity. His theory expands the dyadic, child-object relation to one that includes the role of the other (i.e., a triadic, child-object-other relation). However, Vygotsky does not address in detail the intersubjective, subject-subject relation, particularly those aspects of relational interactivity that make it possible for one to be other to oneself (i.e., self-awareness). Martin (2005a, 2005b, 2006) recently has attempted to clarify how appropriation, internalization, and the relational context in which they occur give rise to self-reflexivity. Building on the work of social psychologist George Herbert Mead (1938, 2002), Martin suggests that learning to take the perspectives of others is a vital aspect in the emergence of a reflexively capable, self-interpreting agency. It is by entering into perspectives sustained relationally within the social world that we are able to understand and interpret ourselves as both subjects and objects.

According to Mead, a perspective is an orientation associated with acting in a particular context. Perspectives, as orientations to action, manifest both perceptual and conceptual features. Although perspectives are formed within specific sequences of social interactivity, they are not fixed to the present. Once experienced, they can be employed imaginatively as well as actually, thereby granting increasingly complex, differentiated, and abstracted forms of activity. Under this construal, perspective-taking is not simply an epistemological capacity to know what we or others are thinking. Rather, perspectives have ontological force. Psychological reality is perspectival in that all phenomena (objects, events, selves, others, ideas, theories) emerge in the relation of persons with the contexts in which they act. Further, perspectives are both real and corrigible (when found to be incompatible with relevant biophysical and sociocultural reality). Perspectives, and the language used to express them, are not exhausted by ideas and words, but are situated and rooted within the world of everyday human activity. It is only those perspectives that achieve adequate degrees of functionality and agreement within the real world that operate effectively as constraints and enablements for our worldly endeavors. Thus, perspectives themselves are both enabled and constrained within sociocultural, discursive practices and contexts.

The key to comprehending the importance of perspectives in the development of reflexive psychological agency resides in the possibility of the simultaneous positioning of an individual within two or more perspectives. This possibility, promoted by a sociocultural context of relational interactivity, provides for experiences and memories that become ontologically transformative in psychological development. As young children gain experience in various kinds of social interactions, they become increasingly capable of discerning, remembering, integrating, and coordinating the different perspectives associated with the positions or roles that are differentiated within social interactions. Martin, following Mead, makes the case that the developing child's ability to take different perspectives on him- or herself and to react to those perspectives is required for attaining reflexive self-awareness.

By repeatedly taking up the different social positions that comprise conventional social interactions, the child comes to remember something of these positions and his or her experience of them. For example, by repeatedly offering and receiving food or an object, and by playing the roles of hider and seeker in games of hide-and-seek, the child gains the experiences and memories of the different social positions of giver and receiver, or hider and seeker. These experiences and recollections of them make it possible for the child to occupy one social position while simultaneously remembering and anticipating occupying another. For instance, in a game of hide-and-seek, the seeker may recollect a successful experience as a hider, and search in that same location for her hiding playmate. Through repeated and graduated participation in routine, everyday interactions with others (including play and games), children take various positions, roles, and perspectives, and eventually become capable of simultaneously entering into and occupying plural perspectives.

However, for an individual to become an object to herself, it is not sufficient for her just to be able to take up the perspectives of others. It also is necessary that she react to the understanding she has of herself, as this understanding appears in current action and imagination as a consequence of previous engagement with others. With respect to the differentiation and development of the self, the child's experience and memory of different social positions and perspectives includes others' reactions to her. These reactions of others grant an initial means by which one can react to him- or herself. In other words, the self is constituted not only by memories of one's engagements with others, but also by an ongoing, immediate reaction to them. This bifurcation provides for a self that is continually emergent as both subject and object. To use Mead's terminology, there is a fleeting, agentive "I" that reacts to a socially spawned, perspectival "Me" in the immediate moment of action. This reaction of the "I" to the "Me" produces changes to the perspectival structure of the "Me" and results in a reconstructed "Me" of the next moment to which an immediately future "I" will respond. The "I," which is present only in the immediate moment of action, leaves a trail of "Me's" in its wake. All that can be known of the self is the "Me" that is constituted of memories and acts of past "I's." While the "Me" can be comprehended in memory, the "I" exists only in the moment of action. The "I" cannot know itself in the present, nor exactly what it will do in the future.

Importantly, as Mead noted, the child's self-development is fueled by her reactivity not only to the reactions of particular others with whom she has interacted, but also to more abstracted and generalized others extracted from her broader experience of those social, cultural, and linguistic practices that subsume her overall social interactivity. Equally importantly, the child's reactions to her self do not simply reflect the perspectives of others that she has experienced and recalled. The child also reacts to those perspectives and to salient features of her social situations. As her social experience and linguistic capabilities extend, additional resources for her self-development become available through her ongoing immersion in more diversified interactions that reflect broader sociocultural practices and perspectives of selfhood and personhood which she also can take up and react to. For example, the adolescent's reading of novels and viewing of films may provide narrative content that assists her to reorganize, elaborate, differentiate, and integrate perspectives and self-perspectives in ways that go well beyond her immediate, everyday experiences. Formal and informal educational experiences may themselves be interpreted as containing a wide variety of perspectives that hold significant possibilities for further self-development and realization.

Martin's incorporation of Mead's insights into the overall program of work described in this essay is important in three major respects. First, Mead's work illustrates how the attitudes, actions, and perspectives of others, discerned through coordinated interactivity with those others within sociocultural practices, serve as vehicles of appropriation and internalization for the emergence of reflexive self-awareness. Second, it enables us to establish that such emergence requires a specifically human context of relational interactivity. Third, it demonstrates that even though psychologically capable persons are constituted by taking on the perspectives of others, each individual is unique, not only with respect to their physical embodiment, but also in the first-person perspective that defines them individually. This follows from the inevitable uniqueness of the totality of social involvements and interactions of a single person over time, but it also is a consequence of the emergent, intersubjective nature of both sociality and the psychological self as a reflection of and reaction to that sociality. All social situations and the various selves they spawn are undetermined and unpredictable to some degree, because of the multiple perspectives that social individuals can occupy and because of the necessary uncertainty of the "I," as discussed above. The perspectival complexity of individual self-understanding is an inevitable feature of social life. Dealing with other people is fraught with uncertainty and discord precisely because it demands negotiation and compromise among constantly emerging perspectives that fail to fit together seamlessly, but rather are disparate and frequently conflicting.

Persons as Agents in Relation

In addition to Mead, a theorist whose ideas we find insightful in revealing the unique ontological features of personal existence and psychological development is the twentieth-century Scottish philosopher John Macmurray (1957, 1961). Although relatively unknown by psychologists, Macmurray's work is expansive, reaching into metaphysics, epistemology, developmental psychology, moral and political philosophy, ethics, and theology. For our present purposes, however, we touch on two themes of particular relevance to our thesis. First, emphasizing the agency of persons, Macmurray asserted the metaphysical and epistemological primacy of action over reflection. Second, he located the emergence of psychological capacities in the active and differentiating agentive engagement of persons with each other. In Macmurray's view, personal existence is never private. It is a relational becoming, ongoing agentive activity in which we are constituted mutually by and with each other as persons. We discover and realize our personhood in a pervasive relational dynamic of self-revelation by which we become present to ourselves though the actions of others.

Cartesian philosophy is premised on the ideas that mental experience is self-evident, and that we can grasp our nature as thinking beings directly in reflection. But building metaphysics on the foundation of a reflective self, Macmurray claimed, overamplifies the importance of thought and, in so doing, creates a host of intractable dualisms (e.g., mind and body, mind and matter, subjective and objective, and the mystery of other minds) that separate the self from its embodied dealings in the everyday world of practical reality. The solution Macmurray proposed is to reverse the relation between reflective subjectivity and agency by giving precedence to action. If we examine the phenomenology of immediate experience, knowledge of ourselves as active agents interacting dynamically with each other and with the world is at least as well founded as knowledge of ourselves as thinking subjects for whom the world is an object. It is action, not thought, that is self-evident to a human agent existing in the world.

Human existence, Macmurray insisted, is foremost and always action. Agency encompasses thinking, and involves intention and choice, not as antecedent mental events that preface and cause what we do, but rather as necessary features of action. Moreover, intentionality is unique to human agents, and marks a crucial difference between material or organic events and human acts. Persons not only are capable of acting, but they also have an awareness of their actions as having real causal force in the world, and of making choices and forming intentions accordingly.

For Macmurray, agency is a definitive feature of personhood. However, equally significant is his claim that personal existence can be realized only in dynamic relation with others. It is not simply that persons are agents, but also that personhood is created mutually in interactions with other agents. All of our uniquely human capacities for knowing and understanding, including self-understanding, arise from our immersion and participation in a world of personal relations. Macmurray rejected the view that psychological development is driven by biological impulses or evolutionary forces that emphasize "survival of the fittest" at the level of the individual. Persons do not begin as infantile organisms that develop by surviving and adapting to their environments. Quite conversely, it is our total inability to survive and adapt on our own that creates a relation of dependence on others that then steers the course of development. Our survival and development take shape within a relation of dependence inscribed by others' individual and collective intentions. Every aspect of the form and direction of infant life is initiated and guided by others, who equip us not simply to survive as organisms, but to take our place as members of a personal community. From birth, our caregivers understand and respond to us as persons and, by so doing, initiate us into personhood.

Knowledge is acquired by making discriminations. Initially, however, knowledge of the caregiver is not discriminated as a correlate of the infant's activity. The caregiver is undifferentiated in the stream of infantile experience. Awareness of the caregiver first appears to the infant in the presence and absence of care. The intermittent tactual presence in response to the infant's cries registers a very basic recognition of the caregiver's repetitive pattern of withdrawal and return. This seeds the development of memory and expectation. As the infant's awareness grows, the presence of the caregiver becomes an expectation stirred by memory.

In time, there is further discrimination of the different persons who interact with the child and with each other. This array of persons takes on the character of a community to which the child senses herself belonging. The differentiation of things from persons, ensuing much later, follows from the discrimination of persons and only when the child's capacities have been augmented significantly by speech. The point is that we do not arrive at knowledge of persons from the personification of the nonpersonal. It is from knowledge of an originary personal world that we come to depersonalize and discriminate inanimate things. Initially, material objects are perceived as extensions or attributes of persons, and it is some time before they are understood as having an existence of their own and indifferent to us. In short, what Macmurray recognizes is that the world into which we are born is a distinctively personal world and all knowledge and understanding is made possible only through relations with others.

Self-consciousness is created via the ongoing and ever-present dynamic exchange by which we make ourselves present to each other. According to Macmurray, self-consciousness emerges and develops as a kind of mutual self-revelation that occurs only within the context of relationship. By revealing and contrasting ourselves in relation, we convey our appreciation of others' unique significance to us, and thereby participate in their self-constitution. The caregiver interacts with the child not simply as a being requiring the fulfillment of needs, but as a being of value: a person. The child becomes present to herself through the actions of the caregiver, who communicates the nature and significance of the child's presence to the child. At the same time, the child responds to the caregiver with love, and in the child's expressions the caregiver is informed of her significance and value as caregiver. It is not simply that our personhood is constituted in relation with others. It is constituted in the mutuality of self-revelation. The mutuality of self-revelation extends developmentally well beyond the caregiver-child dyad. It permeates individual development throughout the many and varied relations we encounter over the course of our lives.

Macmurray's arguments further support both the irreducibility of human agency and its primacy as a feature of persons. His work also is helpful in comprehending how the perspectives of others are involved in self-interpretation. Our psychological development as persons consists largely in expanding the reach of our agency by attempting to know the nature and value of our encounters in the world. Personal life involves the mutual interrogation and exploration of individual and collective possibilities in various settings of dialogical interaction with others. This includes discovering, realizing, questioning, and reformulating the significance of our own unique agentive personhood. Akin to Mead's views, Macmurray's notion of the mutuality of self-revelation suggests that it is through others that we are introduced to new possibilities of being and understanding. In other words, understanding others is to be looked on less as an epistemological problem (e.g., a Cartesian divide to be bridged), and more as a developmental opportunity. In the light of Macmurray's and Mead's insights, openness to otherness is simultaneously openness to possibilities in oneself.

Implications of Agentive Hermeneutics

A psychology informed by agentive hermeneutics presents a view of psychological phenomena that is strongly at variance with the ways in which such phenomena have traditionally been conceived and studied by the discipline. First, agentive hermeneutics accepts the distinctive ontological status and reality of both psychological and sociocultural phenomena. The phenomena psychologists study are not universal, nor do they remain fixed, unchanging, and resistant to human history. Sociocultural and psychological phenomena are created and transformed dynamically as a consequence of individual and collective human activity over time. However, just because these phenomena are socioculturally and psychologically (as well as biophysically) constituted, and constantly evolving, does not mean that they are not real. Sociocultural and psychological phenomena are real. They exert undeniable influence in human life, and both enable and constrain themselves and our interpretations of them. Such influence, while not concretely tangible or fixed, cannot be dismissed, even if this means that psychology never will possess laws and theories that transcend historical and/or cultural boundaries and lay claim to universality. Forms of personhood, like forms of life, have an emergent and evolving, yet real and discernible ontology.

Second, human action and experience unfold within a specifically human life-world, and our activities and experiences can be comprehended only against and within a sociocultural background of the meanings, values, conventions, and practices that constitute us as self-interpreting beings. Much of what we humans share in common is not a definable essence or a discoverable nature, but rather the existential condition of preexisting societies and cultures into which we are born, develop, and act. In this light, any psychology adequate to the task must expand its purview beyond the study of the individual to include the full scope of human historical and sociocultural endeavor. Enlarging the subject matter of psychology in this way would seem to require a different kind of education of psychologists than is now advocated and practiced by most organizations and departments of psychology. However, instituting a broader liberal education in the humanities, sciences, and social sciences also might challenge psychology's status as a separate and readily identifiable discipline in its own right. Amending its subject matter in this way may threaten to subordinate psychology to historical, political, and cultural studies.

Third, in recognizing the constitutive force of historical traditions and sociocultural practices in the expression of human agency, agentive hermeneutics opposes the naturalism and reductionism common to much mainstream psychological theory and research. Once the psychological importance of historical sociocultural contexts is grasped, the belief that human psychology is reducible to neurophysiological blueprints is simply not defensible. There are neurophysiological, chemical, and biological requirements necessary to psychological development. But as we have argued, requirement is not identity.

At the same time, while agentive hermeneutics emphasizes the historical and sociocultural constitution of psychological phenomena, it also affirms their irreducibility. As agents, human beings are able to exercise some degree of self-determination. Once a psychologically capable person has emerged developmentally, his or her interpretations will be active in the further constitution of his or her personhood. Individuals' interpretations can create possibilities for present and future understanding and action that are not entirely constrained by past and present sociocultural circumstances. By championing psychological agency in this way, agentive hermeneutics opposes the hard determinism that has been, and continues to be, a foundational assumption of scientific psychology for many psychologists.

Fourth, from the perspective of agentive hermeneutics, psychological study is an interpretive practice. Psychological phenomena cannot be understood apart from the history of interpretations and descriptions given them. But not only the objects of psychological study are constituted interpretively. So too are the methods of study. Psychological inquiry depends on our ability to recognize that knowledge is made possible by a shared background of living. It is only by virtue of participating in human life as self-interpreting beings that we can make sense of it. Psychologists also are self-interpreting, and psychological study is possible only because its practitioners are "insiders" who already possess the meanings and values they seek to interpret. However, for many psychologists, the idea that psychology is one among many formal and informal practices through which we attempt to understand ourselves erodes the status of psychology as a domain of particular expertise that somehow stands apart from—and is therefore uniquely capable of objectively evaluating—other practices of human self-understanding.

Fifth, while psychological study is inherently interpretive, this does not mean that psychological phenomena can be interpreted in any manner whatsoever. Interpretations are subject to the historical and sociocultural perspective of the interpreter and others. As such, they are always perspectival, partial, and fallible, and never final or absolute. There is always room for reinterpretation. However, interpretations are grounded in social, cultural, linguistic, and historical conventions and traditions, and must make sense within these contexts. Not all interpretations are equally viable. They must cohere with what we already know, and resonate with our self-understandings, and they must function within those traditions and conventions of sociocultural practice by which we coordinate our activities and lives with others.

It is also the case that our individual and collective interpretations can transform our understandings of ourselves and engender different or new possibilities for thinking, acting, and experiencing for both ourselves and others. For instance, one need not look very far to see the powerful influence disciplinary psychology has exerted on the ordinary language contemporary persons use to describe and understand themselves. Of course, underlying this interpretivist, perspectivist, fallibilist, and transformative view of knowledge is a commitment to, and valuing of, understanding itself as a human achievement and tool that carries ontological, epistemological, and moral force. That understanding in general, and psychological understanding in particular, is always an inherently value-laden and moral enterprise has proven especially difficult for many scientifically minded psychologists to accept.

Finally, interpretation is the central means of psychological study. In our view, psychological inquiry consists in offering interpretations of phenomena of interest, and developing or critiquing them by appeals to further interpretations. Psychological study is the attempt to devise language that articulates our understanding of the human existential condition, complete with the possibilities and constraints supplied by our history, societies, and cultures. The merits of our interpretations rest largely on the clarity, cogency, and coherence with which they are expressed, the degree to which others find them compelling and informative with respect to shared concerns in living, and the extent to which they may be applied productively within the life-world to advance our purposes and enrich our existence. This explicit recognition of the inevitably rhetorical and pragmatic bases for the pronouncements of scientific and professional psychology has also been difficult for many traditionally minded psychologists to sanction.

The work described in this chapter reflects an ongoing concern with the ways psychologists conceptualize the ontological status of personhood, selfhood, agency, and other psychological phenomena. The central thesis of agentive hermeneutics is that persons are self-interpreting human agents who are constituted biophysically and socioculturally, but who are not fully reducible to these determinants. Persons are capable of taking up sociocultural practices as psychological resources and wielding these in a reflective, deliberative manner. But moreover, even as persons continue to be constituted by sociocultural practices, they have a capacity, albeit limited and provisional, to transcend those practices. They are capable of revising their purposes and ends, questioning convention, evaluating and reevaluating their practices, remaking their identities, toppling consensus, and reorienting traditions. Persons are socioculturally embedded yet agentive beings, and our capacity for self-critical questioning of our place and time is what liberates us from being merely the passive victims of biology, culture, and history.

If our thesis is correct, psychological phenomena are indeed real and ontologically exceptional, and psychology is warranted as a distinct and bona fide discipline. However, at the same time, the implications of agentive hermeneutics necessitate that psychologists rethink their commitments and assumptions regarding issues such as the nature of reality, reductive strategies modeled after those of the natural sciences, repertoires of knowledge relevant to their disciplinary subject matter, and interpretive aspects of their inquiries. Our hope is that our program of work will encourage other psychologists to take up the challenge of redirecting the discipline in ways that properly address the texture of psychological existence.

References

Gergen, K. J. 1994. *Realities and Relationships: Soundings in Social Construction.* Cambridge, MA: Harvard University Press.

Macmurray, J. 1957. *The Self as Agent.* London: Faber and Faber; repr., Atlantic Highlands, NJ: Humanities Press, 1991.

——. 1961. *Persons in Relation.* London: Faber and Faber; repr., Amherst, NY: Humanity Books, 1999.

Martin, J. 2002. Hermeneutic psychology: Understandings and practices. In S. P. Shohov, ed., *Advances in Psychology Research* 14:97–118. New York: Nova Science.

——. 2005a. Real perspectival selves. *Theory & Psychology* 15:207–224.

——. 2005b. Perspectival selves in interaction with others: Re-reading G. H. Mead's social psychology. *Journal for the Theory of Social Behaviour* 35:231–253.

——. 2006. Re-interpreting internalization and agency through G. H. Mead's perspectival realism. *Human Development* 49:65–86.

Martin, J., and J. Sugarman. 1996. Bridging social constructionism and cognitive constructivism. *Journal of Mind and Behavior* 17:291–320.

——. 1997. Societal-psychological constructionism: Societies, selves, traditions, and fusions. *Journal of Theoretical and Philosophical Psychology* 17:120–136.

——. 1998. Dynamic interactionism: Elaborating a psychology of human possibility and constraint. *Journal of Mind and Behavior* 19:195–214.

——. 1999a. *The Psychology of Human Possibility and Constraint*. Albany: State University of New York Press.

——. 1999b. Psychology's reality debate: A "levels of reality" approach. *Journal of Theoretical and Philosophical Psychology* 19:177–194.

——. 2001a. Is the self a kind of understanding? *Journal for the Theory of Social Behaviour* 31:103–114.

——. 2001b. Interpreting human kinds: Beginnings of a hermeneutic psychology. *Theory & Psychology* 11:193–207.

——. 2002. Agency and soft determinism in psychology. In H. Atmanspacher and R. Bishop, eds., *Between Chance and Choice: Interdisciplinary Perspectives on Determinism*, 407–424. London: Imprints Academic.

——. 2003. A theory of personhood for psychology. In D. Hill and M. Kral, eds., *About Psychology: Essays at the Crossroads of History, Theory, and Philosophy*, 73–87. Albany: State University of New York Press.

Martin, J., J. Sugarman, and J. Thompson. 2003. *Psychology and the Question of Agency*. Albany: State University of New York Press.

Mead, G. H. 1938. *The Philosophy of the Act*. Ed. C. W. Morris. Chicago: University of Chicago Press.

——. 2002 [1932]. *The Philosophy of the Present*. Amherst, NY: Prometheus.

Sugarman, J. 2008. Understanding persons as relational agents: The philosophy of John Macmurray and its implications for psychology. In R. Frie, ed., *Psychological Agency: Theory, Practice and Culture*, 73–94. Cambridge, MA: MIT Press.

——. 2006. John Macmurray's philosophy of the personal and the irreducibility of psychological persons. *Journal of Theoretical and Philosophical Psychology* 26:172–188.

Sugarman, J., and J. Martin. 2005. Toward an alternative psychology. In B. Slife, J. Reber, and F. Richardson, eds., *Critical Thinking About Psychology: Hidden Assumptions and Plausible Alternatives*, 251–266. Washington, DC: American Psychological Association.

Vygotsky, L. S. 1978. *Mind in Society: The Development of Higher Psychological Processes*. Ed. M. Cole, V. John-Steiner, S. Scribner, and E. Souberman. Cambridge, MA: Harvard University Press.

——. 1986 [1934]. *Thought and Language*. Trans. A. Kozulin. Cambridge, MA: MIT Press.

Wundt, W. 1973 [1897]. *The Language of Gestures*. The Hague: Mouton.

Part III

Dialogical Approaches

The mind needs not only itself but also the other person, not only the other person as an outside reality but also the other as a necessary and innovative force in the self.　　　　　　　　　　　　　　　　　　　*—The authors of the present essay*

8　The Dialogical Self as a Minisociety

Hubert J. M. Hermans and João Salgado

In the course of history, various philosophical thinkers have arrived at the insight that the human mind is not visible to itself in one single inclusive glance. Instead, the mind needs itself to reach a decision, to arrive at a conclusion, or to develop an innovative plan. When the mind presents a thought to itself, it is rarely perfect, finished, or ready-made. Rather, it serves as a moment in a process that we usually call "thinking." The mind is used to react not only to the outside world, but also to its own lack of completion. As Gadamer said, "the imperfection of the human mind consists in its never being completely present to itself but in being dispersed into thinking this or that" (1989:425; see also Blachowicz 1999). Plato also touched this imperfection by conceiving the process of thinking in dialogical terms:

> I have a notion that, when the mind is thinking, it is simply talking to itself, asking questions and answering them, and saying yes or no. When it reaches a decision—which may come slowly or in a sudden rush—when doubt is over and the two voices affirm the

We thank Mick Cooper for his editorial comments on an earlier version of this chapter.

same thing, then we call that "its judgment." (*Theaetetus* 189ᵉ–190ᵃ, in Plato 1961; see also Blachowicz 1999)

This quotation from Plato's work includes several elements that are indispensable to a theory of the dialogical self: not one voice but many voices are active and involved in sign-mediated exchange with each other; there is a temporally ordered turn-taking process of question and answer, and agreement ("yes") or disagreement ("no"); a certain amount of doubt or uncertainty is inherent in this interchange, leading to a "resolution" in terms of a decision or judgment. All these elements are necessary for an adequate understanding of the dialogical self. Yet it should be emphasized that the dialogical self, as it is articulated today, is more than internal thinking or internal speech (Lysaker 2006). For a more comprehensive view of the full theoretical scope of the dialogical self, four central concepts are necessary: (a) the-other-in-the-self; (b) the mutually inclusive opposition between multiplicity and unity; (c) the role of power and relative dominance; and (d) the spatial and embodied nature of the self.

The-Other-in-the-Self: Toward a Conception of Self-Otherness

A truly dialogical self can exist only on the supposition that the other person is not purely outside, but simultaneously part of the self and even constitutive of it. The self is reduced to a solipsistic monadic existence if the other is seen as something that "influences" or "determines" an otherwise socially isolated self. The "social" or "intersubjective" is not something that is "added" to a self that, in its preexisting state, has an existence separate from the other. The self can be properly understood only when social interchange and intersubjectivity are considered as intrinsic to its nature. An adequate way to clarify the dialogical disposition of the self is to consider the role of imagination and imaginary figures.

The Role of Imagination in the Self

In most psychological theories imaginary phenomena are rather peripheral, as Watkins (1986) has argued. The existence of actual and real others in particular is given clear ontological priority, with imaginary figures and conversations seen as derivative from and subordinate to them. Nevertheless, imaginary dialogues play a central role in the daily lives of most people: interwoven with actual interactions, they constitute an essential part of our narrative construction of the world. There are many moments when we are outwardly silent, but find ourselves communicating with our parents, critics, opponents, our consciences, our gods, the photograph of someone we miss, with our reflection in the mirror, with a figure from a movie or a dream, with our babies, or with our pets (Watkins 1986).

From the perspective of social anthropology, Caughey (1984) has considered the role of "imaginary social worlds," both in Western and in non-Western cultures. His fieldwork was conducted in Fáánakker, a Pacific island in Micronesia, and in the Margalla Hills of Pakistan. Here, he observed that imaginary interactions are in no way restricted to non-Western cultures. He divided imaginary (or semi-imaginary) figures into three groups: (a) purely imaginary figures created in dreams and fantasies; (b) media figures with whom the individual engages in imaginary interactions; and (c) imaginary replicas of lovers, parents, friends who are treated as if they were really present. Like Watkins (1986), Caughey demonstrated that imaginary dialogues and interactions exist side-by-side with real interactions (e.g., "If my wife could see me now . . ."), and are often intensely interwoven with reality.

The other-in-the-self can be recognized as part of everyday life. When another person is of great value or significance for me, he or she can be experienced as "deeply inside me," "cherished in my heart," or as "a treasure that I carry within myself." In those cases, the other has received a highly valued and precious place in the self, as we see when people memorialize, for example, an "inspiring teacher," a "beloved friend," a "lovely grandparent," or a meeting with a person who was "deeply impressive" and who have evoked, since then, inner conversations at unexpected moments.

Otherness and Alterity in the Self

The dialogical self, inspired by thinkers such as Vygotsky (1986), Bakhtin (1981), and James (1890) emphasizes the self as partly decentered and permeated by otherness, yet having a significant degree of agency. This human agency exercises a high degree of individual responsibility and is, at the same time, intimately woven into the fabric of culture and history. Richardson, Rogers, and McCarroll put special emphasis on the ethical dimension of the dialogical notion: "Dialogical relations are always fundamentally ethical because in them we always are either acknowledged or ignored, understood or misunderstood, treated with respect or coerced" (1998:510). As being different from the self, the other needs to be recognized and valued in his or her alterity. It is a central feature of a dialogical relationship that every party involved in the process of interchange receives a voice to speak from his or her specific point of view and is given the space to express his or her concern in its particularity and uniqueness. Conceived in this way, dialogical relationships require the responsibility of all parties involved in the relationship to contribute to a democratic society in such a way that voices are not silenced, denied, or suppressed on the basis of race, gender, age, or any other social or personal characteristic.

In an analysis of the contemporary literatures on alterity, Cooper and Hermans (2006) observe that the concept of otherness or alterity is intimately linked to the existence of an actual, physical other. Otherness, in the tradition of the founding philosopher of alterity, Emmanuel Levinas (1969), is often equated with the face of another human being, while the internal sphere of the self is characterized by sameness and identity (e.g., Williams and Gantt 2002). However, such an association between self and sameness would not sufficiently account for the differentiation, diversity, and even oppositions of a multivoiced, dialogical self with its relatively autonomous parts characterized by otherness and alterity (Cooper and Hermans 2006).

In the context of a theory of a dialogical self, the notions of "difference," "otherness," and "alterity" can be usefully extended from the interpersonal realm to the intrapersonal one in such a way that an intersubjective viewpoint is preserved. "Otherness" can be experienced not only between the self and the actual other, but also within one's own self, in which the other is intrinsically present; therefore, a concept of self-otherness can serve a valuable psychological function (Cooper and Hermans 2006).

To introduce the notion of self-otherness is not to suggest that this alterity exists within a self-contained, isolated monad. Rather, it is to emphasize that this otherness penetrates the self from the most explicitly "external" realms to the most seemingly "internal" ones, whether carried in the voices and images of actual others or in those of imaginary others (Hermans, Kempen, and Van Loon 1992). When the notion of self-otherness is seen as an extension of "other-otherness"—more than as an alternative to it—it can contribute to further intersubjective thinking, not only by showing that intrapersonal processes result from an internalization of interpersonal existence (cf. Vygotsky 1962), but also by revealing that even the most "internal" self-experiences are infused with something non-self (Cooper and Hermans 2006).

Multiplicity-in-Unity

Inspired by the founding work of James (1890) and Bakhtin (1973 [1929]), Hermans, Kempen, and Van Loon (1992) criticized the assumption that the self is organized around *one* center or core. The dialogical self, instead of being regarded as one centralized author with a unifying view on the world, was conceived in terms of a dynamic multiplicity of relatively autonomous "I-positions" organized in an imaginary landscape. These I-positions are involved in processes of mutual dialogical relationships that are intensely interwoven with external dialogical relationships. In this conception, the "I" is always bound to particular positions in time and space but has the ability to move from one position to the other in accordance with changes in situation and time. The "I" fluctuates among different and even opposed positions, and has the capacity to imaginatively endow each position with a voice so that dialogical relations between positions can develop. The voices behave like interacting characters in a story, involved in a process of question and answer, agreement and disagreement. Each of them has a story to tell about their own experiences from their own perspective. As different voices, these characters exchange information about their respective "Me's," creating a complex, narratively structured self. In this multiplicity of positions, some positions are more dominant than others, so that the voices of the less dominant positions are subdued (Hermans 1996a, 2001a).

In psychological discussions, the question is often posed as to what implications the multivoiced dialogical self has for psychological health. The implicit view behind this question is that multivoicedness may be detrimental to the prevailing notion that the self is an indivisible unity and centered in itself. In these discussions, unity is typically perceived as a desirable end-state or even as a starting point, rather than as a dynamic process. Fragmentation, as its opposite, is generally perceived as an aberration. The guiding idea is that healthy self-development requires the fostering of unity and the avoidance of fragmentation. The term "I-position," however, allows the *inclusive* opposition between unity and multiplicity instead of the *exclusive* opposition between unity and fragmentation. Whereas the latter opposition bears a strong evaluative connotation (unity is good, fragmentation is bad), the former assumes that the two principles, unity (expressed in the dialogical movements between different positions) and multiplicity (expressed in the diversity of positions), are equivalent and even presuppose one another as complementary and dynamic aspects of the self. The hyphenated "multiplicity-in-unity" adds to a better understanding of the connection between notions of multivoicedness and dialogicality as basic properties of subjectivity. When multiplicity is conceived of as multivoicedness, then unity is created as a result of dialogical relationships between the voices. It should be noted that in this conception unity does not exist without multiplicity (Salgado and Hermans 2005).

Discussions regarding the unity of the self also refer to the distinction between the normal functioning of the multivoiced, dialogical self and the controversial clinical dysfunction *Multiple Personality Disorder* (MPD), more recently called *Dissociative Identity Disorder* (DID). These clinical categories describe the serious impediments in the dialogical relationships between the "host personality" and a diversity of "alters." Typically, the alters represent "rejected parts of the original self" (Carson, Butcher, and Mineka 1996:267). The difference between a multivoiced self and dissociative phenomena, however, can be fully grasped only if one takes into account the insight that the dysfunctional aspects of MPD and DID are not primarily in the parts but in their organization. In the dissociative self there is an inability to move flexibly from one position to another and the dialogue between positions is impeded. Moreover, in cases of dissociation, the different voices are not in line with the requirements of the situation at hand. Indeed, in our own research on opposite trait pairs as voices in the self, we observed that normal subjects were able to move from, for example, an open to a closed position and back (Hermans and Kempen 1993). Of course, there may be an experience of opposition or conflict between the positions, but this conflict can be understood as the result of an active shifting between the positions rather than of their separation and fragmentation. In the dysfunctional organization of the self, however, one alter dominates the total experiential field, with a simultaneous impairment of the possibility to move flexibly to other alters (although some people with this dysfunction may learn to invite different alters to enter into mutual conversations). Watkins (1986) concluded that dissociative phenomena are characterized by a sequential, monological succession of personalities rather than by a simultaneous, cooperative, and dialogical relationship between different subselves. (For research and treatment of a client with DID, see Hermans and Hermans-Jansen 1995:187–195.)

Dominance and Social Power

Contemporary theories of the self, particularly those that put a strong emphasis on unity, often lack insight about the intense interplay between dominance relations in the society at large on the one hand, and dominance relations in the "minisociety" of the self on the other. In a review of the literature on the self, Callero (2003) listed a number of concepts that are of central concern to mainstream psychology: self-enhancement, self-consistency, self-monitoring, self-efficacy, self-presentation, self-verification, self-knowledge, self-regulation, self-control, self-handicapping, and self-deception. In his critical comment on these concepts, he raised the issue of social power:

> The self that is socially constructed is never a bounded quality of the individual or a simple expression of psychological character-istics; it is a fundamentally social phenomenon, where concepts, images, and understandings are deeply determined by relations of power. Where these principles are ignored or rejected, the self is often conceptualized as a vessel for storing all the particulars of the person.   (Callero 2003:127)[1]

In apparent contrast to theories built on the notion of self-contained individualism, dialogical self theory proposes a conception of self and dialogue in which social power and dominance play a role in everyday life. This can be demonstrated in an analysis of turn-taking behavior. In an investigation of participants involved in conversation, Linell (1990) argued that an asymmetry between the speakers is present in *each* individual act-response sequence. Involved in a process of turn-taking, speakers can only communicate in comprehensible ways if they are able to take initia-tives and display their own points of view. The actors continually alternate the roles of speaker, in which they are more dominating, and listener, in which they are less dominating of the content and course of the conversa-tion. In various ways one of the parties can control the "territory" shared by the participants in communication. One of the parties can be more dominant by just speaking more than the other party (amount of talk), or may take the most initiatory moves (interactional dominance), introduce topics and new perspectives on topics (topic dominance), or make the most strategic moves (strategic dominance). These examples indicate that relative dominance is an intrinsic feature of turn-taking behavior and not something that is in contradiction with dialogue or alien to its nature. In the service of a well-ordered verbal or nonverbal dialogue, some organization is needed, making relative dominance indispensable.

When comparing internal and external dialogues, we should take into account that, in the typical case, internal dialogues are less systematic, less organized, more abbreviated, and more impulsive than external dialogues. Wiley (2006) has observed that inner speech is both more simple and more complex than outer speech. It is simpler in both semantics and syntax, using fewer words and fewer parts of speech. On the other hand, inner speech incorporates so many extra-linguistic elements—visual imagery, tactile sensations, emotion, kinaesthetics, smells, tastes, and sounds—that it is more complex than outer speech. Although there are significant differences between internal and external dialogues, the basic similarity is that voices play a central role in both forms of dialogue. Voices are basic in both external and internal dialogue. One voice is stronger, louder, and more influential than another. Like external voices, internal ones may be silenced, suppressed, or marginalized (see also Blachowicz 1999 for the basic similarity of internal and external dialogues).

The Importance of Collective Voices

Power differences in society and in the minisociety of the self refer to the importance of collective voices in the self. As Bakhtin (1986) argued, an individual speaker's utterance is not coming simply from an isolated, decontextualized voice speaking in a neutral space. Rather, individual voices are deeply penetrated by the cultures of the institutions, groups, and communities in which they participate, including their power differences. Collective voices, also described as "social representations" (Markova 2006), form, together with "ego" and "alter," a basic triadic structure of dialogical relationships. Collective voices—as expressed in professional jargon, sociopolitical ideologies, authorities, social circles, dialects, national languages, and social expectations—partly constitute what the speaker's individual voice is saying. In terms of dialogical self theory, power differences between the collective voices in a particular community appear as power differences or power struggles between positions in the self.

An illustrative example of power struggles between collective voices and their reflection in individual selves is provided by the postcolonialist writer Edward Said (1999), who was born a Palestinian, educated in an English school in Egypt, and later immigrated to the United states (for a more extensive discussion, see Bhatia 2002). The colonial school in Egypt where Said received his training was run entirely by British staff who viewed the Arab boys as delinquents who needed discipline and punishment. The teachers had a handbook with rules that were intended to make Arab students like the British. Said explained how the boys resisted the colonial rules of the handbook by invoking their Arab position:

> Rule 1 stated categorically: "English is the language of the school. Anyone caught speaking other languages will be severely punished." So Arabic became our haven, a criminalized discourse where we took refuge from the world of masters and complicit prefects and anglicized older boys who lorded it over us as enforcers of the hierarchy and its rules. Because of Rule 1 we spoke more, rather than less, Arabic, as an act of defiance against what seemed then, and seems even more so now, an arbitrary, ludicrously gratuitous symbol of their power.   (Bhatia 2002:184)

As this excerpt suggests, power struggles between collective voices on the level of the community have their impact on the dialogues between the members of a minority group and also between opposing positions in the self ("I as born as an Arab" vs. "I as educated in an English school"). As a result of oppression on the level of the institution, the Arab position in the self of the boys was not simply repressed but rather emphasized as a counterposition that had to be defended and maintained for its own value.[2]

The Spatial and Embodied Nature of the Self

A central feature of the dialogical self is its combination of temporal and spatial characteristics. Advocates of a narrative approach in psychology, like Sarbin (1986), Bruner (1986), and Gergen and Gergen (1988), have emphasized the temporal dimension of narratives. This emphasis is nicely illustrated by Bruner's (1986) sentence "The king died, and then the queen." The two parts of this sentence represent two successive phases in an irreversible time sequence. Certainly, dialogical self theory acknowledges the temporal dimension as a constitutive feature of narratives. Without time, there can be no story. However, time and space are of equal significance to the narrative structure of the dialogical self. The spatial nature of the self is expressed in the terms "position" and "positioning," terms that are, moreover, more dynamic and flexible than the traditional term "role" (cf. Harré and Van Langenhove 1991). The spatial term "position" can be determined only by its relationship with another position. Of particular importance are "counterpositions" (Leiman 2002), which assume the existence of other positions that are located somewhere else, creating a dynamic field in which dialogical relationships may emerge.

It is even possible to translate temporal relations into spatial structures by "juxtaposition" of different periods in our life, as Bakhtin (1973 [1929]) described. Whereas temporal sequences are irreversible, spatial positions are reversible. In real and imaginary space, one can move from the present to the past or to the future, *and back*. When the person moves back to the present, he or she has, more or less, been changed by the dialogical process itself. People can imaginatively move to a future point in time, and then speak to themselves about the sense of what they are doing *now* in their present situation. This position, some point in the future, may be very helpful and meaningful for evaluating one's present activities from a long-term perspective, as Oles (2005) has empirically demonstrated.

The Body in the Mind

In his book *The Body in the Mind*, Johnson started with three provocative statements: "Without imagination, nothing in the world could be meaningful. Without imagination, we could never make sense of our experience. Without imagination, we could never reason toward knowledge of reality" (1987:ix). Because the faculty of imagination plays a central role in the dialogical self, we refer to the phenomenon "image schema"—or "metaphor" as described by Johnson (1987)—as an exemplification.

An image schema serves as a frame for orienting ourselves in a great variety of situations on the basis of the form of our body. A "verticality schema" is used to employ an up–down orientation so that our experience can be meaningfully organized. We stand "upright" or "lie down," climb a staircase, wonder about the level of the water, and ask how tall our child is.

However, the image schema is more than a purely corporeal structure. It is also used as a metaphor for organizing our more abstract understanding. In the estimation of quantities, we understand them in terms of verticality. We say: prices are going up; someone's gross earnings fell; and we turn down the heat. We assume that "more is up" although we are not aware of that. We use a verticality structure as a physical base for our mental understanding, although there is no intrinsic reason why "more" should be "up." Apparently, a given image schema emerges first as a structure of our body, and is then figuratively developed as a meaning structure at more abstract levels of cognition.

The concept of imagination as inherent to the dialogical self can only be properly understood if one realizes that the body is *in* the self. Moreover, in apparent contrast to Cartesian philosophy, spatial structures are not simply external to the self, but *in* the self.

The Dialogical Brain

The notion of embodiment is central to the functioning of the dialogical self in another sense also. Researchers are interested in exploring the relationship between the dialogical self and the functioning of the brain. Lewis (2002), for example, observed that children and adults, when faced with stress, want to return to "ordinary" self-positions that offer sufficient safety, security, and relaxation to keep a feeling of continuity of the self. This observation raises the question of whether dialogue is possible if the person continuously and automatically wants to return to one position or a few positions that fulfil this desire. In an attempt to answer this question, Lewis analyzes phrases like "That was stupid" or "You are dumb" that the person (or an imagined other) is saying to him(self) or her(self) while performing a task. In such situations of internal dialogue, Lewis observes that there is neither a clear-cut other voice nor much turn-taking or an explicit sequence of question and answer. In such cases, internal "dialogues" are usually inchoate and sublingual and there is not much elaboration and development of a dialogue with another voice. On this sublingual level, we are more conservative and monological than innovative and dialogical.

Elaborating on these observations, Lewis presents a model that is based on neuroscientific evidence and, at the same time, compatible with dialogical self theory. In our daily lives, he reasoned, we are involved in a dialogical relation with an anticipated, almost-heard other represented in the self as a familiar and continuous I-position. This model is consistent with Schore's (1994) work on the relationship between the dialogical self and the functioning of the (higher) orbitofrontal cortex, which produces, in its linkage to the lower (conservative) subcortical limbic system, an affectively charged, gist-like sense of an interpersonal respondent, which is based on stabilized expectancies from many past interactions. Lewis' and Schore's models have the advantage that they show how relatively stable, sublingual voices put constraints on the linguistic, dialogical processes. Such limits are not necessarily a disadvantage, because the automatic responses that are inherent to sublingual voices may contribute, in specific situations, to our action readiness and behavioral efficiency.

Brief History and Contemporary Work

The main purpose behind work on dialogical self theory was to bring together two familiar concepts, dialogue and self, and combine them in such a way that a more extended view of the possibilities of the mind becomes visible. The theory is rooted in two traditions: the notion of self was inspired by the groundbreaking work of William James (1890) and George Herbert Mead (1934), main representatives of American pragmatism, while the notion of dialogue was instigated by the pioneering work of the Russian literary scholar Mikhail Bakhtin (1973 [1929]), the main representative of what is called "dialogism." The first psychological publication on this topic appeared in 1992 in the *American Psychologist*, authored by Hubert Hermans (personality psychologist), Harry Kempen (cultural psychologist), and Rens van Loon (philosopher). Such an exploration of the "composite concept" of the dialogical self was stimulated by discussions of the "individualism" and "rationalism" of Western culture. Such discussions challenge psychologists, in the words of Spence, "to attempt to rise above their own culture" (1985:1286).

After the beginning writings on the dialogical self in the 1990s, further publications appeared, primarily in special journal issues in which authors combined their efforts in order to tackle a specific subject area.

In *Culture & Psychology* (7 [2001]: 243–408), a more elaborated theory of personal and cultural positioning was exposed and discussed. In *Theory & Psychology* (12 [2002]: 147–280), the dialogical self was related to a variety of fields: developmental psychology, psychotherapy, psychopathology, brain sciences, cultural psychology, personality psychology, Jungian psychoanalysis, and semiotic dialogism. In the *Journal of Constructivist Psychology* (16 [2003]: 89–212), the focus was on the implications of the dialogical self for personal construct psychology, on the philosophy of Martin Buber (1958), on the rewriting of narratives in psychotherapy, and on a psychodramatic approach in psychotherapy. The notion of mediated dialogue in a global and digital age was the subject of a special issue in *Identity: An International Journal of Theory and Research* (4 [2004]: 297–405). Finally, in *Counselling Psychology Quarterly* (19 [2006]: 1–120), the dialogical self was applied to a variety of topics, such as the relationship between adult attachment and working models of emotion, narrative impoverishment in schizophrenia, paranoid personality disorder, and the significance of power in psychotherapy. Special attention was devoted to the "self-confrontation method" (Hermans and Hermans-Jansen 1995) as informed by dialogical self theory. The same issue includes an autobiographical sketch of the first author of the present essay, who, during his scientific and professional career, was moving through three paradigms: individual differences, narrative psychology, and dialogical psychology (Hermans 2004b).[3]

Recently, attention has been devoted to the experience of uncertainty in the context of the accelerated processes of globalization and localization (Hermans and Dimaggio 2007). In this research, an attempt is made to combine theoretical, empirical, and ethical approaches in the study of self-extension in space and time. For further on the tension between global and local positions in a psychology of globalization, see Arnett 2002.

Illustrative Research Examples

In what follows we present examples of two types of research that are based on dialogical theory. One is the case study approach, which has the advantage that it is sensitive to the complexity of the individual and highly suitable for studying the nature of changes of the self over time. The second looks at experimental research as a more recent development in the field.

Dominance Reversal of I-Positions

The phenomenon of dominance reversal among I-positions reflects a radical change of the self. In a project on changes in the organization of the dialogical self (Hermans and Kempen 1993), a research participant, Alice, a twenty-eight-year-old woman, was invited to mention two parts of her self that were opposite to each other, with the one part more or less dominating the other part. Alice said that she saw a dominant "open side" of her personality and she added that other people also saw her as an open person ("friendly," "helpful," and "sociable"). She reported, however, that she also had another part, less acceptable to herself and less visible to others, that often was in conflict with her open part. In the next step of the investigation, Alice was invited to tell a story about her past, present, and future from the two I-positions successively. First, she told about her past, present, and future as an "open person" and then as a "closed person." From her open position she told primarily stories that referred to the unproblematic relationship with her mother and a very positive relationship with her boyfriend. From the perspective of her closed side, however, she largely referred to the problematic relationship with her father and expressed doubts about the future with her boyfriend. In fact, the stories were clearly different and even opposed to each other.

After the investigation, Alice was requested to rate her stories (summarized in a number of sentences) on two variables: relative dominance ("How dominant was this aspect of your life during the past week?") and meaningfulness ("How meaningful was this aspect of your life during the past week?"). Surprisingly, it was found that, over the three-week period, the story parts of her closed position became more dominant than the story parts of her open position, whereas the stories of the latter position receded to the background. This change represents a clear example of a "dominance reversal," also mentioned in another study (Hermans 1996b)[4]

In the same period, the meaningfulness of the stories from Alice's closed position increased strongly, whereas the meaningfulness of the stories from her open position strongly decreased. This suggests that the increasing dominance of her closed position was experienced as very meaningful, although this position was associated with a great deal of negative emotion. From her diary notes, which she made accessible to the researcher after the period of investigation, it was concluded that the increase of the meaning of her closed position could be understood as bringing hitherto neglected or suppressed experiences to the surface, giving her a sense of unity or synthesis in her life as a whole. At the same time, this helped her to improve the relationships with her father and other family members.

The study on dominance reversal brings together several elements that are central in dialogical self theory, as discussed earlier in this essay: the other in the self (e.g., mother, father, boyfriend), multiplicity of internal I-positions (e.g., "open" vs. "closed," including their dialogical conflict and disagreement), relationships of relative dominance (dominance reversal), and both spatial (position and opposed position) and temporal relationships (changes in the self over time). Note that research on different or opposed I-positions can also be applied to cultural positions as parts of the self in a globalizing world (e.g., I as an Iranian vs. I as a citizen in UK, each with their specific experiences and stories).

In the present research example there are only two positions. For the study of more positions, a specific method is devised for assessing the content and organization of the "personal position repertoire" (PPR-method; Hermans 2001b). In this method, the client is provided with a prestructured list of positions that refer to the internal domain of the self (e.g., "I as a professional," "I as a mother," "I as a perfectionist," "I as dependent," "I as an enjoyer of life") and positions that refer to the extended or external domain of the self, the domain that includes persons or groups that we have described as "others in the self" (e.g., "my father," "my mother," "my friends," "my colleagues," "my opponent"). Part of the procedure is to ask the client to add positions in his or her own idiographic terms (e.g., "I as a career woman," "I as an elephant maker, making an elephant from a mosquito"). The procedure is based on a stage metaphor: from one side internal positions enter the stage, from the other side external positions appear. On the stage they meet each other so that dialogical relationships may develop. In order to study the relative prominence of the positions, a matrix is used, on which the participant or client fills in to what extent (on a 0–5 Likert scale) a particular internal position has become prominent in relation to a particular external position. On the basis of the matrix, with its prominence scores, a series of quantitative indices can be calculated that give information about the organization of the position repertoire.

Experimental Research Into Dialogical Relationships

Another type of research, emerging from dialogical self theory, is focused on experimental manipulation of variables that refer to central elements of the theory. For example, Stemplewska-Zakowicz, Walecka et al. (2005) asked students to discuss the question of whether psychological knowledge could be helpful in passing exams and invited them to chat with each other about this topic. In one experimental condition, students were instructed in such a way that they believed themselves to be in the position of an expert; in another, students believed that they were in the position of a layperson. Moreover, in some experimental conditions, students were placed in the position of expert or layman in a *direct* way (both participants received the explicit instruction that they were expert or layperson), whereas in other conditions they were positioned in an *indirect* way (their interlocutor was instructed that they were an expert or layman on the topic, but they themselves did not receive this instruction). The purpose behind this procedure was that in the latter condition the participants did not see themselves as expert or layman, but they were perceived as such by their interlocutors. The results confirmed one of the basic premises of dialogical self theory: that different positions produce different narratives. In fact, the students positioned as experts gave more advice than those positioned as laypersons. Even when the students were positioned in an indirect way, the same effect was found, although to a minor degree: students positioned as experts by their interlocutor but not by themselves gave more advice than those that were positioned, in an indirect way, as laypersons. (For a more extended experiment with similar outcomes see Stemplewska-Zakowicz, Walecka, and Gabinska 2006.)

The running of experiments like those above has the advantage that insight is gained not only into conscious processes, typical of most dialogical self research, but also into nonconscious processes. Moreover, this type of research provides an avenue for finding linkages with research performed in the field of interpersonal cognition. As Sakellaropoulos and Baldwin said:

We believe that to further increase the understanding of both interpersonal cognition and dialogical science, researchers should strive to incorporate each area's fundamental principles into the other. Although research into interpersonal cognition has progressed significantly in the last decade, much work remains. Despite dialogue being a core component of self and identity, a dialogical component to interpersonal cognition is essentially lacking. . . . On the other hand, dialogical science, still a relatively recent enterprise, could benefit greatly from the methods and findings already available in the interpersonal cognition literature.   (2006:63)

Indeed, dialogical self theory is constantly seeking to cross the boundaries of existing (sub)disciplines, because the field is topic-oriented rather than discipline-oriented. We agree with Côté (2001), who criticized disciplinary boundaries as creating an insularity that separates scientists from others who are ostensibly interested in the same phenomena. This insular attitude has the disadvantage of giving rise to a dogmatic insistence that each discipline's definition and preferred methodology is the right one and that other approaches are misguided. This attitude results in a scholarship that is fragmented and scattered into various perspectives or paradigms, a phenomenon that can lead to indifference or even aversion to "intruders" and evoke defensive reactions against attempts to critically analyze such paradigms. In dialogical self research, it is an explicit purpose to profit from other approaches that study similar phenomena or have the potential to innovate existing insights or methods of investigation in our own field. When disciplines and subdisciplines work in dialogical ways, they are mutually complementing and fertilizing rather than developing in isolation.

Promises and Problems

One of the promises of dialogical self theory, as we envision it, follows from its radical extension. It proposes a conception that goes far beyond the limits of any self-contained identity, so typical of many contemporary conceptions of the self (Callero 2003) and even a basic feature of our Western culture (Sampson 1985). It is our conviction that a contemporary theory of the self needs to take into account the processes of globalization and localization (Hermans and Dimaggio 2007). We each of us no longer live within the confining limits of one culture. Different cultures are crossing the boundaries of existing communities. More significantly, different cultures are living in one and the same person. Dialogical self theory takes these developments into account by conceiving cultures as positions in the self, involved in mutual dialogues. Dialogues have the benefit that they foster understanding not only between different individuals, groups, and cultures but also between different cultural positions within one and the same individual. It is expected that the improvement of self-understanding will stimulate or facilitate tolerance and cooperation between different cultural groups in a globalizing world (Hermans and Kempen 1998).

Another promise of dialogical self theory is that it allows for the study of inner multiplicity and multivoicedness without giving up the notion of a substantial self. As Falmagne (2004) recently explained, some social-constructionist conceptions of the self have led to the radical rejection of a substantial self and have embraced a nonsubstantial, fluid notion of subjectivity. For some social constructionists, the self is decentralized to the utmost so that nonhomogeneity and contingency in discursive positioning are taken as reasons to reject the self as a theoretical notion. In agreement with Falmagne, we argue for a conception of the self that is distributed yet substantial. We see distribution, multiplicity, uncertainty, and fluidity not as an impasse for a theoretical notion of the self, but as intrinsic aspects that are "owned" by an embodied and agentic self (Salgado and Hermans 2005).

Dialogical self theory also has the advantage that it can bring together theory and practice of scientist and practitioner. We believe that the optimal place for meaningful change is the interface between internal and external dialogues. This is most visible in the field of psychotherapy. Psychotherapeutic assistance can be seen as an intersubjective enterprise in which insights and behavioral modifications emerge from the external dialogues between client and psychotherapist, with the simultaneous inclusion of these exchanges into the internal dialogues of client and psychotherapist. This principle applies to a variety of psychotherapeutic approaches. In a recent publication (Hermans and Dimaggio 2004), representatives of different therapeutic traditions (cognitive, constructivist, process-experiential, narrative, psychodynamic, psychodramatic, person-centered, and cognitive-analytic) demonstrated that many of their therapeutic tools exemplified some basic principles of dialogical self theory. The authors showed that they assisted their clients with proper attention to multivoicedness, dialogical relationships, and the organization and reorganization of the clients' selves. They demonstrated that such theoretical principles had direct repercussions for their practical interventions.

Although dialogical self theory shows different promises, it is not without problems. One of the main risks is in its breadth. As we said earlier in this contribution, the theory crosses the borders of disciplines and subdisciplines and attracts scholars and practitioners from diverse backgrounds. Moreover, their interest and theoretical scope motivates dialogical scholars to contact colleagues from different cultures and countries, in order to discuss challenges and problems emerging at the interface of different cultures and their implications for self and identity. The interdisciplinary and intercultural orientation of dialogical self theory requires, on the one hand, a conceptual system that is broad enough to serve as a meeting point for scholars from different disciplinary and cultural backgrounds, but, on the other hand, a conceptual system that offers sufficient precision and constraints to avoid the pitfall that "dialogue" and the "dialogical self" mean everything. In our view, this problem can be tackled by creating sufficient interfaces, in the form of international conferences and journal activities, where such issues can be discussed and their consequences explored. The problem is not that parties disagree or have different interpretations of the same theory, but that they don't know on which issues they agree or disagree. Science and practice can profit from disagreement and even conflict, under the condition that they stimulate a creative learning process and innovate existing theory.

Dialogical self theory is a relatively young field that seeks its direction(s) in the context of an enormous diversity of scientific, professional, and cultural influences. Crucial for its further development are an exploring attitude and an open mind that are willing and able to deal with uncertainty at the interface of an increasing diversity of voices, so typical of a globalizing society.

Notes

1. See also Sampson's (1985) criticism of "self-contained individualism" in psychological theories of the self in the West.

2. For another example of power differences between collective voices and their influence on the dialogical self see Van Meijl's (2006) discussion of Maori youngsters. These young people are placed in a field of tension between the classic model for a Maori identity, which prescribes that they embrace traditional culture, on the one hand, and their personal identification as outcasts in the daily practices of New Zealand society, on the other hand. For a discussion of collective voices as reflected in family cultures (the culture of father's family vs. the culture of mother's family), and their power differences in the self of the children, see Hermans 2004a.

3. In order to stimulate theory, research, and practice, biennial conferences on the dialogical self have been organized, the first taking place in Nijmegen, the Netherlands (2000), the second in Ghent, Belgium (2002), the third in Warsaw, Poland (2004), the fourth in Braga, Portugal (2006), and a fifth at Cambridge University, UK (2008). The conferences are organized by the International Society for Dialogical Science (ISDS), established in 2002. This society publishes an electronic, peer-reviewed, open-access journal: the *International Journal for Dialogical Science* (*IJDS*) (first issue, spring 2006).

4. Note that James (1982) described many examples of this type and made it clear that such radical changes occur in a period in which the self is in a state of "unstable equilibrium."

References

Arnett, J. J. 2002. The psychology of globalization. *American Psychologist* 57:774–783.

Bakhtin, M. 1973 [1929]. *Problems of Dostoevsky's Poetics*. 2nd ed. Trans. R. W. Rotsel. Ann Arbor, MI: Ardis.

——. 1981. *Speech Genres and Other Late Essays*. Trans. V. M. McGhee. Austin: University of Texas Press.

Bhatia, S. 2002. Acculturation, dialogical voices, and the construction of the diasporic self. *Theory & Psychology* 12:55–77.

Blachowicz, J. 1999. Dialogue of the soul with itself. In S. Gallagher and J. Shear, eds., *Models of the Self*, 177–200. Thorverston: Academic.

Bruner, J. S. 1986. *Actual Minds, Possible Worlds*. Cambridge, MA: Harvard University Press.

Buber, M. 1958. *I and Thou*. Trans. R. G. Smith. 2nd ed. Edinburgh: T. and T. Clark Ltd.

Callero, P. L. 2003. The sociology of the self. *Annual Review of Sociology* 29:115–133.

Carson, R. C., J. N. Butcher, and S. Mineka. 1996. *Abnormal Psychology and Modern Life*. 10th ed. New York: HarperCollins.

Caughey, J. L. 1984. *Imaginary Social Worlds: A Cultural Approach*. Lincoln: University of Nebraka Press.

Cooper, M., and H. J. M. Hermans. 2006 Honoring self-otherness: Alterity and the intrapersonal. In L. M. Simão and J. Valsiner, eds., *Otherness in Question: Labyrinths of the Self*, 305–325. Greenwich: Information Age Publishing.

Côté, J. 2001. Editor's note: The hope and promise of identity theory and research. *Identity: International Journal of Theory and Research* 1:1–3.

Falmagne, R.J. 2004. On the constitution of "self" and "mind": The dialectic of the system and the person. *Theory & Psychology* 14:822–845.

Gadamer, H.-G. 1989. *Truth and Method*. 2nd ed. Trans. J. Weinsheimer and D. G. Marshall. New York: Continuum.

Gergen, K. J., and M. M. Gergen. 1988. Narrative and the self as relationship. *Advances in Experimental Social Psychology* 21:17–56.

Harré, R., and L. Van Langenhove. 1991. Varieties of positioning. *Journal for the Theory of Social Behaviour* 21:393–407.

Hermans, H. J. M. 1996a. Voicing the self: From information processing to dialogical interchange. *Psychological Bulletin* 119:31–50.

——. 1996b. Opposites in a dialogical self: Constructs as characters. *Journal of Constructivist Psychology* 9:1–26.

——. 2001a. The dialogical self: Toward a theory of personal and cultural positioning. *Culture & Psychology* 7:243–281.

——. 2001b. The construction of a personal position repertoire: Method and practice. *Culture & Psychology* 7:323–365.

——. 2004a. Introduction: The dialogical self in a global and digital age. *Identity: An International Journal of Theory and Research* 4:297–320.

——. 2004b. Moving through three paradigms, yet remaining the same thinker. *Counselling Psychology Quarterly* 19:5–25.

Hermans, H. J. M., and G. Dimaggio, eds. 2004. *The Dialogical Self in Psychotherapy*. New York: Brunner and Routledge.

——. 2007. Self, identity, and globalization in times of uncertainty: A dialogical analysis. *Review of General Psychology* 11:31–61.

Hermans, H. J. M, and E. Hermans-Jansen. 1995. *Self-Narratives: The Construction of Meaning in Psychotherapy*. New York: Guilford.

Hermans, H. J. M., and H. J. G. Kempen. 1993. *The Dialogical Self: Meaning as Movement*. San Diego, CA: Academic Press.

——. 1998. Moving cultures: The perilous problems of cultural dichotomies in a globalizing society. *American Psychologist* 53:1111–1120.

Hermans, H. J. M., H. J. G. Kempen, and R. J. P. Van Loon. 1992. The dialogical self: Beyond individualism and rationalism. *American Psychologist* 47: 23–33.

James, W. 1890. *The Principles of Psychology*, vol. 1. London: Macmillan.

——. 1982. *The Varieties of Religious Experience: A Study in Human Nature*. Gifford Lectures on Natural Religion delivered at Edinburgh, 1901–1902. New York: Penguin.

Johnson, M. 1987. *The Body in the Mind: The Bodily Basis of Meaning, Imagination, and Reason*. Chicago: University of Chicago Press.

Leiman, M. 2002. Toward semiotic dialogism: The role of sign-mediation in the dialogical self. *Theory & Psychology* 12:221–235.

Levinas, E. 1969. *Totality and Infinity: An Essay on Exteriority*. Trans. A. Lingis. Pittsburgh: Duquesne University Press.

Lewis, M. D. 2002. The dialogical brain: Contributions of emotional neurobiology to understanding the dialogical self. *Theory & Psychology* 12:175–190.

Linell, P. 1990. The power of dialogue dynamics. In I. Marková and K. Foppa, eds., *The Dynamics of Dialogue*, 147–171. New York: Harvester Wheatsheaf.

Lysaker, J. 2006. "I am not what I seem to be": Commentary on Wiley. *International Journal for Dialogical Science* 1:41–45.

204 DIALOGICAL APPROACHES

Markova, I. 2006. On "the inner alter" in dialogue. *International Journal for Dialogical Science* 1:125–148.

Mead, G. H. 1934. *Mind, Self, and Society.* Chicago: University of Chicago Press.

Oles, P. K. 2005. The dialogical self: Cognitive inspirations and preliminary results. In P. K. Oles and H. J. M. Hermans, eds., *The Dialogical Self: Theory and Research,* 169–182. Lublin, Poland: Wydawnictwo KUL.

Plato. 1961. *Collected Dialogues.* Ed. E. Hamilton and H. Cairns. Bollingen series. New York: Pantheon.

Richardson, F. C., A. Rogers, and J. McCarroll. 1998. Toward a dialogical self. *American Behavioral Scientist* 41:496–515.

Said, E. W. 1999. *Out of Place: A Memoir.* London: Granta.

Sakellaropoulos, M., and M. W. Baldwin. 2006. Interpersonal cognition and the relational self: Paving the empirical road for dialogical science. *International Journal for Dialogical Science* 1:47–66.

Salgado, J., and H. J. M. Hermans. 2005. The return of subjectivity: From a multiplicity of selves to the dialogical self. *E-Journal of Applied Psychology* 1:3–13.

Sampson, E. 1985. The decentralization of identity: Toward a revised concept of personal and social order. *American Psychologist* 11:1203–1211.

Sarbin, Th. R. 1986. The narrative as a root metaphor for psychology. In Th. R. Sarbin, ed., *Narrative Psychology: The Storied Nature of Human Conduct,* 3–21. New York: Praeger.

Schore, A. N. 1994. *Affect Regulation and the Origin of the Self: The Neurobiology of Emotional Development.* Hillsdale, NJ: Erlbaum.

Spence, J. 1985. Achievement American style: The rewards and costs of individualism. *American Psychologist* 40:1285–1295.

Stemplewska-Zakowicz, K., J. Walecka, and A. Gabinska. 2006. As many selves as interpersonal relations or maybe even more. *International Journal for Dialogical Science* 1:71–94.

Stemplewska-Zakowicz, K., J. Walecka, A. Gabinska, B. Zalewski, and H. Zuszek. 2005. Experiments on positioning, positioning the experiments. In P. Oles and H. J. M. Hermans, eds., *The Dialogical Self: Theory and Research,* 183–199. Lublin, Poland: Wydawnictwo KUL.

Van Meijl, T. 2006. Multiple identifications and the dialogical self: Urban Maori youngsters and the cultural renaissance. *Journal of the Royal Anthropological Institute* n.s. 12:917–933.

Vygotsky, L. S. 1986. *Thought and Language.* Cambridge, MA: MIT Press.

Watkins, M. 1986. *Invisible Guests: The Development of Imaginal Dialogues.* Hillsdale, NJ: Erlbaum.

Wiley, N. 2006. Inner speech as a language: A Saussurean inquiry. *Journal for the Theory of Social Behavior* 36:320–342.

Williams, R. N., and E. E. Gantt. 2002. Pursuing psychology as science of the ethical: Contributions of the work of Emmanuel Levinas. In E. E. Gantt and R. N. Williams, eds., *Psychology for the Other: Levinas, Ethics, and the Practice of Psychology,* 1–31. Pittsburgh: Duquesne University Press.

9   Theorizing Cultural Psychology in Transnational Contexts

SUNIL BHATIA

In her memoir Meena Alexander, a poet of South Asian origin, reflects on her ethnicity as an Indian-American and states that she is a woman "cracked by multiple migrations," with many selves born out of broken geographies (1993:3). Her narrative foregrounds the struggles with self and identity that many transnational immigrants face as they try to find a place in contemporary U.S. society. Transnational practices and diaspora communities have become important sites for the reconstruction of culture, identity, diversity, and difference. In these sites, personhood acquires hybrid, creolized, hyphenated cultural properties and is transformed into an "other" with multiple, shifting, and conflicting identities.[1] The politics of race, gender, and class are intertwined with multiple migrant identities, incompatible cultural positions, and a fluctuating sense of self. How do we understand the complex and multilayered psychological processes involved in the acculturation of these transnational migrants?

We live in an age where transnational immigration, border crossings, and global media are proliferating at an increasing rate. Discussions about the self—which are further intensified by issues of race, gender, class, sexuality, ethnicity, and nationality—challenge the grand narratives of the stable, bounded, contained, and Cartesian identity. Acquiring knowledge about issues of self and identity becomes all the more critical in the face of sweeping demographic changes in the United States and Europe, where encounters with diverse histories, languages, religions, and ethnicities have emerged as central to the daily lives of those inhabiting many urban, metropolitan cultural spaces.

This chapter provides a cultural psychology framework for rethinking how postcolonial migrants maintain, resist, and reinvent their identities in the wake of enormous cultural change and conflict. My aim here is to add to the critical impulse that initially defined the vision of cultural psychology, by analyzing how transnational diaspora communities have become new sites for the rethinking of core concepts, such as culture and identity. I use migrant narratives from the Indian diaspora in the United States to show how contemporary notions of culture and identity within cultural psychology can be reexamined within the context of transnational movements and diaspora cultures. Given the conceptual nature of this article, my objective is to present an argument supported by selected auto-biographical accounts of migrants from the Indian diaspora. First, I provide a brief summary of the main concepts of cultural psychology. Second, I examine three autobiographical narratives of first-generation Indians living in southeastern Connecticut in the United States; their discourses about 9/11 have implications for understanding the hybrid intersections between race, culture, and nation. I conclude with some notes on the importance of adding a transnational orientation to cultural psychology.

Identity in Cultural Psychology

The vision of key cultural psychology theorists (Bruner 1992; Cole 1996; Shweder 1991) is broad enough in its scope to include those critical definitions of culture that have been discussed by scholars in cultural anthropology and diaspora studies in order to address conflicting and contested notions of culture and identity. The key arguments of this chapter fall within the overarching framework and vision of cultural psychology, but my larger aim is to push its horizon and theoretical scope to include an analysis of migration, diasporic cultures, and global identities.

I take as my point of departure Hermans' (2001) proposal that the notions of travel, diaspora, and immigration require that we come up with a dynamic and multivoiced notion of self. Hermans and Kempen (1998) emphasize that universal notions of culture and self fail to explain the challenges accompanying the acculturation process in a world where cultures are mixing and moving and the local and the global are merging and creating new "contact zones" between different cultures. As a consequence, Hermans makes a call to those scholars who study the relationship between culture and human development by asserting that the field of "developmental psychology is challenged by the increasing necessity to study a variety of developmental trajectories in the contact zones between cultures" (Hermans 2001:28). This essay can be construed as an answer to that call.

The last two decades have witnessed several movements in psychology that aim to understand how the self is constituted by society, culture, and history. For example, the field of cultural/sociocultural psychology has played a significant role in emphasizing how culture shapes human development and mediates the psychological functioning of individuals in their societies (Bruner 1986; Cole 1996; Rogoff 1990; Shweder 1991; Valsiner 1998; Wertsch 1991). The field of cultural psychology has made progress in demonstrating how the self is embedded in the topography of culture. Several proponents of cultural psychology imagine it as an interpretive discipline that uses methodologies from the social sciences and the humanities. These theorists focus on symbolic meanings, practices, and activity contexts; more recently, a few researchers in psychology have been using a cultural psychology framework to discuss the implications of transnationalism, migration, and creation of diaspora communities for the concepts of culture, identity, and difference (Bhatia 2007; Hermans and Kempen 1998; Mahalingam 2006).

It is important to mention at the outset that there is no single theoretical agenda or camp into which one can put the work of contemporary cultural psychologists. The cultural psychology movement does not signal one unified field of research or theory. More broadly construed, its vision represents the "road not taken" (Cole 1996:101) almost a century ago. Cole argues that the current cultural psychology movement came into being as a result of dissatisfaction with the way the concept of culture was incorporated in both cross-cultural and mainstream psychological research. The term "cultural psychology" began to be used around the 1980s. It was Stephen Toulmin who prodded psychologists to "reconsider Wundt's proposal for a *Volkerpsychologie*, which he translated as 'cultural psychology'" (Cole 1996:101–102).

Shweder believes that cultural psychology is "heretical" in its approach; he is opposed to formulating a cultural psychology that is based on "pure psychological laws or unmediated stimulus events" (1990:24). He writes that "cultural psychology is far more heterodox vis-à-vis the canon of psychic unity, and thus it differs from cross-cultural psychology" (p. 13). Humans as intentional beings are constituted by intentional worlds and embody their desires and goals through art, discourse, institutions, and religious practices. The aim of cultural psychology, according to Shweder, is "to imaginatively conceive of subject-dependent objects (intentional worlds) and object-dependent subjects (intentional persons) interpenetrating each other's identities or setting conditions for each other" (p. 25). Bruner writes that "cultural psychology, almost by definition, will not be preoccupied with 'behavior' but with action, its intentionally based counterpart, and more specifically with situated action in a cultural setting and in the mutually interacting intentional states of the participants" (1990:19). In short, Burner is concerned with how people use canonical and ordinary understanding of events to interpret and give "narrative meaning" to breaches, deviation, and other extraordinary mitigating conditions in everyday, cultural life.

A cursory examination of the vision of cultural psychology offered by some of the prominent practitioners of cultural psychology tells us that they are all concerned with explaining how culture—conceived as a system of everyday practices, customs, traditions, and artifacts—shapes the contours of human identity and thinking. Additionally, their focus is on delineating the social and cultural foundations of human development and the joint and co-constructed nature of all human action. The basic ideas of cultural psychology offered above go well beyond the mechanistic and central processing metaphor employed by general psychology to explain human action. Cultural psychology thus transcends the Platonic universalism of both cross-cultural psychology and general psychology and gives us a dynamic, situated, practice-based, and mediated notion of culture. It focuses on the creation of symbolic meaning as grounded in everyday life and seeks to explain the constructed, mediated, and relational nature of all human activity.

The vision of cultural psychology offered by some of these theorists can be extended to include how transnational practices mediate the formation of culture and cultural identities. The new cultural psychology movement began as a critique of general psychology, mainstream developmental psychology, and cross-cultural psychology. These theorists have given us a starting point for a cultural psychology that is spacious enough to include conflicting and contested notions of culture and identity—specifically notions of culture and identity that emerge from the formation of transnational diasporas across "First World" metropolitan cities and suburbs.

9/11 and Narratives of Identity from the Indian Diaspora

The interviews that are analyzed here are part of a larger study that looks at how members of the first-generation Indian diaspora respond to the varying levels of racism and discrimination they experience in their communities and workplaces (Bhatia 2007). I draw on a small subset of three interviews that specifically show how the events of 9/11 made many Indians rethink the status of their assimilation process and their place in the American culture.

I conducted fieldwork in this Indian diaspora for sixteen months between February 2000 and June 2001. From August 2001 to January 2002 I conducted in-depth interviews with thirty-eight first-generation Indian migrants and twenty second-generation migrants. Most of my participants worked for the local ABC Computer company and lived in the mostly white suburbs of East Lyme and Old Lyme, Connecticut. Since the 1960s these migrants have lived in small cities and suburbs of southern Connecticut, such as Groton, Ledyard, East Lyme, Norwich, Noank, New London, Old Lyme, and Waterford. Most of my interviews for this qualitative study were conducted in the immediate aftermath of the events of September 11, 2001 (henceforth, 9/11). I asked all of my participants to define "Indianness'" or what it means to be an Indian in the United States. Several participants talked about their Indianness within the context of the events of 9/11 and used this particular event to reconstruct and reexamine their cultural and racial identity.

My first interview with Neelam and her husband, Ranjit, occurred about three weeks after 9/11. Neelam was a professor of sociology at a local university and her husband worked as a vice president of finance for a local multinational company. I asked Neelam to describe her reaction to the events of 9/11. She observed, "But if this incident, which happened recently, is any indication, a lot of people in our neighborhood didn't even REALIZE that we are any different." The interesting part of this narrative is that their sense of difference suddenly emerged after 9/11, when Ranjit told his neighbor that they were being cautious about going out in public places. Neelam recalled:

NEELAM: And when Ranjit told them, "We are being careful not to go to other places, just to be on the safe side," they all were very embarrassed because they all, said, "Oh, we never thought that you could be considered . . ." And then they looked at him. "Yes, you *could* be, couldn't you?" (*laughing*). So, that was in fact, that was a very hard [xxx] to us, because it did not, so many of them, they all kept, came and said, "We are so sorry, but we just, it never occurred to us."

INTERVIEWER: That's right.

NEELAM: And that was, I think probably to me, that was much more of an acceptance . . .

INTERVIEWER: Um hmm, uh hmm . . .

NEELAM: "You know, we know that you are not terrorists" (*laughing*).

The most important part of the conversation occurs when the neighbors look at Neelam and Ranjit and say, "Yes, you *could* be, couldn't you?" The question is what the neighbors meant whey they said, "Yes, you could be, couldn't you?" What do Neelam and Ranjit represent in this context? It suddenly dawns on their neighbors that both Neelam and Ranjit could possibly be mistaken for being Arabs and that that mistaken association could invite harm to them. The neighbors apologized to Ranjit and Neelam because they would not go out in pubic due to the possible threat of their being identified as terrorists. Why did the neighbors apologize? On whose behalf were they apologizing? Ranjit and Neelam's cultural identity suddenly moves into the zone of being different, even though they were always different. What is this new sense of difference that emerges from their "old" sense of being different? How is it that prior to 9/11 Ranjit and Neelam's "Indianness" was not considered foreign by their neighbors? Why did Ranjit and Neelam's neighbor apologize and then reassure them that "You know, we know that you are not terrorists."

The answers to these questions can be found in the next excerpt from the interview.

RANJIT: And I would say for the first time since I joined, came to this country, sixteen years, not even during the Gulf War, *after these attacks was the first time that I felt I was not white. For the first time. And it's a very bad feeling.* [italics for emphasis]

INTERVIEWER: Why did you feel bad?

RANJIT: You know it's hard to explain, I honestly don't know. It's not that anybody even noticed. And in fact people are surprised I even told them, so it's really more of a fear inside me than anything else. And it's not even a fear, it's just that I felt different, a discomfort. And I felt if I go to the candlelight vigils and things which I felt very strongly for that people will look at me and I didn't go. So for the first time . . .

INTERVIEWER: Now that's interesting because you so identify with this unity but . . .

RANJIT: *For the first time EVER that came to me, and it wasn't because anybody said anything or looked anything or did anything. I felt I was different for the first time, it's a very bad feeling. Yes it is, it's a very bad feeling.*

INTERVIEWER: Did you feel like that sense of belongingness was shaken?

RANJIT: It was definitely shaken, and hopefully not shattered but definitely shaken. And it's nothing we did. . . .

In this excerpt, Ranjit makes it clear that during his sixteen years in the United States he had always considered himself as white. Now, in the light of the events of 9/11, his racial self-identification as a "white American" was under interrogation. He was interested in participating in the 9/11 candlelight vigils that were being held in his suburban town, but he would not go to these vigils because he feared that people might "look at him" differently. Ranjit assumed that his neighbors would consider him as a nonwhite person—a foreigner, an Arab, a Muslim, or a terrorist. He was afraid that his identity as a nonwhite person would suddenly become more visible and that this would shatter his sense of belonging in his community.

The events of 9/11 had played an important role in the lives of several other participants in my study of the Indian diaspora. Priya, a forty-six-year-old woman, is an infectious disease specialist at a local university. During our interview, I asked Priya to recall one moment that made her feel different in the past twenty years of her life in the United States. Priya replied:

You know and some of these were subtle and some of these were not subtle, but the most scary thing that comes to mind happened very recently actually after 9/11—umm, I think it was the beginning of October and I had gone to drop my son who's at B.C. to the railway station. . . . You know, he's going to Boston by Amtrak. And, umm, you know he's got long hair that he ties at the back a little bit of a beard and stuff—and suddenly I saw and we were waiting—his train was a little late and I saw two "American young men" who were about the same age as my son—he was sort of standing with his back towards them and I was facing these kids—or young men—and you know one of these young folks was draped in the American flag or so it seemed to me and, you know, sort of very nationalist in attitude. And, you know, the whole fervor was against anybody who looked different—was sort of at a peak. And I just remember being very uncomfortable and I stared right back at those kids because I . . . these are the kind of kids my sons had played with, gee!—They come to my house—they play hockey, you know—and in a way I—I knew who these boys were, but for that one moment I felt very different.

This excerpt reveals how 9/11 produced "scary moments" for some members of the Indian diaspora. At the railway station, Priya felt extremely threatened and uncomfortable in front of the two men who had visited her house on several occasions, Priya recognized these two young men immediately as they were her son's school friends and yet she feared that these men might mistake her son for a Muslim and may harm him:

And I felt very concerned for my son's safety. You know, so I told him—when he got off the train to take a cab and go back to college and, you know, not to wander around and *I've been trying to tell him since then to take his beard off—it looks very Muslim and stuff, so I would say that was one of the more overt memories I have*—but at subtler levels I'm sure there are things that have happened that probably somebody like V. S. Naipaul can probably articulate a lot better than I can, but at an overt level—no.

Priya was afraid that her son might be mistaken for a Muslim, and so she had repeatedly asked him to shave his beard. Priya explained to me that her son's face "looks very Muslim."

Ranjit, Neelam, and Priya's narratives force us to reexamine the contours of cultural psychology. Their narratives of race, place, and belonging compel us to rethink how we should conceptualize the development of migrant identity from the viewpoint of diaspora cultures and acculturation.

Culture and the Politics of Acculturation

Cultural psychology imagines itself to be concerned with study-ing the mediations of self through traditions, history, practices, and con-text—as exemplified in the type of identity negotiations undertaken by Ranjit, Neelam, and Priya. What cultures do Neelam and Ranjit repre-sent? What is their cultural identity from the point of view of cultural psychology? Typical cross-cultural theories of self would posit that Ranjit and Neelam are Indians living in the United States. Their nationality is foregrounded and the culture they bring with them from their homeland is assumed to be their lived culture in this country. What is missing in such theories is how the "here" and "there" are connected and how identi-ties are constructed out of shifting, contested, and incompatible notions of culture.

These post-9/11 narratives from the Indian diaspora spell out the con-tradictions, tensions, and the cultural specificities involved in the experi-ences of diasporic immigrants living with multiple cultures and histories that seem incompatible with one another. Additionally, these narratives show how various structural and sociological forces influence the psycho-logical positions of feeling *simultaneously* assimilated, separated, and mar-ginalized. Recall that Ranjit feared that after 9/11, he might be mistaken for an Arab and his sense of being white in the community would come under question.

Several scholars working in the area of Asian-American studies and sociology have shown that after 9/11 many South Asian American citi-zens who resembled the enemy were racialized and constructed as non-American (Maira 2004; Purkayastha 2005). In particular, they have shown that the post-9/11 period has created a new category of identity in the USA that perceives Arabs, Muslims, and Middle Eastern men as disloyal and nonpatriotic citizens or as individuals who are part of terrorist networks (Maira 2004). I find sociologist Bandana Purkayastha's research useful because it provides an analytical framework for understanding the larger structural forces that shaped my participants' responses to the events of 9/11.

Since 9/11 there has been a conflation of South Asian Muslims and Arabs with terrorism and "Islamic fundamentalism"; regardless of their nationality or religion, many South Asians are being categorized as sus-picious and having links to terrorists. Purkayastha notes that those who are perceived as having non-American traits during a sustained period of conflict and political crisis can face extremely dangerous consequences. U.S. foreign policy toward the Middle East has often provided a framework and a justification for the direct and indirect racial profiling of South Asian Muslim youth and adults in the United States. She writes:

> When other countries are seen as "threatening" to the United States, politically or economically, racialized individuals who look like "the enemy" to sections of the majority group are subjected to higher levels of discrimination and hate. Becoming visible is akin to having a spotlight turned on members of the group. Those caught in the spotlight remember their vulnerability at being under a significant level of public scrutiny, while those who turn on the light do not hold the impression beyond the moment.   (Purkayastha 2004:42)

The various responses of my participants—Ranjit, Neelam, and Priya—reveal the vulnerabilities they experienced when they suddenly became visible under the spotlight of the media and attacks from the majority.

In her research, Purkayastha (2004) cites several examples of how this vulnerability was experienced by several other South Asians in the post-9/11 period. The Sikh males in the South Asian community became hypervisible because of their beards and turbans and were victims of several hate crimes across the nation. The hate crimes were further legitimized when some radio stations described Sikh men as wearing "towels," or as "diaper heads" and "cloth heads." Many South Asians expressed a sense of dread or an impending fear as they traveled in public places, such as when taking the subway or buying groceries. Several South Asian American women were reminded by their friends and family members to stop wearing *saris* or *salwar khameezes* (traditional clothing) and were also asked to "lay low" so that they don't make themselves visible during the post-9/11 times. Purkayastha illustrates the consequences of "looking like the enemy" during heightened political conflict via an exchange between an Indian woman, Mallika, and a young white male. She writes:

> Mallika described an incident that occurred in October 2001. She was working out in a gym with a friend when a young white male came up to her friend and said threateningly, "You look like you could be Osama bin Laden's sister." Her friend tried to explain that she was an Indian, not Saudi Arabian. Mallika realized that even

though she and her friend were Americans, this was no longer relevant to the conversation. She felt she could not say they were American or South Asian American. Emphasizing their Indianness, with
its association of a mainly Hindu identity, seemed to be the only way
of proving their nonthreatening character. She later reflected that
their responses denied Pakistani and Bangladeshi South Asians the
rights to use their parents' country of origin as a safety shield in a
similar situation.   (Purkayastha 2004:45)

It is interesting to note here that Mallika's place of birth and American
citizenship were not relevant factors in this conversation. What mattered
to the young male was that she looked like she could be "the enemy's" sister; this projection of Mallika belonging in the enemy's camp is another
clear example of how the process of racialization works in everyday life in
the United States.

Mallika was reflective about the fact that she could strategically position herself as a Hindu Indian, but none of my three participants articulated the level of hostility, threat, and intimidation that other South Asian
Muslims and Arab-Americans experience on an everyday basis. Their
narratives were about the sense of otherness and un-belonging that they
had experienced, but evidently these narratives were also about indirectly
distancing themselves from a Muslim cultural identity.

Racial Identity and Modes of Belonging

The participants in my study were subjected to racial discrimination, yet they were reluctant to see themselves as having a racial identity or a racial subjectivity. Recall Ranjit's interview where he expressed
his new discomfort with being nonwhite. Ranjit and Neelam lived in an
upper-class suburb of Connecticut. Husband and wife were successful
professionals who had many friends in the mainstream, white community. They went on summer vacations with their white friends and
had regular social interactions with their neighborhood friends. Ranjit and Neelam's daughter had regular sleepovers at their neighbor's
house. In short, Ranjit and Neelam had worked hard at integrating
into their community as white Americans. In the wake of 9/11, Ranjit's
sense of identity was shaken and his place in the community was in
doubt. It is important to mention here that none of Ranjit's friends or

neighbors had made any comments about his cultural identity or his sense of belonging in the community.

On the contrary, Ranjit and Neelam's friends were being "extra-friendly" to them and were aware there could be a public backlash against Ranjit and Neelam because they looked "Middle Eastern." Ranjit acknowledged that 9/11 has made him realize that he is actually different from his neighbors and that he is not a white American. Ranjit and Neelam had been Indians living in a white suburban neighborhood who felt sure that they had assimilated in American society, but 9/11 had made them realize that they did not fully belong to mainstream, white America. Ranjit remarked that prior to 9/11 he had never considered himself as a "foreigner" or an "outsider" in the United States, but the events of 9/11 had ruptured his self-perception as a white person and his perceived proximity to whiteness was now under interrogation. The crucial question here is: Why did Ranjit feel that he was white when he is actually racially identified as brown?

Ranjit had achieved what Purkayastha describes as "structural integration," a type of integration that can be defined by one's level of access to economic and educational opportunities. Many Indians living in the United States earn high salaries, own large homes, live in middle-class suburbs, and have access to the same kinds of economic and educational opportunities as many white Americans. However, their status as racial minorities prevents them from adopting the "racially neutral" language that is often used by their white peers and friends. Their racial status still marginalizes them and marks them as culturally and ethnically different. Living in affluent suburbs with mostly white Americans, many Indian migrants believe that the American dream can be acquired by working hard, and on the basis of personal merit. They often operate under the unconscious assumption that their middle-class standing makes their racial identity irrelevant and protects them from discriminatory incidents.

Ranjit had defined himself as a white American primarily because of his structural or economic assimilation in the middle-class white suburbs. The post-9/11 months made his racial position much more visible, however, and his phenotypic similarities to "Arab" terrorists prompted his neighbors to remark, "Yes, you *could* be, couldn't you?" The post-9/11 spotlight on people who looked Arab/Muslim/Middle Eastern made Ranjit realize that he could be perceived as being in the enemy camp; his structural integration or assimilation in American society was thus being challenged from multiple directions.

The same kind of analytical framework can be used to explain why Priya, immediately after 9/11, felt threatened at the railway station by the young men who had been her son's childhood friends. At the railway station, Priya identified these men as "American young men" rather than just "young men." She called them "American young men" to clearly demarcate the cultural identity of her son and herself from these patriotic American youth. What is omitted in this excerpt is that Priya's son is born and raised in the United States—at that moment his "Americanness" or his "American citizenship" seemed to have been erased and his "Indianness" stood out, evinced by his black hair and beard. Priya's emphasis on her son's "black hair and beard" essentially points to the fact that in that moment she focused on her son's "Indian" and "brown" attributes rather than his American citizenship. She feared that his external racial similarities to Arab men would put him under the spotlight and make him vulnerable to attacks from the public.

Priya, Neelam, and Ranjit's interviews reveal that all three of them had acculturated in America as "model minorities" in white middle-class suburbs, and prior to 9/11 they believed in the idea that their status as middle-class professionals would make their racial identities irrelevant. These individuals had perceived themselves as having a strong "cultural identity" but not a "racial identity." The events of 9/11 had elevated the otherness of these three individuals and had revealed a sense of ambiguity that they had experienced with regard to their racial identity. Their difference, which was previously neutralized, hidden, or erased, was now suddenly recast as a nonmainstream, marginal cultural identity that was perceived to pose a threat to the larger culture. The external and internal reconstructions of identity that occurred after 9/11 among the members of the Indian diaspora ruptured the participants' sense of race, place, and acculturation into American culture.

The acculturation process of middle-class Indians in the United States reveals that they have some ambivalence toward their racial identity; this point has been well documented by several scholars (George 1997; Maira 2004; Prashad 2000). By employing and constantly reproducing the model minority discourse, many professional, post-1965 immigrants make attempts to reposition their difference as being the same as or equal to the dominant majority. This attempt to establish sameness by using a model minority discourse also means that many participants are reluctant to see themselves as a racially distinct community that is different from white America. Other scholars have pointed out that since the model

minority stereotype focuses on the achievements of Asians, their success
also invites resentment and hostility from mainstream America (Kibria
2002). With respect to the Chinese-American diaspora, the model minority stereotype represents the opposite meaning of the image of "yellow
peril." Kibria notes that "in both the model minority image and that of
yellow peril, Asian achievement takes on inhuman, even species-different
character" (Kibria 2002:133). Indian-Americans are comfortable with the
idea that they differ from mainstream America in terms of culture and
ethnicity, but not in terms of racial identity (George 1997). George writes
that most South Asians have been reluctant to cast their identities in racial
terms. She explains:

> What is refused by nearly all upper and middle class South
> Asians is not so much a specific racial identity but the very idea
> of being raced. The only identity that is acknowledged is the cul-
> tural and ethnic one of being no more and no less than "Indian-
> American."   (George 1997:29)

George asserts that many South Asians living in the United States want
to make themselves racially invisible. Constructing one's personhood in
terms of class and cultural formations makes the move toward invisibility.
For example, there is a tendency among many Indian-Americans to represent themselves to Americans as being from the glorious ancient Indian
civilization, the spiritual and cultural East, or from the pure Aryan race.
Mazumdar's (1989) pioneering article, "Racist Responses to Racism: The
Aryan Myth and South Asians in the United States," analyzes the phenomenon in which South Asians insisted on seeing themselves as "Ary-
ans of pure stock," even though the dominant majority perceives them to
be black or people of color. Within the context of the Indian migration to
the United States, she cites the case of Bhagat Singh Thind, who was a
Hindu born in Punjab and came to America in 1913. Thind argued in the
Supreme Court that under the 1906 naturalization law, he was Caucasian,
therefore white, and thus entitled to U.S. citizenship.

Prashad's insights on the reasons for Desis'[2] ambivalence toward race
help us understand the participants' responses in my study. He notes:

> Desis realize they are not "white," but there is certainly a strong
> sense amongst Desis that they are not "black." In a racist society, it
> is hard to expect people to opt for the most despised category. Desis

came to the United States and denied their "blackness" at least partly out of a desire for class mobility (something, in the main, denied to blacks) and a sense that solidarity with blacks was tantamount to ending one's dream of being successful (that is, of being "white").   (Prashad 2000:94)

An examination of the "acculturation" experiences of Priya, Neelam, and Ranjit as individuals living in the diaspora allows us to examine the distinct racialized experiences of non-Western/European immigrants. Moreover, given the existence of racial prejudice in American society, non-European immigrants have been more likely to face exclusion and discrimination than their European counterparts. When new immigrants—whether Caribbean, Chilean, Chinese, Indian, Mexican, or Vietnamese—enter the United States, they are introduced to the stories, legacies, and immigration heritage of their respective ethnic group. Subsequently, through personal remembering and shared histories, tales of discrimination, hardships, and sheer exploitation are kept alive in most non-European immigrant communities.

Toward a Transnational Cultural Psychology

Neelam, Ranjit, and Priya's narratives illustrate that transnational, diaspora, and immigrant identities require that we come up with a dynamic and multivoiced notion of self. Their stories show that contemporary notions of culture and self in psychology fail to explain the challenges accompanying the acculturation process within a diasporic world where cultures are mixing and moving, and the local and the global are merging and creating new hyphenated identities. How do we create a new vision for cultural psychology that pays attention to these new subjects of a global world?

Bruner's (1986, 1990) vision is primarily concerned with examining the "folk psychology," or the "folk human science," of how people with desires, beliefs, goals, and intentional states inhabit symbolic worlds and use narrative to make meaning and interpret their experiences. About two decades ago, Bruner outlined a vision for cultural psychology in stating that psychology must move away from being preoccupied with "behavior" and shift its focus to how we make meaning of our "actions" as intentional agents located in cultural practices and socially situated settings (1990:19).

Bruner writes that "cultural psychology, almost by definition, will not be preoccupied with 'behavior' but with action, its intentionally based counterpart, and more specifically with situated action in a cultural setting and in the mutually interacting intentional states of the participants (1990:19)." In short, Bruner is concerned with how people use canonical and ordinary understanding of events to interpret and give "narrative meaning" to breaches, deviation, and other extraordinary mitigating conditions in everyday, cultural life. The focus here is not only on understanding cultural meaning systems through sense and reference, but on how individuals use narratives to make sense of the cultural events around them. The use of narrative as a way of knowing the world, according to Bruner, is "one of the crowning achievements of human development in the ontogenetic, cultural, phylogenetic sense of that expression" (p. 67).

If cultural psychology is to be relevant in the contemporary world then it must investigate the phenomena in which modes of othering and racialization are inseparable from the everyday experiences of transnational migrants. My analyses of narratives from the Indian diaspora illustrate that when referring to an immigrant's acculturation process, we need to be attentive to issues related to the race, gender, and power status of that immigrant both before and after migration to the host country. The acculturation process within the United States takes on a different developmental trajectory, if, say, the migrant had been part of a powerful center or majority in his/her local milieu prior to migration, and after migration, finds himself or herself to be a part of a minority living on the margins. As Frankenberg and Mani (1993) allege, race and gender are crucial signifiers that mark our locations and positions in the center or at the margins. Through these signifiers we identify ourselves and our selfhood, and we become identified by others as well. In other words, our identities, as Frankenberg and Mani point out, are both "relational and situated" (p. 278).

The concepts of culture and self need to be reconfigured within the context of a global and transnational cultural psychology. The field of psychology has focused on the mutual constitution between culture and self, but has not yet investigated the complexities associated with the formation of selves and identities that are created in the borderland and the postcolonial diasporas. According to Gupta and Ferguson (1992), the idea of a transnational sphere makes any narrow, atomistic, and bounded notion of a community and culture outdated. Diasporas have led to the articulation of news forms of selfhood, community, and solidarity that are not based on the concept of space, where "contiguity and face-to-face contact are paramount" (Gupta and Ferguson 1992:8). According to van der Veer (1992:1), in the early 1990s about 8 million South Asians, 22 million Chinese, 11 million Jews, 300 million people of African descent, and 350 million Europeans were living as migrant populations.

Contemporary global movements and globalization impulses (variously motivated) force us to abandon seamless conceptions of similarities and differences between national cultures in favor of hybridized, diasporized, and heterogeneous notions of culture (Hall 1993:356). In other words, "culture"—however we wish to understand it—cannot be understood as contained and circumscribed by national boundaries. To posit such static, immovable, immutable constructions of culture is a convenient fiction that allows us, as Hall (1991) acerbically remarks, "to get a good night's sleep." For it allows us to believe that, in spite of the fact that history is "constantly breaking in unpredictable ways, . . . we somehow go on being the same" (p. 43).

Conflating culture with nation is an extremely problematic position. Anderson (1991:3) has famously argued that nation, nationality, and nationalism are notoriously difficult to define, let alone analyze. To posit that the "nation" can be understood as a durable, ontological, material, geopolitical concept ignores the counternarratives, the contested identities, and the historical inventions that continuously challenge any unified understanding of a nation. A nation is more than a geographically identified space; rather, it is what Anderson terms an "imagined community," what Renan (1990:19) calls a "spiritual principle" constituted by memories that swallow up discordant details, and what Bhabha (1994:297) refers to as a series of narrations constructed by "scraps, patches, and rags."

Moreover, when we consider the history of colonialism, we are forced to abandon national-level classifications of culture. Postcolonial writers have persistently sought to demonstrate how formerly colonized cultures bear indelible, imperial inscriptions. As Spivak (1993:48) comments, the "subject-position of the citizen of a recently decolonized 'nation' is epistemically fractured," and can "inhabit widely different epistemes, violently at odds with each other." The now infamous, but once celebrated, *Macaulay Minute* stated with imperial certitude that: "We [the British] must at present do our best to form . . . a class of persons, Indian in blood and color, but English in taste, in opinions, in morals and in intellect" (Macaulay 1972:249). So if history and culture are inseparably tied to the construction of self, then, for example, any discussion with regard to an

Indian immigrant must account for the cultural genealogy of "English India," which, according to Suleri (1992:3), is extensive enough to include both colonial and postcolonial histories.

From the formation of the modern nation-state, which is deeply intertwined with colonial and imperialist policies, to the vast flows of migration from "Third-World" postcolonial societies to the "First World," the idea that culture can be circumscribed and defined by national boundaries is highly debatable. As Hermans and Kempen argue, equating culture with the geographic space of the nation does not fully capture the complex relationship between global cultures and the construction of self (1998:1117). They note that globalization has led to a hybridization of cultural practices and meanings that

> may create such multiple identities as Mexican school girls dressed in Greek Togas dancing in the style of Isadora Duncan, a London boy of Asian origin playing for a local Bengali cricket team and at the same time supporting the Arsenal football club, Thai boxing by Moroccan girls in Amsterdam, and Native Americans celebrating Mardi Gras in the United States.   (p. 1113)

Ranjit, Neelam, and Priya's interviews point to the construction of identities through the intermingling, mixing, and moving of cultures. Such a description of culture broadens contemporary understanding of culture and contributes to the growing body of knowledge in cultural psychology. After 9/11, Ranjit feared that he might be mistaken for an Arab and that his sense of being white in the community would come into question. The events of 9/11 elevated the otherness of these individuals and revealed the sense of ambiguity they felt with regard to their racial identity. Their difference, which was previously neutralized, hidden, or erased, was now suddenly recast as a nonmainstream, marginal cultural identity that was perceived to pose a threat to the larger culture. The external and internal reconstructions of identity that occurred in the Indian diaspora after 9/11 had ruptured the participants' sense of race, place, and acculturation into American culture. These members of the diaspora had assumed that they were not only assimilated into American society, but were *also* able to integrate both American and Indian cultures. However, the events of 9/11 clearly showed that the construction of these identities is connected to cultural practices that are mediated by shifting notions of race and nationality.

A transnational cultural psychology needs to rethink concepts of culture and identity within the context of migration, displacement, and transnational diasporas. Given the increasing discursive and material emergence of the diaspora, cultural psychology can no longer insist on thinking about culture as contained by national boundaries or of cultures as reified, polarized entities. Scholars studying issues related to the diaspora make us confront questions about the status of "culture" in global, transnational, diasporic societies: Is there anything such as a univocal, monolithic, American, English, or Indian culture? What does it mean to have hyphenated identities, such as African-American, Asian-American, or Mexican-American, in the larger American society? How do "Third-World," postcolonial immigrants residing in "First-World" societies and countries negotiate their identities in relation to both Western/European/"First-World" settlers *and* to other non-European/"Third-World" immigrants? These new immigrants often find themselves struggling with asymmetrical cultural positions, racially charged contexts, and an oppressive political rhetoric. Additionally, in contrast to their turn-of-the-century European counterparts, new immigrants have far better access to transatlantic travel and can take advantage of accelerations in global communication technology.

Glick-Schiller, Basch, and Szanton-Blanc define the new immigrants as "transnationals" whose lived experiences and everyday activities are shaped by multiple connections and linkages to several nations and cultures through travel, technology, and media (1995:48). The web of contradictory discourses related to race, community, ethnicity, and loyalty experienced by the new immigrants as well as their children demand that we rethink our traditional notions of immigrant adaptation and acculturation. The narratives of the first-generation Indian diaspora show how they have negotiated their hybrid sense of self in such a context of cultural difference and racial politics (Bhatia and Ram 2001a, 2001b, 2004; Bhatia 2002).

The new diasporas have both created and transformed social networks, circuits of capital and commodities, and cultural practices and rituals that exist in the country of their settlement and in their home society. These immigrants now live in dual societies and inhabit multiple homes, roles, identities, and languages. Their networks and ideas of belonging transcend national boundaries and bring together the local and the global, and the home and host country, into a single "social field." Glick-Schiller, Basch, and Szanton-Blanc (1995) define the new immigrants as transmigrants whose patterns of activities are structured around multiple and continuous linkages across national borders.

Indeed, many of the transmigrants living in diasporic communities do adapt and become incorporated into the social fabric and the political institutions of America. However, at the same time they remain invested in the everyday events of their home country and retain a strong identification with their homeland. Clifford (1994) notes that "diaspora cultures thus mediate, in a lived tension, the experience of separation and entanglement, of living here and remembering/desiring another place" (p. 311). Glick-Schiller, Basch, and Szanton-Blanc (1994) thus argue that "in identifying a new process of migration, scholars of migrations emphasize the ongoing and continuing ways in which current-day immigrants reconstruct and reconstitute their simultaneous embeddedness in more that one society." How is this simultaneous linkage and embeddedness of self and identity in multiple social fields constituted and reconstituted? Clifford (1994) argues that the new transnational migration has realigned the conception of majority and minority communities, and the concomitant concepts of assimilation, resistance, adaptation, and ethnicity that are associated with it. He distinguishes diasporas from immigrant communities by arguing that the latter are often described as temporary communities, whose inhabitants do feel the loss of their homeland, but essentially follow a linear assimilation narrative in which the typical three generations, through hard work and struggle, attain the identity of an ethnic American and build a new home in a new world. Nations that follow the assimilationist ideology, he points out, employ such narratives to appeal to the immigrant community as opposed to those migrants who live in diasporic communities.

Cultural psychology needs to expand its boundaries and study various modes of belonging and identifying in the diaspora. The emphasis should be on studying how cultures, selves, and identities are connected and shaped by the politics and cultures of homeland and hostland, by the larger forces of globalization, media, cable, and modern transportation, by communication technology, and by the virtual and actual back and forth movement between two or more societies.

Notes

1.   What I want to emphasize here is that diasporic identity is not just about abstract concepts—it is rooted in lived experiences of difference and otherness.

The construction of diasporas reminds us again and again, according to Hall (1991:9), that we cannot go on defining identities "as two histories, one over here, one over there, never having spoken to one another, not having to do with one another." Such a definition of identity, he proclaims, "is simply not tenable any longer in a globalized world. It is just not tenable any longer." This new type of transnational selfhood, along with the experiences accompanying it, forces us to "reconceptualize fundamentally the politics of self, community, solidarity, identity, and cultural difference of living in a global world" (Hall 1991:9).

2.   *Desi* is a colloquial Hindi word that is etymologically connected to the word *Desh. Desi* refers to first- and second-generation families who have origins in South Asia (India, Nepal, Maldives, Pakistan, and Sri Lanka). See Bahri 1996 for a detailed discussion of the changing conceptions of the label "South Asians" in the United States.

References

Alexander, M. 1993. *Fault Lines*. New York: Feminist Press at the City University of New York.

Anderson, B. 1991. *Imagined Communities: Reflections on the Origin and Spread of Nationalism*. London: Verso.

Bahri, D. 1996. Coming to terms with the "postcolonial." In D. Bahri and M. Vasudeva, eds., *Between the Lines: South Asians and Postcoloniality*, 137–164. Philadelphia: Temple University Press.

Bhabha, H. 1994. The Location of Culture. New York: Routledge.

Bhatia, S. 2002. Acculturation, dialogical voices, and the construction of the diasporic self. *Theory and Psychology* 12:55–77.

———. 2007. *American Karma: Culture, Identity, and Race in the Indian Diaspora*. New York: New York University Press.

Bhatia, S., and A. Ram. 2001a. Rethinking "acculturation" in relation to diasporic cultures and postcolonial identities. *Human Development* 44:1–17.

———. 2001b. Locating the dialogical self in the age of transnational migrations, border crossings, and diasporas. Commentary on H. J. M. Hermans' "The dialogical self: Toward a theory of personal and cultural positioning." *Culture & Psychology* 7:297–309.

———. 2004. Culture, hybridity, and the dialogical self: Cases from the South-Asian diaspora. *Mind, Culture, and Activity* 11:225–241.

Bruner, J. 1986. *Actual Minds, Possible Worlds*. Cambridge, MA: Harvard University Press.

———. 1990. *Acts of Meaning: Four Lectures on Mind and Culture*. Cambridge, MA: Harvard University Press.

Clifford, J. 1986. Introduction: Partial truths. In J. Clifford and G. E. Marcus, eds., *Writing Culture: The Poetics of Ethnography*, 1–26. Berkeley: University of California Press.

————. 1994. Diasporas. *Cultural Anthropology* 9:302–338.

Cole, M. 1996. *Cultural Psychology: A Once and Future Discipline*. Cambridge, MA: Harvard University Press.

Frankenberg, R., and L. Mani. 1993. Crosscurrents, crosstalk: Race, "postcoloniality," and the politics of location. *Cultural Studies* 7:292–311.

George, R. M. 1997. "From expatriate aristocrat to immigrant nobody": South Asian racial strategies in the southern Californian context. *Diaspora* 6:27–59.

Glick-Schiller, N., L. Basch, and C. Szanton-Blanc. 1995. From immigrant to transmigrant: Theorizing transnational migration. *Anthropological Quarterly* 68:48–63.

Glick-Schiller, N. G., and G. E. Fouron. 2001. *Georges Woke Up Laughing: Long-Distance Nationalism and the Search for Home*. London: Duke University Press.

Gupta, A., and J. Ferguson. 1992. Beyond "culture": Space, identity, and the politics of difference. *Cultural Anthropology* 7:6–23.

Hall, S. 1991. Old and new identities, old and new ethnicities. In A. D. King, ed., *Culture, Globalization, and the World-System: Contemporary Conditions for the Representation of Identity*, 41–68. Binghamton: State University of New York Press.

————. 1993. Culture, community, nation. *Cultural Studies* 7:349–363.

Hermans, H. J. M. 2001. Mixing and moving cultures require a dialogical self. *Human Development* 44:24–28.

Hermans, H. J. M., and H. J. G. Kempen. 1998. Moving cultures: The perilous problems of cultural dichotomies in a globalizing society. *American Psychologist* 53:1111–1120.

Hernandez, D. J. 1999. Children of immigrants, one-fifth of America's children and growing: Their circumstances, prospects, and welfare reform. Master lecture presented at the biennial meeting of the Society for Research in Child Development, Albuquerque, NM.

Kibria, N. 2002. *Becoming Asian American*. Baltimore: John Hopkins University Press.

Macaulay, T. B. 1972 [1835]. Minute on Indian education. In J. Clive, ed., *Selected Writings*, 237–251. Chicago: University of Chicago Press.

Mahalingam, R. M., ed. 2006. *Cultural Psychology of Immigrants: An Introduction*. Hillsdale, NJ: Erlbaum.

Maira, S. 2004. Imperial feelings: Youth culture, citizenship, and globalization. In M. Suarez-Orozco and D. Quin-Hilliard, eds., *Globalization: Culture and Education in the New Millennium*, 203–234. Berkeley: University of California Press.

Mazumdar, S. 1989. Racist responses to racism: The Aryan myth and South Asians in the United States. *South Asia Bulletin* 9:47–55.

Prashad, V. 2000. *The Karma of Brown Folk*. Minneapolis: University of Minnesota Press.

Purkayastha, B. 2005. *Negotiating Ethnicity: Second-Generation South Asian Americans Traverse a Transnational World*. New Brunswick, NJ: Rutgers University Press.

Renan, E. 1990. "What is a Nation." In H. Bhabha, ed., *Nation and Narration*, 9–22. New York: Routledge.

Rogoff, B. 1990. *Apprenticeship in Thinking: Cognitive Development in Sociocultural Activity*. New York: Oxford University Press.

Rogoff, B., J. Mistry, A. Göncü, and C. Mosier. 1993. Guided participation in cultural activity by toddlers and caregivers. *Monographs of the Society for Research in Child Development* 58.7, serial no. 236.

Shweder, R. A. 1991. *Thinking Through Cultures: Expeditions in Cultural Psychology*. Cambridge, MA: Harvard University Press.

Spivak, G. 1993. *Outside the Teaching Machine*. New York: Routledge.

Suleri, S. 1992. *The Rhetoric of English India*. Chicago: University of Chicago Press.

Valsiner, J. 1989. *Human Development and Culture: The Social Nature of Personality and Its Study*. Lexington, MA: Lexington Books.

———. 1998. *The Guided Mind*. Cambridge, MA: Harvard University Press.

van der Veer, P. 1992. Introduction: The diasporic imagination. In P. van der Veer, ed., *Nation and Migration: The Politics of Space in the South Asian Diaspora*, 1–16. Philadelphia: University of Pennsylvania Press.

Wertsch, J. V. 1985. *Vygotsky and the Social Formation of Mind*. Cambridge, MA: Harvard University Press.

———. 1991. *Voices of the Mind: A Sociocultural Approach to Mediated Action*. Cambridge, MA: Harvard University Press.

Part IV

Neo-Vygotskian Approaches

10 Cultural-Historical Activity Theory

*Foundational Worldview, Major Principles,
and the Relevance of Sociocultural Context*

ANNA STETSENKO AND IGOR M. ARIEVITCH

In this chapter, we outline the foundations and the major principles of cultural-historical activity theory (CHAT)—a theoretical perspective that suggests a unique way to conceptualize human development and has much to offer for finding solutions to the conundrums of today's social sciences. While many of the debates in these sciences remain stalled between the two extremes of naïve positivism on the one hand and laissez-faire constructivism and relativism on the other, CHAT represents a well-grounded alternative (in both the natural sciences, such as biology and physiology, and critical-humanistic perspectives) that capitalizes on the social and relational nature of human development and at the same time does not eschew human subjectivity and agency. Developed in the early twentieth century, this perspective offers a new vision of the most profound questions pertaining to human development and human "nature," also suggesting a new mission for psychology as a discipline that can be put to use for the betterment of the human condition and of society as a whole. Specifically, we argue that CHAT offers a dialectical and nonreductionist, yet consistently materialist (i.e., nondualist), vision of human nature and development as rooted in, derivative of, and instrumental in the material collaborative social practices of people (i.e., human goal-directed, purposeful, collaborative activities) aimed at transforming their world. These practices produce and engender social interactions and human subjectivity, and (at mature stages of development in history and in ontogeny) are themselves reciprocally produced by these interactions and subjectivity.

We are not suggesting that CHAT—or any other theory from the past, for that matter—can be mechanically transposed into contemporary debates and used to address today's challenges. Such a position would go against the most basic tenet of CHAT itself, which emphasizes the profoundly situated and historicized nature of mind and its products such as knowledge and systems of thought. By expanding CHAT to the analysis of science, however, it can be suggested that knowledge and science are direct outcomes of and contributors to social practice (a) that are entwined with the practical, political, and value-laden contexts of their creation and (b) that embody this practice in the very fabric of knowledge claims, concepts, and theories. The relevance of CHAT, therefore, does not inhere in its having discovered some ahistorical "timeless truths" about human development; rather, it has to do with the continuing relevance of the goals that CHAT represents—the goals of struggling for a humane society built on the foundations of social justice and equality. It is this ideologically nonneutral, political, and ultimately practical project, stretching far beyond the confines of science as an academic enterprise, that gave rise to CHAT and itself became enriched by and embodied in it. It is also the profound saturation of CHAT by the goals of social transformation that marks its uniqueness and ultimately explains its vast appeal (especially to scholars who realize the urgency of addressing social injustice in today's world).

A specification of the term "CHAT" is needed before we proceed. Although this is a relatively new term, various meanings have become associated with it in recent literature, for example, relating it to contemporary works that use Vygotsky and Leontiev as their foundation and are sometimes referred to as a "third-generation" CHAT (e.g., Cole and Engeström 1993; Engeström 1990). We use CHAT here in a more narrow sense, to refer to a project launched by Lev Vygotsky in the 1920s–30s in collaboration with Leontiev and Luria (and several other scholars) and later continued (after Vygotsky's untimely death in 1934) and expanded within what became known as Vygotsky's school. This school united scholars from diverse areas in psychology (e.g., developmental, neuropsychology, social, educational, organizational, comparative), the majority of them working at the Moscow State University, the true hot-bed of CHAT; most prominently, and in addition to the famous "tro-jka" (Vygotsky–Leontiev–Luria), these were D. Elkonin, P. Galperin, A. Zaporozhets, L. Bozhovich, L. Lisina, P. Zinchenko, and V. Davydov. At the peak of its influence (from the 1960s to the early 1980s), this school represented one of the dominant research directions in psychology in the Soviet Union (though in constant and quite fierce competition with other approaches, such as the traditional positivist ones [e.g., Lomov]). The work of this school shaped many of the theoretical debates of the time, producing noteworthy findings, attracting a wide following, and affecting many applied fields, including education and neurological diag-nosis and treatment, and perhaps most remarkably embodied in reha-bilitation programs for deaf-and-blind children (work by Mesheryakov and Sokolyansky). A vast body of literature was produced in these years, still not all known in the West, though partly available through *Soviet Psychology* (at present, the *Journal of Russian and East European Psychol-ogy*), in large part due to the efforts of Michael Cole, who for many years served as its editor.

It should be noted that Vygotsky's school today has, largely and regrettably (though, we are convinced, temporarily), lost its appeal for most Russian scholars. This situation needs to be understood in the context of a dramatic sociocultural and political reshuffling that took place after the demise of the Soviet Union and was accompanied by a drastic, and not always well-balanced, reconsideration of this coun-ty's recent past, including in academic domains. However, in a more positive development, the tradition associated with Vygotsky's school has moved to international quarters, where a growing global commu-nity of researchers (from countries as diverse as Finland, Brazil, the United States, Hong Kong, Canada, Denmark, South Africa, and Cuba) is now applying and further developing it. The internationalization of CHAT, especially evident in the last ten–fifteen years (e.g., influential works including Cole 1996; Engeström, Miettinen, and Punamaeki 1999; John-Steiner, Panofsky, and Smith 1994; Moll 1992; Wells 1999; Wertsch 1988; and several volumes published during the past few years, e.g., Hedegaard 2001; Karpov 2006; Lantolf and Thorne 2006; Robbins and Stetsenko 2002; Rogoff 2003; Sawchuk, Duarte, and Elhammoumi 2006) happened gradually and progressed from an initial interest focused on Vygotsky's works (and, in a separate vein, on those by Luria), largely fueled by the seminal efforts of Western scholars such as Jerome

Bruner, Michael Cole, Vera John-Steiner, Sylvia Scribner, and James Wertsch. Since then the internationalizing of CHAT has been gradually expanded, especially by Yrjo Engeström, to reflect contributions by this school's other representatives, such as Leontiev and Davydov. Today's "internationalized" CHAT is playing a prominent role in areas such as communication studies, education, human–computer interaction, literacy, and organizational studies. However, in other areas with goals and orientations highly commensurate with CHAT—such as critical theory and pedagogy, feminist and science studies—the ideas and premises of this approach have not yet been discovered, which is unfortunate, especially given that cross-fertilization among these frameworks could be mutually beneficial.

While the works of recent years in the CHAT tradition—since its internationalization—are of great interest and value, we confine ourselves to analyzing the original "Russian" version of CHAT—Vygotsky's school—for several reasons. First, restoring the original CHAT and addressing the context that gave rise to it can help to understand its uniqueness, especially as associated with the historical and sociocultural context of its creation, and thus help reveal how this approach is relevant in today's context. Second, going back to the roots of any phenomenon, including theoretical systems, is a methodology highly consistent with CHAT, which strongly asserts, among its core principles, the importance of historically reconstructing the development of phenomena (starting from their incipient forms) as a way to understand them. Third, because CHAT is a system of ideas not without some gaps and imbalances, such reconstruction can serve the much-needed function of repairing some cracks in its foundation (addressed below) and, as a consequence, also mitigate some gaps in today's applications of this approach. Among these gaps, we will address the still-persisting dualism of social versus individual forms of activity and the related disregard of "traditional" psychological matters, such as mind, agency, and human subjectivity, that continue to be associated with mentalist and individualist premises.

In what follows, we first chart the foundational premises of the Vygotsky–Leontiev–Luria system of thought and then offer a brief exposition of how these premises were developed in Vygotsky's school; we next address some gaps that, in our view, need to be bridged for this system to serve as a viable foundation for social sciences that concern themselves with issues of social justice and transformation.

Foundational Worldview and Premises of CHAT

Transactional Worldview

In today's literature CHAT in general and Vygotsky's works in particular are often associated with two core premises—the centrality in human development of (a) sociocultural contexts and (b) cultural mediation. CHAT fully acknowledges the sociocultural and mediated origin and nature of human development and subjectivity (i.e., the broadly conceived psychological processes that include cognition, self-regulation, emotion, and the self). The grounding premises of CHAT, however, are much broader.

At its most fundamental level—and drawing on groundbreaking advances in natural sciences in the late nineteenth and early twentieth centuries—CHAT bases itself on the premise that living organisms exist only as part of a dynamic system that connects them with the environment (note the similarity with recently influential developmental systems theories in biology, e.g., Oyama 2000, and dynamic systems in psychology, e.g., Thelen and Smith 1998). It is the open-ended, ongoing, dynamical, and bi-directional relationship with the environment that constitutes, according to CHAT, the foundation of life and ultimately defines all characteristics of organisms, such as their structure, functioning, morphology, and development (including in evolution). In this view, no organism exists outside of or prior to a dynamical relationship with its environment and organisms can be neither studied nor understood in abstraction from this relationship.

Crucial to Vygotsky and his followers' adoption and further elaboration of the relational and dynamical worldview was their acquaintance with and enthusiastic reception of Darwin's ideas about animate nature as a process imbued with *collective, relational, and historicized dynamics*. This idea marked a dramatic departure away from the notions of life processes as immutable and predetermined (intractable and fixed) and of organisms as simple mechanisms that exist separately from each other and independent of the world and its history—two pillars of the mechanical worldview. Continuing this profound insight, CHAT views processes in the animate world as being in constant flux and subject to change, variation, chance, and development—thus entailing the position that neither do these processes have predestined constraints nor follow preprogrammed paths, algorithms, and ordered stages. This is a point that often goes unnoticed in many accounts of Darwinism in biology and especially in the sociobiological incarnations of (pseudo)-Darwinism, such as the recently popular brands of evolutionary psychology where the immutability, linearity, and determinacy of life processes serve as central theoretical postulates.

The emergence of this worldview has been a complex and lengthy development that included the merger of evolutionary thinking with the growing knowledge about the physiology of the nervous system and the brain (e.g., Helmholtz, Sherrington, Sechenov, and, later, Ukhtomskij, Pavlov, Bekhterev, and Bernstein). In this worldview, the complex dynamics of self-evolving activities of organisms in their real life environment, and the notion of organism-environment as a unified system, emerged in opposition to the view of the universe as composed of separate, discrete entities. Thus, the stage was set for the CHAT founders to attend to questions about the place and role of mind in the broader context of life (i.e., in regulating activities of organisms in their environment), rather than in the workings of physiological processes or narrowly defined behavior. The next task for these scholars was to conceptualize mind as being a part of this organism-environment nexus, rather than existing in organisms taken in isolation. Vygotsky's early works can be interpreted as focused on elaborating a dynamical notion of development consistent with the relational worldview (bearing much resemblance to Deweyan transactionalism).

In ways similar to those adopted by Dewey, Vygotsky expanded insights about the open-ended, fluid, and dynamical character of natural processes into the realm of psychology, essentially defining mind as representing part of nature. For both scholars, mind evolves from matter and can be seen as involved and immersed in life activities of organisms-in-environments. This dynamical process of interrelations with the environment calls for and gives rise to regulatory mechanisms that allow it to be carried out. This idea, formulated in its incipient form by Vygotsky, became central to Leontiev (e.g., 1981) and Galperin (e.g., 1976) in their works on the phylogenetic origins of the mind. Much of CHAT is devoted to exploring how more and more refined mechanisms of regulation, in the form of increasingly complex psychological processes, have emerged in phylogeny as a result both of increasingly complex exchanges between organisms and their environments and of evolutionary pressures to adapt to the ever more complex demands of life associated with growing levels of unpredictability and uncertainty.

Conceptualizing the mind as inherent in the activities of living organisms within their environment (under its constraints and challenges, as well as related to the organisms' own needs and goals) entailed a number of strong implications of a principled nature. Some of these have been well assimilated in recent expositions of Vygotsky's approach and CHAT, while others remain relatively unnoticed (at least in part because they were not explicitly and consistently spelled out by the CHAT founders; also, some works purportedly conducted in Vygotsky's school did in fact operate within the traditionally dichotomous worldview).

First and most significantly, CHAT offered a way to overcome the Cartesian gap between the subject (the living organism as agent) and the object (the world), between the knower and the known that characterized systems of thought developed from within the atomistic, entities-based worldview. Because the activity of relating to and engaging with the world was taken by CHAT scholars (with varying degrees of explicitness) to be the principal foundation of life, constitutive of all of its expressions, the emphasis shifted away from analyzing (a) any properties of individual organisms such as their inherent proclivities and characteristics and (b) any properties of the environment taken in isolation from organisms acting in them, toward analyzing the "third reality"—the *evolving dynamics of activity* that connects the two in a constantly unfolding, ever-shifting, give-and-take, dynamical interrelation.

Second, in a related conceptual move, this approach implied that the human mind and its development are fully and profoundly embedded (or situated) within the environment, yet are not directly and immediately determined by its effects. In other words, this approach implied a strong contextualist position in that it necessitated scrutiny of environmental demands, constraints, and affordances, yet did not reduce human development to a process driven by environmental influences per se, taken in abstraction from organisms uniquely situated in a given environment and engaged in an active interaction with it. According to CHAT, the mind is profoundly sociocultural and historical not simply because it is somehow "situated" (or embedded) in a sociocultural world, but because it is produced from within, out of, for the sake of, and as driven by the logic of evolving activity that connects individuals to the world, other people, and themselves.

Third, understanding mind as a relational act in the world meant that the mind did not need to be itself related, by some sort of a mechanism or a process, to the environment because it itself exists as a form of relation; it itself *is* a relation to the world (in contradistinction to the theme of relating psychological processes to cultural, institutional, and historical contexts as found in some recent interpretations of Vygotsky and his school).

Fourth (perhaps the most contentious and least understood premise of Vygotsky's school), given CHAT's emphasis on activity as the foundation and source of human development, this perspective offered a vision more subtle and, we would argue, more advanced than the currently popular version of bio-socio-cultural co-determinism. This latter approach represents a progressive step compared to the narrowly one-sided perspectives that pit biology against culture as two independent forces and then attempt to calculate their relative impact (e.g., by suggesting that variations in such processes as intelligence are due to both the genetic inheritance *and* environmental influences). However, even these progressive co-determinist approaches sometimes tacitly operate under the old notions of nature and culture, i.e., as the pool of genetic inheritance internal to organisms and the equally static pool of cultural artifacts external to them, respectively; as such, these approaches do not completely break away from two-factorial models that have been in circulation since the nineteenth century. In contrast, the original CHAT resolutely dismisses the traditional distinction between biology and culture, not simply by assuming that the two somehow interact or blend, but by fundamentally reconceptualizing their role in human development. In particular, CHAT puts at the core of development the processes of activity as a *reality sui generis* belonging to neither culture nor nature (if these are understood in reified ways as forces acting on organisms). Instead, activity is viewed as a unique level of reality—a unique "fabric" of life—beyond the distinction of culture versus nature by way of dialectically negating their direct influence on development. That is, activity is seen as forming a new level of self-regulated and self-determined processes (where the "self" relates to organism-in-activity and not to an agent taken separately from interactions with the world) unique to living beings. The mind therefore is not a mere ramification of either social or biological forces, or their combination, that act upon individuals; rather, the mind is inherent in the activities of an organism that, while making use of cultural and natural resources and also being constrained by these resources and conditions, nonetheless develops according to these activities' own regularities and dynamics.

Leontiev's (1981) example of a child born with a physical feature such as a hip anomaly illustrates this point. Although such a feature can dramatically influence development, its effects are neither direct nor predetermined. Rather, they only come about through particular constellations of activity carried out by the child herself. Thus, as a result of this physical feature a child might not be able to participate in everyday activities with peers and instead become prone to engage in alternative endeavors such as academic pursuits. The nature of these pursuits is greatly influenced by social forces, such as access to cultural resources and parental influences. However, the patterns of activities that the child engages in, although initially influenced by the presence of a certain physical feature and by diverse social forces, gradually evolve into a complex reality, with its own logic and internal dynamics, that ultimately shapes developmental outcomes.

The tacit but important distinction between accepting that both culture and nature influence development (as conceptualized in various two-factorial models), on the one hand, and the focus on the emergent dynamics of activity on the other (the point that the CHAT scholars constantly struggled to elucidate), continues to be in need of elaboration and integration with contemporary research. Today's debates between proponents of preformist views (e.g., behavior genetics) and advocates of the dynamic system approach (for a review, see Lickliter and Honeycutt 2003) constitute an arena where CHAT stands to make a useful contribution. In particular, CHAT's insistence on the centrality of organisms' activity in development—as the superordinate reality that absorbs the biological and environmental "givens" by transforming their effects on its own grounds—still represents an original idea that can greatly enrich epigenetic approaches (which for the most part ignore this level and, with it, the individual as such).

Finally, in CHAT the mind and other forms of psychological processes are understood to be realized as *bodily* processes, enacted in and through real-time activities of whole organisms, always anew—under ever-changing conditions and in view of dynamically unfolding goals of activity—rather than as separate mental and ultimately mysterious processes emanating from some ephemeral "internal depths" and not of much practical import in life. This premise reflects the CHAT commitment to a holistic, embodied, and dynamic concept of mind similar to that represented by recent works on embodied cognition (e.g., Clark 1997).

In the light of these principles, we think one can argue that CHAT has substantially predated many of today's cutting-edge approaches in psychology, such as distributed and situated cognition, constructivist epigenesis, embodied enactment, and dynamic systems theories. However, this meta-theoretical (worldview) foundation of CHAT, though highly original for its time and still progressive today, does not fully explain the truly revolutionary import of this approach.

Human Development as a Collaborative Process of Transforming the World

The truly original contribution of CHAT, we argue, begins where the transactionalist, situated cognition, constructivist, and dynamic systems theoretical approaches exhaust their explanatory potential. This originality resides in a unique conceptualization of the relation that links humans to their world and therefore lies at the foundation of human development. Whereas, for example, both Dewey and Piaget (and their contemporary followers) remained firmly within the Darwinian mode of thinking and treated human beings as not much different from other biological organisms—in keeping with the notion that "nature makes no drastic leaps"—Vygotsky and his followers postulated precisely such a leap and turned to exploring its implications. In doing so, these scholars primarily aligned themselves with the dialectical materialist view, according to which the "base for human thinking is precisely *man changing nature* and not nature alone as such, and the mind developed according to how man learned to change nature" (Engels, quoted in Vygotsky 1997:56; italics in the original). According to this view, the advent of humans has to do with a uniquely human relation to the world—goal-directed, collaborative activity aimed at changing and essentially creating their environment anew. This new relation to the world, precisely as a *new form of life*—the sociocultural, collaborative, transformative practice of people unfolding and expanding in history—brings about the emergence of human beings, through whose activities the "eternal laws" of nature are transformed into historical laws. This transition supercedes adaptation and natural selection and instead involves cultural-historical development in its unity of history, society, and culture. It is a change that signifies the end of biological evolution and entails a transition to human development, which now takes place in the realm where cultural-historical social forces reign. This extension by the CHAT scholars is truly dialectical because it posits that human development is both continuous with and radically different from processes in the rest of the animate world. Human history and life entail a radical break with nature, while at the same time continuing it. Exploration into implications of this view constitutes an important contribution of Vygotsky's project to today's sciences of mind, human development, and education.

While Dewey insisted that a state of imbalance in organic-environmental interactions and in the goals of adaptation explains the genesis of psychological processes, including those of humans, and Piaget adopted a very similar perspective, the CHAT scholars considered adaptation, disequilibrium, and other purely biological mechanisms to be of limited use in explanations of human development. Instead, the emphasis in their approach was placed on humans *transforming their world through collaborative, goal-directed activity*. Collaborative social practice (involving development and the passing on, from generation to generation, of collective experiences reified in tools, including language) represents a form of exchange with the world that is unique to humans—the social practice of labor, or human activity. In these social and historically specific processes, people not only constantly transform and create their environment; they also create and constantly transform their very life, changing and de facto *creating* themselves while, in the process, gaining self-knowledge and knowledge about the world. Therefore, human activity—material, practical, and always by necessity social collaborative processes aimed at transforming the world and people themselves—is taken in CHAT to be the basic form of human life, by which is created everything that is human in humans, including knowledge produced by them.

Because human labor inevitably entails the collective efforts of people, its development is prepared by and gives rise to increasingly complex social exchanges (in the form of social structures such as family and other social institutions) and to individual mechanisms (in the form of various psychological processes such as mind and the self). All of these forms, at both societal and individual levels, emerge precisely because they are needed to regulate the collective material production of human life. It was arguably the greatest insight of Marx that the social (inter-subjective) and the individual (intra-subjective) forms of human life became demystified as being derivative from (though not reducible to) the processes of material production. However, whereas Marx focused primarily on the dynamics of, contradictions within, and transformations between the material production of human existence, on the one hand, and the emerging collective forms of its regulation (i.e., human society), on the other, the Vygotskian project addressed two other forms of interdependency critical for human development.

Specifically, Vygotsky (e.g., 1987, 1997, 1999) focused on exploring the functioning of, and transformations between, the societal and the individual forms of life, relatively (and inevitably) neglected in Marxist philosophical and economic analyses. The idea that became pivotal for Vygotsky was that social exchanges between people were at the foundation of all intrasubjective processes, as the latter originate from the former in both the history of civilization and individual life (see the famous law of development, Vygotsky 1999). For Vygotsky, the transitions from inter-subjective to intra-subjective psychological processes by means of cultural mediation became the focus of analysis. In later stages in the development of CHAT, Leontiev (e.g., 1978) and other colleagues of Vygotsky focused relatively more on how the material forms of activity and practice are transformed into intra-psychological processes (in what became termed "activity theory" but which represents, in our view, the logical extension of Vygotsky's works—see Stetsenko 2005; Stetsenko and Arievitch 2004a).

Thus Vygotsky and his colleagues were arguably the first psychologists to expand the Marxist approach to further unravel the centuries-old mystery of human subjectivity—by revealing its origination from the processes of material production and social exchanges, instead of viewing it as an ephemeral phenomenon detached from these exchanges and evolving on its own mentalist grounds. In the Vygotskian project, the genuinely constructive and collaborative, practical and historically evolving processes of materially transforming the world were conceptualized as giving rise to the dialogical and dynamical realm of human interactions that, in tandem, engendered increasingly complex forms of human subjectivity. However, the question of how exactly, and through which mechanisms, material processes of collaborative production engender the human mind and other forms of subjectivity remained largely unanswered, although Vygotsky acknowledged the critical role of speech in this process, devoting his last works (e.g., 1987) primarily to this issue. In the next section, we discuss one crucial, and as yet underappreciated, aspect in the development of CHAT after Vygotsky's death—namely, the work of Piotr Galperin, who made a substantial contribution to precisely this intractable question.

From Practical Object-Related Activity to the Mind

Vygotsky made an important step in resolving one of the key problems of psychology—how to overcome the centuries-old dichotomies of "external versus internal" and "individual versus social." For him, the structure of human social interaction as mediated by cultural tools and symbols was the "material" that was appropriated from the social into the individual domain. Vygotsky's closest co-workers, especially Leontiev (e.g., 1978, 1981), expanded this insight and made a further contribution by capitalizing on the genetic and structural interrelation between external material (object-related, in their terminology) activity and mental processes. The ontological significance of this step by the founders of CHAT is difficult to overestimate. The impassible barrier between the external world and internal mental phenomena has been broken. The human mind has been conceived of as originating not from the functioning of the brain, and not as something entirely different from human productive activities, cultural practices, and social interactions, but as a direct product and ingredient (or dimension) of these external forms of human life.

However, there remained a great need to further clarify how the transformation of the initially external activity—be it in the form of social interaction or in the form of object-oriented practical activity—into its "internal" form takes place. Neither the communicative aspects of joint activity addressed by Vygotsky nor the powerful impact of material activity on the individual's mental performance explored by Leontiev provided a completely sufficient explanation for this highly significant question.

In this context, an important contribution was made by Piotr Galperin—a member of Vygotsky's project from the 1930s (when he joined the research group headed by Leontiev in Kharkov) through the 1980s. Galperin realized that without a detailed and consistent account of how mental actions emerge out of initially practical and collaborative, humanly meaningful activity, the whole cultural-historical project would be in constant danger of falling back into the familiar traps of either the old mentalist psychology or one of the many versions of reductionism, such as the physiological or the sociological ones (with many such precedents to be found in today's Vygotsky-inspired scholarship: see Stetsenko 2005; Stetsenko and Arievitch 2004a, b). Galperin devoted his entire career to analyzing the formation of mind—conceptualized as a unique capacity to perform object-related actions on the "internal plane"—within a profoundly sociocultural account of human development.

One needs to note Galperin's general focus, in line with the major premises of CHAT, on viewing the mind not as an isolated reality, but as processes that link organisms and their environments. In furthering this view, Galperin defined psychological processes as specific forms of activity that become necessary as a result of the complexity of environmental demands for which automatic forms of behavior do not suffice. In particular, he argued that the mind gradually arises in development (both phylogenetically and ontogenetically) out of material activity because it serves the need to thoroughly examine emerging, new situations and to anticipate the consequences of actions within these situations prior to their physical execution. To analyze and demystify the process of mental activity issuing from material action, Galperin (1992a, b; for details, see Arievitch and Haenen 2005) developed a stepwise (spiral) procedure framed as a teaching-learning experiment. This procedure entailed carrying out *one and the same* activity first at the material level and then, through its transformations in the symbolic medium of speech, in an abstract and generalized form based on *meanings* (understood as templates of action in which past actions are coordinated with the demands of present conditions and desired future goals)—that is, "in the mind." At the final stage of formation, this activity appeared as a "pure" thought, in which individuals operated with meanings per se, rather than with words.

It turns out that the *quality of the cultural tools* that students employ while learning new activities is critical for these transformations. In particular, advances in activity transformations were contingent on whether cultural tools gave students access to historically evolving meaningful practices (hidden "behind" cultural tools—that is, embodied and reified in them) so that students could engage in, reenact, and ultimately contribute to these practices through their own meaningful activities. That is, the learners' activities with cultural tools—embodying sociocultural activities of previous generations—represented the major pathway through which teaching, learning, and development took place. The centrality of cultural tools, therefore, served to bridge the gap between social and individual planes of development, as well as among the processes of teaching, learning, and development (Arievitch and Stetsenko 2000).

Thus, material external action was shown to be transformed into cognition in a sequence of rather comprehensible, not mysterious, events involving gradual metamorphoses of action from its external into "internal" (abstracted, generalized, symbolized, etc.) modes of existence. Importantly, the focus on the internal plane of action does not imply "mental representation" in its traditional connotation of static images that parade information in front of the subject; rather, acting on the internal plane retains all the characteristics of human real-life activity—it is an active process of solving problems that exist out in the world and of searching for "what is to be done next" given present conditions and future goals. That is, actions performed in abstraction from the physical situation—although termed "mental" in this interpretation—are not some mysterious mental faculties, nor are they a reflection of brain processes. They are object-related actions, as are all other human actions, with the only difference being that mental actions are carried out in the medium of meanings, that is, without a physical execution. Conceptualizing mental activity itself as object-related activity—something that human beings do in pursuing their worldly life-goals with the help of collaboratively created tools—implies that it occurs in the objective, outer world and, as such, is always profoundly situated and distributed. Perhaps most importantly, mental activity is carried out not according to any internal, mysterious "mental" laws of mind, but according to the laws and the "stubborn facts" of the world itself.

The significance of this account can be fully appreciated when it is viewed as a novel attempt to conceptualize mental processes in a *nonmentalist* way. It provides theoretical tools for understanding human development as essentially embedded in sociocultural contexts and intimately connected to collaborative activities, while at the same time leaving room for conceptualizing what traditionally has been described as individual cognition and mind. Although Galperin used many traditional notions and metaphors, such as "internal" action, internalization, and acting "in the mind," his account—firmly grounded in the overall framework of CHAT—was in fact aimed at overcoming the limitations of the traditional concept of mind. In particular, this approach debunked the myth of the mind as an individual internal container or a "mental theater" (for further details, including a critical appraisal, see Arievitch and van der Veer 1995; Vianna and Stetsenko 2006).

To summarize the discussion so far: CHAT can be seen as having much in common with those recent frameworks in the social sciences, including psychology and education, that strive to overcome profound dichotomies and dualisms—of social versus individual, internal versus external, process versus product—that stall progress in theorizing human development and learning. However, unlike many of today's approaches that focus on overcoming these dualisms as their final goal and tend to disregard (or even call into question) the reality of individual mind and knowledge, we do not think that such phenomena have to be eliminated as a price to pay for abandoning dualistic views (Martin 2004; Martin and Sugarman 2000). Instead, CHAT can be understood as suggesting a more dialectical and flexible approach. Namely, after resolutely relinquishing dualistic views, it suggests the next analytical step: to explore the uniquely psychological reality of mind within a profoundly unified view of human life as based in the materiality of people's continuous transformative engagements with their world.

The Relevance of the Sociopolitical Context

It is its inclusion of the wider sociocultural and political circumstances and contexts of knowledge creation that contributes to the uniqueness of CHAT as compared to other, equally transactional and relational but more narrowly and organically based, theories of the time. Both Dewey's and Piaget's approaches were imbued with an essentially biological vision and reflected an environment that knew nothing of "crisis and radical discontinuity," perfectly compatible with the end of nineteenth-century stability and the idea of a continuous societal growth based on the steady progress of science (e.g., Diggins 1994). Vygotsky's project, in stark contrast to these approaches, was imbued with a commitment to radical change, highly consistent with the wider project of social transformation launched by the sweeping revolutionary changes in Russia at the time CHAT was created.

Just as mind in the Vygotskian project can be described as an outcome, vehicle, and embodiment of ultimately practical collaborative engagements of humans with their world, so Vygotsky and his colleagues' own theory needs to be seen as by no means only a reflection and an outcome of their merely intellectual endeavors and commitments (for details, see Stetsenko and Arievitch 2004a). Their approach and the knowledge developed through it were part and parcel of the practical, and simultaneously deeply ideological, project that came out of the drama of their life, not of ideas, and returned to this life to transform it. In other words, CHAT can be seen as a product, and simultaneously a vehicle, of Vygotsky's and his colleagues' collaborative practical engagements with a unique sociohistorical context that presented them with an unprecedented challenge—and opportunity—to devise a new psychology in parallel with creating a new society. It was the goal of creating a psychology for a society that itself needed to be created on the foundation of social justice and equality (all the tragic failings of the larger political project behind CHAT that turned into a dysfunctional regime notwithstanding), and the interpenetration—and even blending—of these two goals and their respective orientations that turned CHAT into an instrument of social transformation and change.

The history of CHAT itself therefore illustrates its own central premise. It provides an example of how the mind and its products, including theories and knowledge, emerge out of unfolding collaborative practices—where individuals position themselves vis-à-vis these practices by committing to meaningful social goals—and then feed back into the world, thereby transforming it and establishing the platform for the next expansive cycles of unending human development. Indeed, Vygotsky's enthusiastic participation in social transformations brought about his theory, in which such processes were seen as constituting the centerpiece of development. In fact, all major concepts in Vygotsky's project reflect its unique orientation toward social transformation. Psychological processes as collaborative pursuits of meaningful, transformative tasks; teaching-and-learning as a social transformative practice that leads to development; the zone of proximal development as a social endeavor in which new horizons of development are collaboratively co-created; new revolutionary methods of understanding and treating disability through alternating social conditions of life; practice being the linchpin of theory—these all are examples of a direct, mirrored congruency between Vygotsky's project's own grounding in social transformative practice on the one hand, and his theory revolving around the notions of social change and transformation on the other. In carrying out their project, the CHAT founders produced knowledge of a radical sort that was instrumental in creating new alternatives for the conditions of social existence. In the process of so doing, they changed and liberated themselves.

However, subsequent sociopolitical developments that took place in the Soviet Union (toward a more and more stifling atmosphere and ensuing political repressions) also played a dramatic role in the fate of CHAT, turning the Vygotskian project into an arrested social movement (cf. Fuller 2000). These social developments quite possibly played a role in Vygotsky's untimely death; suffering from a growing clash between his romantic aspirations and the unfolding ominous reality, he essentially gave in to illness. Many of its progressive ideas gradually receded into the background, or never came to be fully realized in the project's subsequent developments. Most regrettably in our view, the notion of transformative, collaborative practice ceased to be regarded as playing the role of a pivotal, formative principle in human development (although continuing to be mentioned, it served the function of a "décor," rather than a working proposition; see Stetsenko 2005). Today's internationalized versions of CHAT also avoid the notion that people collaboratively transform their world. This notion causes aversion arising from several reasons, including the unwarranted beliefs that it (a) entails a strictly and narrowly economic interpretation of history and human development that is incomplete, unsatisfying, and antihumanist and (b) is associated with the perils of instrumental control over the environment that can only result in its destruction. This latter belief is especially pronounced today when destruction of the environment and the overall ecological crisis have reached epic proportions. It is this notion of collaborative transformation, however, that lies at the core of CHAT's unique views on human development, including anthropogenesis.

The task for today's scholarship in CHAT, we believe, is to restore the centrality of collaborative transformation while unhinging this notion from a narrowly economic interpretation and a pernicious instrumentalism. Instead of this narrow interpretation, collaborative transformation should be integrated with the *ethical dimension* of responsibility and positioning (still largely overlooked in Vygotsky's scholarship) as inherent in human development, understood as an activist project (Stetsenko 2007, 2008). Capitalizing on this dimension should help to bridge the gap between CHAT and critical scholarship (e.g., building on Freire 1970), and to mutually strengthen and perhaps even integrate these approaches. This integration becomes viable in the light of a synergistic emphasis on the pervasive practical relevance of the mind (and other forms of human subjectivity) as always entailing practical ramifications in real life, on the one hand, and on the material processes of practical activity as always imbued with ideology, ethics, and other human dimensions, on the other. In this view, human subjectivity appears as individual and social *at the same time*, because each individual is regarded as part of a larger matrix of society, coming to exist only through engaging in pursuits to collaboratively transform the world, and struggling to contribute to this profoundly social process. This latter struggle is simultaneously a struggle for one's own identity and self, that is, for one's own place in the world of historically unfolding collaborative practices.

It is the notion of individual *contribution to sociocultural practices* as the essence of humanness and self (see Stetsenko and Arievitch 2004b; Vianna and Stetsenko 2006) that is particularly important if CHAT is to be developed into an integral account of human development. We suggest that this notion directly points to a crucially important intersection and essential unity of individual and social planes, and entails viewing individuals as ineluctably social in all of their activities. We believe that advancing this notion and exploring its implications are sorely needed as steps forward to overcome some recent incarnations of individualism—i.e., conceptions that exclude the individual dimensions from relational theories of development and reduce them to collective dynamics, thus firmly (and ironically) remaining in the grip of a vision of individuals as isolated and separate entities. This notion also has a number of advantages compared to the notion of participation currently popular in sociocultural studies (e.g., Lave and Wenger 1991; Rogoff 1990) due to the more agentive character of social contribution—namely, as entailing commitment, ethics, directionality, and determination.

Having established the principal sources of human development and mind in collective material transformations of the world, CHAT resolutely broke with the ontological eclecticism typical of so many previous (and contemporary) accounts. Instead, it predicated itself on a clear commitment to a materialist ontology (not to be confused with the narrow physicalism of today's neuroscience) of human subjectivity—an approach in which subjectivity is understood as issuing from and implicated in material, collaborative practices. At the same time, CHAT also entailed (though less explicitly) a humanist ontology of materialism—the view that human subjectivity constitutes an indispensable element (or dimension) of collaborative practices. This approach, especially if it is expanded to include the notion of contribution to social practice as the essence of humanness (as suggested herein), establishes the dialectical unity of social and individual dimensions as being rooted in, derived from, and instrumental in the production of collective social life and human development. Within this perspective, traditionally mentalist constructs such as the mind and self appear in their practical relevance—as processes that allow people to participate in and contribute to the social collaborative production of their lives. This conceptualization opens ways to develop a consistent and coherent account of human development simultaneously based in scientific and critical-humanist traditions, overcoming their unduly strict dichotomy without falling into the traps of either narrowly positivist views (inherently tied up with the static, mechanistic, and ahistorical worldview), on the one hand, or the postmodernist and inevitably relativist versions of constructivism and social constructionism (in their extreme forms), on the other. Arguably, such a framework could be used to integrate what now appear as many fragmented and disconnected sociocultural perspectives on human development, merging their important insights and inviting a dialogue among them to ultimately enhance their contribution to the world we all live in.

On a final note, we want to emphasize again that Vygotsky's project should not be regarded as providing eternal solutions for the dilemmas of its time, let alone of today. CHAT, to our mind, is indeed a project of great relevance for today's problems and dilemmas, though not because of some static "truths" that can be mechanically transposed into today's debates. Rather, it is the continuing relevance of social goals that Vygotsky and his followers espoused, struggled for, and contributed to (though never fully realized)—the goals of creating a society based on ideals of social justice and equality—that can explain the continuing appeal of CHAT. Because these goals are as urgent today as they were at the beginning of the twentieth century, having never been fully brought to life—either in psychology or in society at large, there is much to be discovered by going back to CHAT's roots. It is in the light of the continuing (and even rising) turmoil and strife in the world today, especially on the global scale, where social inequalities are mounting, that we stand to learn from the CHAT founders and their efforts—efforts which, although incomplete and fragmented, were portents of what appear to be the world's perennial dilemmas and perhaps their future solutions.

References

Arievitch, I. M., and J. P. P. Haenen. 2005. Connecting sociocultural theory and educational practice: Galperin's approach. *Educational Psychologist* 40:155–165.

Arievitch, I. M., and A. Stetsenko. 2000. The quality of cultural tools and cognitive development: Gal'perin's perspective and its implications. *Human Development* 43:69–92.

Arievitch, I., and R. van der Veer. 1995. Furthering the internalization debate: Gal'perin's contribution. *Human Development* 38:113–126.

Clark, A. 1997. *Being There: Putting Brain, Body, and World Together Again.* Cambridge, MA: MIT Press.

Cole, M. 1996. *Cultural Psychology: A Once and Future Discipline.* Cambridge, MA: Harvard University Press.

Cole, M., and Y. Engeström. 1993. A cultural-historical approach to distributed cognition. In G. Salomon, *Distributed Cognitions: Psychological and Educational Considerations*, 1–46. New York: Cambridge University Press.

Collins, C. 1999. *Language, Ideology, and Social Consciousness: Developing a Socio-historical Approach*. Aldershot: Ashgate.

Diggins, J. P. 1994. *The Promise of Pragmatism: Modernism and the Crisis of Knowledge and Authority*. Chicago: University of Chicago Press.

Engeström, Y. 1990. *Learning, Working, and Imagining: Twelve Studies in Activity Theory*. Helsinki: Orienta-Konsultit.

Engeström, Y., R. Miettinen, and R.-L. Punamaeki, eds. 1999. *Perspectives on Activity Theory*. New York: Cambridge University Press.

Freire, P. 1970. *Pedagogy of the Oppressed*. New York: Continuum.

Fuller, S. 2000. *Thomas Kuhn: A Philosophical History of Our Times*. Chicago: University of Chicago Press.

Galperin, P. Ia. 1976. *Introduction Into Psychology* [*Vvedenie v psihologiju*]. Moscow: Moscow University.

———. 1992a [1978]. Stage-by-stage formation as a method of psychological investigation. *Journal of Russian and East European Psychology* 30:60–80.

———. 1992b [1977]. The problem of activity in Soviet psychology. *Journal of Russian and East European Psychology* 30:37–59.

Hedegaard, M. 2001. *Learning in Classrooms: A Cultural-Historical Approach*. Aarhus: Aarhus University Press.

John-Steiner, V., C. P. Panofsky, and L. W. Smith, eds. 1994. *Sociocultural Approaches to Language and Literacy: An Interactionist Perspective*. New York: Cambridge University Press.

Karpov, Y. V. 2006. *The Neo-Vygotskian Approach to Child Development*. New York: Cambridge University Press.

Lantolf, J., and S. Thorne. 2006. *Sociocultural Approach to Second Language Learning*. New York: Cambridge University Press.

Lave, J., and E. Wenger. 1991. *Situated Learning: Legitimate Peripheral Participation*. New York: Cambridge University Press.

Leontiev, A. N. 1978. *Activity, Consciousness, and Personality*. Englewood Cliffs, NJ: Prentice Hall.

———. 1981 [1959]. *Problems of the Development of the Mind*. Moscow: Progress.

Lickliter, R., and H. Honeycutt. 2003. Developmental dynamics: Toward a biologically plausible evolutionary psychology. *Psychological Bulletin* 129:819–835.

Luria, A. R. 1976. *Cognitive Development: Its Cultural and Social Foundations*. Cambridge, MA: Harvard University Press.

Martin, J. 2004. Self-regulated learning, social cognitive theory, and agency. *Educational Psychologist* 39:135–145.

Martin, J., and J. Sugarman. 2000. Between the modern and the postmodern: The possibility of self and progressive understanding in psychology. *American Psychologist* 55:397–406.

Moll, L. C., ed. 1992. *Vygotsky and Education: Instructional Implications and Applications of Sociohistorical Psychology*. New York: Cambridge University Press.

Oyama, S. 2000. *Evolution's Eye: A Systems View of the Biology-Culture Divide*. Durham, NC: Duke University Press.

Robbins, D., and A. Stetsenko, eds. 2002. *Vygotsky's Psychology: Voices from the Past and Present*. New York: Nova Science.

Rogoff, B. 1990. *Apprenticeship in Thinking: Cognitive Development in Social Context*. New York: Oxford University Press.

——. 2003. *The Cultural Nature of Human Development*. New York: Oxford University Press.

Sawchuk, P., N. Duarte, and M. Elhammoumi. 2006. *Critical Perspectives on Activity Theory*. New York: Cambridge University Press.

Stetsenko, A. 2005. Activity as object-related: Resolving the dichotomy of individual and collective planes of activity. *Mind, Culture, and Activity* 12:70–88.

——. 2007. Being-through-doing: Bakhtin and Vygotsky in dialogue. *Cultural Studies of Science Education* 2:25–37.

——. 2008. From relational ontology to transformative activist stance: Expanding Vygotsky's CHAT project. *Cultural Studies of Science Education*.

Stetsenko, A., and I. M. Arievitch. 2004a. Vygotskian collaborative project of social transformation: History, politics, and practice in knowledge construction. *International Journal of Critical Psychology* 12:58–80.

——. 2004b. The self in cultural-historical activity theory: Reclaiming the unity of social and individual dimensions of human development. *Theory & Psychology* 14:475–503.

Thelen, E., and L. B. Smith. 1998. Dynamic systems theories; from W. Damon and R. Lerner, eds., *Handbook of Child Psychology*, 5th ed. In *Theoretical Models of Human Development*, 1:563–634. New York: Wiley.

Vianna, E., and A. Stetsenko. 2006. Embracing history through transforming it: Contrasting Piagetian versus Vygotskian activity theories of learning and development to expand constructivism within a dialectical view of history. *Theory & Psychology* 16:81–108.

Vygotsky, L. S. 1987. Thinking and speech. In R. W. Rieber and A. Carton, eds., *The Collected Works of L. S. Vygotsky* 1:39–288. New York: Plenum.

——. 1997. *The History of the Development of Higher Mental Functions*. In R. W. Rieber, ed., *The Collected Works of L. S. Vygotsky* 4. New York: Plenum.

——. 1999. Tool and sign in the development of the child. In R. W. Rieber, ed., *The Collected Works of L. S. Vygotsky* 6:3–68. New York: Kluwer/Plenum.

Wells, G. 1999. *Dialogic Inquiry: Towards a Sociocultural Practice and Theory of Education*. New York: Cambridge University Press.

Wertsch, J. V. 1988. *Vygotsky and the Social Formation of Mind*. Cambridge, MA: Harvard University Press.

11　Vygotsky and Context

Toward a Resolution of Theoretical Disputes

MICHAEL COLE AND NATALIA GAJDAMASCHKO

The publication of English versions of a large portion of Lev Vygotsky's writings, supplemented by a number of excellent scholarly examinations of both his ideas and their relationship to antecedent and contemporaneous thinkers, has enormously expanded the horizons of our knowledge about the work of Vygotsky and his immediate colleagues (Vygotsky 1987, 1997, 1998; van der Veer and Valsiner 1991; Wertsch 1985). Simultaneously, there has been a rather broad recognition of the pitfalls of the intercultural appropriation of Vygotsky's ideas. The resulting difficulties require a critical approach to all claims of authenticity about adherence to presumed originals or fidelity in application of these ideas in contemporary scholarship on learning and development (Cole and Gajdamaschko 2007; Karpov 2005; Kozulin, Gindis et al. 2003).

This chapter is intended to contribute to this ongoing process of critical reappraisal. We focus on a comparison of Vygotsky's use of the concept of "context," along with similar terms, such as "environment" and "situation," with the interpretations of such terms by Americans who believe they are following the teaching of Vygotsky and his students. Our goal is to enable a better understanding of competing interpretations of performance differences between children of different ages from the same culture, people of the same age from different cultures, and the developmental consequences associated with school attendance in societies that lack universal formal schooling (so that some children attend school while others do not). We believe that disagreements between Russian and American psychologists with respect to these issues go beyond the area of cross-age and cross-cultural research to touch upon general questions of the role of culture and context in the development of human mental functioning. Seeking ways to resolve differences with respect to these issues is an important task of contemporary followers of Vygotsky's tradition.

Context: Variations in Meaning

Contemporary ideas about context vary enormously across national traditions, disciplines, and individual users. For example, the definition of "context" in the 1958 *Dictionary of the Russian Language* is: "the boundaries of a fragment of written language that makes it possible to establish the meaning of a word or a phrase within those boundaries" (Barkhudarov et al. 1958). By Anglo-American standards, "context" extends well beyond written text. For example, the Oxford English Dictionary defines context as "the connected whole that gives coherence to its parts," a definition that applies across a wide range of culturally mediated phenomena. Clearly, we need to be cautious at the outset in comparing American and Russian ideas with respect to the key concept of our concern here.

American Uses of "Context"

Among American psychologists, "context" is ordinarily used in three general ways. First, it appears as a rough equivalent of the term "environment," referring to a set of circumstances, at different levels of scale, within which children interact with the artifacts and people that are said to influence the child in various ways. Thus, it is common to encounter articles that speak of the influence of family or classroom contexts as the proximal environment of children's behavior or the "social-interactional context" (Winegar and Valsiner 1992).

Wertsch employs a closely related concept of context when he argues that any social interaction has to be considered in "the broad sociocultural context in which it occurs [because] any episode of human action must occur in a specific cultural, historical, and institutional context, and this influences how the [interpersonal] action is carried out" (200:18). This approach, which conceives of children "in" a context, naturally invokes the image, made famous by Bronfenbrenner (1979), of context as a nested set of socio-ecological arrangements. Various interpersonal relationships occur in proximal "contexts" (family, home, church, etc.) embedded in successively more inclusive "sociocultural contexts." Wertsch suggests that linkages between the levels of context thus interpreted can best be understood in terms of the cultural tools (language, counting systems, writing, maps, etc.) that are provided within the sociocultural context and used by individuals in the interpersonal context. Reciprocally, mastery of the use of cultural tools in the proximal contexts allows children to generalize what they have learned from one social-interactional context to another context, a process that is central to overcoming the apparently "context-bound" nature of young children's thought processes.

Finally, although less commonly, psychologists use the term "context" in a manner consistent with the dictionary definition given above, as a "whole in relation to its parts." This relational notion of context harkens back to the Latin origins of the term, *contexere,* meaning "to weave together," as when the warp and woof of different colored threads on a loom are woven together to create a meaningful pattern. From this perspective, we find one point of agreement: the "text" and what accompanies the text (the "con"-text) are inextricably co-constitutive (Cole 1996; McDermott 1983) (note that in this respect the American and Russian notions of context are quite similar). The difficulty of moving from this theoretical agreement, and (as we shall see) its elision in practical uses of the term, bespeaks an incompletely understood conceptual problem.

Vygotsky's Use of "Context" and Associated Terms

The topic for which Vygotsky most explicitly evokes the use of the "context" is his discussion of the relationship between sense and meaning (Vygotsky 1987). However, unlike the compilers of the Russian dictionary, he goes beyond written language to consider spoken language:

Meaning is only one of these zones of the sense that the word acquires in the context of speech. In different contexts, a word's sense changes. In contrast, meaning is a comparatively fixed and stable point, one that remains constant with all the changes of the word's sense that are associated with its use in various contexts.

Moreover,

> The actual meaning of the word is inconstant. In one operation, the word emerges with one meaning; in another, another is required. . . . Isolated in the lexicon, the word has only one meaning. However, this meaning is nothing more than a potential that can be realized in living speech, and in living speech meaning is only a cornerstone in the edifice of sense. (1987:276)

The example Vygotsky uses to illustrate the way in which linguistic context conditions the relation of sense to meaning involves a fable by Krylov (an example from written language).

> The word "dance" with which the fable ends has a definite and constant meaning. This meaning is identical in all contexts. In the context of this fable, however, it acquires a much broader intellectual and affective sense. It simultaneously means "be merry" and "die." This enrichment of the word through the sense it acquires in context is a basic law of the dynamics of meaning. The word absorbs intellectual and affective content from the entire context in which it is intertwined. (1987:276)

When he moves beyond the domain of language, Vygotsky appears to prefer to use other terms, such as "situation" or "environment," rather than "context" as a reference term. For example, an important concept in Vygotsky's thinking about development is the "social situation of development." By this Vygotsky meant "the relations between the personality of the child and his social environment at each age level" (1998:198). According to Vygotsky,

> at the beginning of each age period, there develops a completely original, exclusive, single, and unique relation, specific to the given age, between the child and reality, mainly the social reality that surrounds him. The social situation of development represents the initial moment for all dynamic changes that occur in development during

the given period. It determines wholly and completely the forms and the path along which the social becomes individual.   (1998:198)

Two features of this statement are important. First, Vygotsky is here using "situation" more or less in the sense of "life situation as a whole," not referring to any particular situation (setting/context) that the child might be inhabiting at a particular moment (we will return to examine the consequences of this choice below). We focus now on the second, perhaps related, feature, one that invites a misunderstanding we consider quite widespread—the possibility that Vygotsky assumes that the social-interactional context acts as an external influence on development. Contrary to such an interpretation, Vygotsky wrote with respect to the social situation of development that

> one of the major impediments to the theoretical and practical study of child development is the incorrect solution of the problem of the environment and its role in the dynamics of age when the environment is considered as something outside with respect to the child, as a circumstances of development, as an aggregate of objective conditions existing without reference to the children and affecting him by the very fact of their existence.   (1998:198)

Instead, for Vygotsky, the "social situation of development" is a relational construct in which characteristics of children combine with (are interwoven together with) the structure of social interactions in their proximal environment. The resulting hybrid process is the starting point for a new cycle of developmental changes that will result in a new, and higher, level of development (and a new, relevant, social situation of development).

This relational orientation is highlighted by two well-known Vygotskian principles. First, moving in the direction from adult to child, there is what Vygotsky termed "the general law of cultural development":

> Any function in children's cultural development appears twice, or on two planes. First it appears on the social plane and then on the psychological plane. First it appears between people as an inter-psychological category and then within the individual child as an intrapsychological category . . . but it goes without saying that internalization transforms the process itself and changes its structure

and function. Social relations or relations among people genetically
underlie all higher functions and their relationships.   (1981:163)

Although invocation of the idea that interpersonal functions precede
intrapersonal functions is sometimes taken as evidence that Vygotsky was
a kind of "social learning" theorist who believed that the social environment "causes" development, we believe this interpretation to be a serious misreading. Throughout his writings, Vygotsky insisted that children
do not simply receive cultural tools passively but actively appropriate
them to their own uses, declaring repeatedly that "in the beginning was
the deed."

This belief in the child's active, dynamic participation in creation of the
social situation of development was embodied in the crucial experimental method he constructed as a model of the specifically human "cultural
method of behavior" (Vygotsky 1929), the "method of dual stimulation"
in which children are confronted with tasks that are beyond their present
capabilities. He characterized the essence of this method as follows:

> In such cases a neutral object is placed near the child, and frequently
> we are able to observe how the neutral stimulus is drawn into the
> situation and takes on the function of a sign. Thus, *the child actively
> incorporates these neutral objects into the task of problem solving.* We
> might say that when difficulties arise, neutral stimuli take on the
> function of a sign and from that point on the operation's structure
> assumes an essentially different character.   (1978:74–75)

The active appropriation of stimuli not necessarily or obviously involved
in the problem-solving situation was, in Vygotsky's view, the characteristic that most clearly distinguished human and nonhuman animals. The
development of this "indirect, instrumental, mediated" form of behavior
was the subject matter of many experiments (see Vygotsky 1978, 1997).

For example, he and his colleagues replicated Köhler's famous experiments with apes in studies of young children who wanted to obtain cook-
ies from a jar high on a cupboard. Frustrated by their failures, they engage
in what Vygotsky refers to as "an imbroglio of actions" that at first appear
bewildering to the experimenter. But, Vygotsky writes,

> The child, after having completed a number of intelligent and inter-
> related actions which should help him successfully solve the given

problem, suddenly, upon meeting a difficulty in realization of his plan, cuts short all attempts and turns for help to the experimentalist, asking him to move the object nearer and thus give him the possibility to accomplish his task. . . . [Thus] the child, first separating verbal description of the action from the action itself, crosses the border of co-operation, socializing his practical thinking by sharing his action with another person. . . . The control of another person's behavior becomes, in the given instance, a necessary part of the child's entire practical activity.   (Vygotsky and Luria 1930:117)

This same general pattern of behavior was traced in many experiments involving a variety of psychological functions, including memory and attention. In these latter cases, children were given various possible "neutral" stimuli that might, but did not have to, be used to accomplish the task at hand. With respect to remembering, for example, children were asked to remember a series of words and were given pictures that might be used to remind them of the words. Young children ignored the pictures or failed to use them effectively even if the pictures were pictures of the word's referent (cup, pencil). Somewhat older children could use such transparently related stimuli to help them remember, but they could not use pictures that required them to think of an indirect relationship to the to-be-remembered words (a picture of a pencil as a possible reminder of the word to be remembered—notebook). Still older children could effectively use even the obscure auxiliary stimuli to help them remember, a form of behavior that Vygotsky likened to tying a string around one's finger in order to remember something; the string in this case is clearly an arbitrary, neutral stimulus with respect to the to-be-remembered action.

Of course, in everyday interactions between children and their social worlds, the objects (cultural tools) that are introduced by others are not neutral; rather, they are selected for what people take to be their appropriateness to the circumstances. But the essential point is that children, no less than their social interlocutors, are actively appropriating cultural tools and each other's behavior into their own actions to the best of their abilities, creating what has come to be termed a "co-constructional" account of the cultural mediation of development (Wozniak 1992). This double-sided dialogic process clearly highlights the fact that at least in terms of face-to-face interactions, contexts/situations/environments were, for Vygotsky, the emergent outcome of the weaving together of separate "threads of history."

Finally, there are many places in his writing where Vygotsky invokes what Wertsch refers to as "the broad sociocultural context," which, characteristically, he conceived of in cultural-historical terms. So, for example, in *Studies in the History of Behavior* (1993 [1930]), Vygotsky and Luria trace a general line of historical development beginning with "primitive man" (which they take to be an abstraction that provides a hypothetical starting point for historical development). They saw the advent of writing as a particularly important cultural advance because it made the fixation of past experiences more reliable and, as a consequence, accelerated the development of culture. Cross-cultural research within this framework seemed to provide a promising way to recover the psychological state of primitive man and thereby to be able to trace the process of psychological/cultural evolution, improving on the past to create ever-more-developed modes of life.

In another publication written about the same time, Vygotsky reasserts the basic Marxist position that human consciousness depends upon human beings' ways of life in their society and underscores what he then believed to be a fundamental change in human personality that accompanies the transition from a capitalist to a socialist way of life (Vygotsky 1934).

Differences in Conceptions of Context Reviewed

In surveying the growing interest in the cultural-historical approach of Vygotsky and his followers some two decades ago, one of the present authors noted that what appeared to be taking place at the time was a fusion of the Russian emphasis on diachronic (historical) variation with an American emphasis on synchronic, "contextual" heterogeneity. In principle, he argued, the cultural-historical approach, with its emphasis on the social environment and the centrality of tool mediation to human psychological development, required that cultural-historical psychologists pay close attention to synchronic variation:

A focus on tool-mediated action as a central mechanism of development implied some degree of context-specificity. In their quite correct insistence on the mediated nature of the mind and the instrumental aspect of mediation, embodied in the notion of psychological tools, the founders of the sociohistorical school neglected the cardinal fact that there is no universal, context-free tool. Rather, all tools embody simultaneously a theory of the activity they have been designed to fulfill and a theory of the human beings who must carry out the activity. Tools vary from highly specialized to relatively general with respect to the tasks they can fulfill. . . . But the dream of a context-free tool . . . completely misinterprets the relationship between human beings and the world, denying the mediated, and always incomplete, nature of human knowledge.   (Cole 1988:148)

We have little doubt that Vygotsky and his colleagues would have agreed with this general point. But in our reading of their work, synchronic variability of behavior "across contexts/situations/activities" was muted in comparison to their emphasis on diachronic, developmental change.

As noted earlier, from an American perspective, what is striking about Vygotsky's characterization of the social situation of development, in addition to its rejection of the environment as an external influence on children in favor of an "interweaving," co-constitutive interpretation, is that he writes as if there existed only one social situation of development for a given child at a given age period. This seeming uniformity is highlighted, for example, when he claims that the social situation of development is an "exclusive, single, and unique relation, specific to the given age, between the child and reality" (1998:198). In contrast, Americans who invoke context emphasize the heterogeneity of the many "social-interactional contexts" (social situations of development?) that children inhabit and the heterogeneity of levels of development that accompany their varied modes of participation. In short, Vygotsky is not using the concept "situation/ context" in a manner similar to its usage in Anglo-American psychology.

This divergence of views also appears in his treatment of the "larger sociocultural context," leading James Wertsch (1991) to comment that for the Russian cultural-historical psychologists, cross-cultural work was essentially cross-historical. We will return to address these issues after reviewing two lines of research where different ideas about context/situation and development lead to competing interpretations of what appear to be the same psychological phenomena.

Interpreting Cross-Cultural Variation: Developmental Advances and Contextual Variation

One illustration of the kinds of disagreements that can arise from Russian and American psychologists' differing conceptions of context concerns cross-cultural research in which both cultural-historical and ontogenetic variations play a prominent role. A famous case in point concerns the research conducted by Alexander Luria and his colleagues on the modes of thinking of people living in rural Uzbekistan and Kirghizia in the early 1930s when those areas had recently been incorporated into the then–Soviet Union (Luria 1976). Many of these people were illiterate and had never attended school. Some had a few years of schooling and had worked for a time on the newly collectivized farms that had been imposed upon the rural population of the USSR a few years earlier. After presenting Luria's research and conclusions, we will examine research conducted by Michael Cole and his colleagues in Liberia, West Africa, in the late 1960s at a time when roads were being built into the interior of the country and schools were introduced in some of the towns along those roads (Cole, Gay et al. 1971).

Luria's Research in Central Asia

When Luria undertook his research in Central Asia, he assumed that the cultural-historical change from pastoral herding to involvement in industrialized farming, combined with the acquisition of literacy in school, would cause a general change in modes of thought. He phrased his understanding of this change in the following terms:

> Conceptual thinking involves an enormous expansion of the resultant forms of cognitive activity. A person capable of abstract thought reflects the external world more profoundly and completely and makes conclusions and inferences from perceived phenomena on the basis not only of his personal experience but also of schemes of logical thinking that objectively take shape in a fairly advanced stage of development of cognition activity.
>
> The appearance of verbal, logical codes enabling one to abstract the essential features of objects and thus assign these objects to general categories leads to the formation of a more complex logical apparatus. This apparatus permits conclusions to be drawn from given premises without having to resort to immediate graphic-functional experience, and makes it possible to acquire new knowledge in a discursive and verbal-logical fashion. This is what provided the transition from sensory to rational consciousness, a

phenomenon that the classics of Marxism regard as one of the most important in history.   (Luria 1976:100–101)

Luria assessed the evidence for this kind of transition in a wide variety of psychological domains: responses to perceptual illusions; classification of objects by color and shape; categorization of verbally presented sets of objects (hammer–saw–log–hatchet); judgments of similarity of verbally presented objects (chicken/dog, water/blood); deduction and inference (using syllogisms); and solution of verbally presented problems ("It takes twenty hours to go on foot to Dzhizak, or five times faster on a bicycle. How long will it take on a bicycle?").

His conclusion for each of these domains was the same: there is a major historical shift in the form of consciousness from a situation-bound, practical form of cognition in which language is not used in an abstract, theoretical way to a form of consciousness in which language operates more abstractly to isolate crucial features of stimuli presented—be they pictures of objects in the color-and-form studies or verbal stimuli in many of the other studies—thereby, in his terms, leading to a "more advanced kind of cognitive activity."

Not only Luria but also his student Peeter Tulviste (1991) and, most recently, Yuri Karpov (2005) interpreted these results as support for the proposition that the new form of activity associated with participation in socialist modes of production, literacy, and formal schooling combined with the more advanced forms of social life of which they are a part give rise to an historically new form of thought, one which Luria referred to as "theoretical" or "verbal logical" and Karpov refers to as "formal-logical." This mode of thought is assumed to replace the prior, situation-bound, practical, functional-graphic mode of thought. It is assumed to be pervasive in industrialized societies and is considered to be developmentally more advanced, historically and ontogenetically, than the mode that precedes it (see, however, Tulviste's somewhat different interpretation at the end of this chapter).

Analogous American Cross-Cultural Research

Cole and his colleagues also studied the ways that nonliterate and schooled people responded to a variety of tasks; some of these task categories overlapped closely with those used by Luria (the syllogism problems), and some involved memory, verbal concept formation, and inferential reasoning and used procedures that deviated from Luria's. Like Luria, the researchers often found that involvement in schooling (they worked with children and adults who had experienced different amounts of schooling) was associated with a marked shift in performance in modes of classification, reasoning, and remembering. But characteristic of their approach was their skepticism about inferring that when a nonliterate person failed to respond to a particular task in the way that their schooled counterparts did, such failure represented a general absence of "abstract thinking" or dependence on "graphical-functional" categorization. Trained in the American experimental psychological tradition, Cole and his colleagues were keenly sensitive to the strong possibility that when local people were presented with tasks in which the contents of the problem were unfamiliar to them—or the researchers were unaware of the conventions of the social interactions comprising the experimental situation, or did not have a sufficiently detailed knowledge of the local language—such factors might negatively influence the subjects' performance and hence lower psychologists' estimates of their psychological capabilities.

Consequently, they began their work by investigating the kinds of activities that Kpelle rice farmers carry out on a daily basis, the ways in which they categorize the objects in their local environment or the varying uses of language in such settings as a court case or storytelling. They also spent time in local schools and interviewed children and youth who had several years of experience of formal schooling. They referred to this enterprise as "ethnographic psychology."

From their investigation of the local language using a variety of anthropological elicitation methods, they found that while people certainly shared a more or less hierarchically organized category of things in the world, the specific categories as well as the extent to which items in those categories were categorized differed somewhat from one elicitation technique to another. They then chose a set of items that everyone appeared to agree upon regardless of elicitation method and for which everyone knew the superordinate concepts (tools, cooking utensils, food, clothing) in order to investigate the conditions under which these categories would be used to structure different kinds of cognitive processes such as those involved in free association, classificatory sorting of the objects, concept learning, and free recall memory. Results appeared to differ according to the specific task used. A few examples will suffice:

- Verbal free associations to items in each of the four categories were predominantly made to other items from the appropriate category, regardless of educational level. But classificatory sorting of objects was relatively weak regardless of educational level.
- In concept identification studies in which members of word pairs were either linked with the same category or linked at random, the uneducated Kpelle subjects learned very quickly while educated American subjects learned very slowly. Why? The reason was that the Americans paid so much attention to the category membership of the materials that they were distracted from noticing the actual pairings, while the uneducated Kpelle subjects simply learned which items were paired together in these particular circumstances and learned quickly.
- When two items from a category were placed on the table and a person was asked to choose an item that went with them from one of three categories (tools, utensils, food), the results depended upon the category involved. When a pair of tools was presented, another tool was always chosen by educated and noneducated groups to go with the tools; when a pair of foods was presented, only high school students, but not second–fifth graders or nonliterates of any age always picked another food to include in the category. When two utensils were presented, the two educated groups always chose another utensil to complete the category, but the two uneducated groups, children and adults, chose foods almost as often as other utensils.

Similar variability according to procedures was found in studies of free recall memory in which the four familiar categories discovered in psycholinguistic analysis were used and contrasted with a set of equally familiar items that formed no known category. Sometimes the words were repeatedly presented for recall in random order. Sometimes the actual objects were displayed. Sometimes the items to be recalled were linked to a physical object, such as a distinctive chair upon which examples of a given category were placed. Sometimes the items were embedded in folk stories in various ways.

For the most part, these studies indicated that schooled subjects were far more likely to use common categorical membership of to-be-remembered materials when seeking to remember the lists, and they soon were able to commit the entire list to memory. In contrast, for many of the procedures, the noneducated subjects appeared to have little idea of how to go about remembering such lists in a systematic way that would lead to mastery. However, this difference disappeared when the items to be remembered were embedded in folk stories. When use of the categorical structure of the list made sense in terms of the stories, this information was used by nonliterate subjects.

When it came to logical syllogisms, the results of Cole and his colleagues replicated those obtained by Luria to an astonishing degree. Noneducated people reasoned in terms of their everyday experiences as if the syllogism was actually an inquiry into empirically encountered phenomena. They even included some fanciful syllogisms about characters used in local stories named spider and black deer, but the fictitiousness of this content produced no change in the tendency of people to reason in terms of everyday experience.

Sylvia Scribner (1977) replicated these findings and showed that when a subject was responding empirically, the correctness or incorrectness of the person's response depended entirely on whether the contents of the problem were counterfactual or not, confirming Luria's conclusions that there was nothing illogical about people's reasoning in terms of their everyday experience. But when, in Luria's terms, they were responding theoretically (e.g., in terms of the verbally given premises) based on contents that had not been experienced by the subjects, their responses were always correct, even if empirically counterfactual. Scribner also pointed out that in all of her studies some noneducated people responded theoretically, although the proportion of people who did so was significantly less than in the schooled group. So it appeared that at least with respect to syllogistic reasoning, Luria had identified a cultural-historical influence of schooling on reasoning of the general sort he had hypothesized. But he was not identifying a rigid cultural-historical dichotomy.

In later studies, Scribner and Cole (1981) found that when problem content referred to matters about which neither the experimenter nor the subject knew much, other than that the problem was about something that existed in nature and was beyond the experience of either (the presence of particular rocks on the moon), noneducated Vai people in Liberia were much more likely to respond theoretically and correctly, although they almost always responded in terms of everyday experience when they were questioned about plausible earthly scenarios. Moreover, when "moon content syllogisms" were mixed with "everyday content syllogisms," the rate of theoretical responding increased for the empirically plausible problems, suggesting that people's interpretation of the task had been modified.

A related series of studies by Paul Harris and his colleagues (e.g., Dias and Harris 1990; Dias, Roazzi, and Harris 2005) found that uneducated adults in nonindustrialized countries also reason accurately from premises and provide "theoretical" justifications for their responses if cued to the fact that the syllogistic problems are hypothetical by ascribing the statements made to life on another planet.[1]

The same sorts of variations in performance have been observed with respect to a wide range of cognitive tasks that serve as the backbone of efforts to characterize cultural variations in cognitive development by other American psychologists. For example, in a series of carefully conducted comparisons of Wolof children of different ages in Senegal who did or did not attend school, Patricia Greenfield (1966) found that many nonschooled children did not acquire the concept of conservation using well-known Piagetian tasks. She concluded that schooling is essential to the development of concrete operations. Greenfield reported one odd observation in this research: conservation was much more likely to be achieved if children were allowed to pour the liquid themselves instead of observing the experimenter. She speculated that this change in procedure reduced the children's tendency to interpret the experiment as something of a magic show, but she did not highlight these findings in her conclusions at the time.

Following up on Greenfield's work among the same population, Judith Irvine (1978) asked her subjects to solve the conservation task and then to play the role of informants whose job it was to clarify, for the experimenter, the Wolof terms for resemblance and equivalence with respect to the task. When confronted with the critical test in which one beaker of water is poured into a narrower, taller beaker, the Wolof children in the role of a subject solving the problem gave the wrong response—they said that the beaker with water higher up its sides contained more liquid. But in their role as "linguistic informants," these same children went on to explain that while level of water was "more," the quantity was the same.

Irvine's and Greenfield's results provide nice examples of the kinds of performance factors that can make it appear that children understand less about the underlying question of interest to the psychologist than they actually do. In seeking to interpret these kinds of variability, Cole and his colleagues concluded that cultural variations as well as school-nonschool variations appeared to have more to do with specifics of the problem contents, modes of discourse that frame the problem, etc., created by the experimental tasks than with the presence or absence of specific cognitive abilities in one group and its absence in the other.

It seemed only natural that subjects who had attended school—where the discourse is often about purely hypothetical, often implausible, topics and where learning how to categorize and memorizing arbitrary materials are ubiquitous practices—would realize what was expected of them in the experimental setting. But it did not seem plausible to attribute the observed differences to a generalized shift in modes of thinking from lower, childlike and situation-bound to higher, adultlike, and generally applicable ("context free").

Soviet/Russian scholars have generally been unimpressed by either the methodological arguments or the data offered by their American counterparts, asserting, for example, that there is no empirical basis for thinking that people without schooling are capable of theoretical thinking (Karpov 2005). In reviewing Cole's work on this topic, Mescheryakov and Zinchenko (2000) even suggested that his approach should be referred to as "anti-historical" psychology rather than cultural-historical psychology. After all, schooling arose relatively late in the history of homo sapiens; it is the breeding ground of science and logic, so to deny the historical supremacy of industrialized societies seems absurd.

Interesting evidence of how differently American and Russian scholars approach the issue of culture and logical reasoning comes from a study of syllogistic reasoning among American college students and the reactions to this work by a Russian proponent of Vygotsky's approach. Roy D'Andrade (1989) described research stemming from studies by Peter Wason (1968) in which British college students were presented seemingly straightforward deductive syllogistic reasoning problems and 80 percent of the students failed to respond correctly. The contents of these problems were not obscure, but they were totally arbitrary (the task was to say which of four cards should be turned over to determine if a machine had erred in putting symbols on the backs or fronts of labels). However, if the content of the problem was changed so that it was meaningful, these same students were overwhelmingly correct.

D'Andrade, who extended Wason's work among American college students, concluded that the variations in problem solving he observed depended upon the extent to which the contents were cognitively well structured in terms of local cultural models. Karpov (2005) rejects this line of reasoning, and ascribes the difficulties of the American college students to the failures of the American school system to teach theoretical thinking. This conclusion seems somewhat odd to us because whatever the shortcomings of the American educational system, it is difficult to believe that students in leading U.S. universities in the 1990s have not achieved the intellectual level of Uzbeki peasants with two years of involvement in schooling and collective farming in the 1930s.

This is not the place to decide who is correct. Addressing that question would require a specialized discussion providing a great deal more about the studies in question and relevant comparative data from Russian colleges. Our point is that the very fact that such arguments can be made indicates the wide gap in ways of interpreting the variations under discussion and the different orientations to the invocation of context to which they are related.

Development of Children Within a Single Culture

Evidence that Russian and American developmental psychologists are using different notions of context also comes from research on developmental change in the United States and Europe. Consistent with the generality attributed to the social situation of development in Russian research, Russian psychologists of the cultural-historical school, very much like psychologists who operate within a Piagetian framework, place a strong emphasis on regular, age/social situation–related developmental stages, each manifesting a characteristic mode of thought. In contrast, and given the narrower interpretation of the "social situation of development" in the American literature, current American research on children's cognitive development places a very strong emphasis on the way in which small particulars of the local activity/social situation of development/experimental setting contribute crucially to the manifestation of various capacities.

Recent American research on children's intellectual development readily acknowledges that children's behavior becomes more complexly mediated and results in higher levels of achievement as they grow older. But this research has simultaneously emphasized that when great care is taken to place children in situations that make "human sense" to them, they display levels of cognitive development that they do not display in less familiar situations (see Cole, Cole, and Lightfoot 2004 for a broad sampling of such research).

For example, Borke (1975) replicated Piaget's famous three mountains problem in which children had to say how a diorama scene looked from various perspectives under two conditions. The first was a replica of Piaget's own materials: a diorama with three mountains, each distinctive in its appearance. The second was a logically isomorphic diorama with characters taken from the popular television program *Sesame Street*, depicting a farm, a lake, and other familiar environmental features. Young children who failed Piaget's version of the task were successful at Borke's version, undermining the idea that young children are generally egocentrically unable to view things from a visual perspective different from their own.

A somewhat different illustration of how familiarity with the objects to be thought about can influence children's apparent level of development comes from a study by de Loache and Brown. They focused on children's ability to remember where an object has been hidden over varying periods of time. In laboratory experiments, young children are notoriously bad at this form of remembering, but when they are asked to remember where a favorite toy was placed many hours previously in their own homes, they show perfect memory for its location (de Loache and Brown 1979).

Familiarity with the forms of discourse that characterize experiments is also extremely important in determining whether children will perform developmentally significant mental actions at the age suggested by norms derived from standard Piagetian stages. A large variety of such examples is to be found in Michael Siegal's work on the forms of conversation embodied in standard experiments (1991).

We do not want to give the impression that there is no mechanism for dealing with variations across contexts/situations/activities in the Russian literature. In one of his late articles, on the role of play in development, Vygotsky developed the idea of activity in a manner that appears to allow the possibility of synchronic variability. In particular, he hypothesized that play is a "leading" form of activity for pre–school-aged children, providing a source of motives and a structure that enables children to behave in a more developed manner than they can when not engaged in play. Play, he wrote, "creates a zone of proximal development of the child. In play a child is always beyond his average age, above his daily behavior; in play it is as though he were a head taller than himself" (1978:103).

Subsequent research by students of Alexei Leontiev demonstrated this activity-dependent form of synchronic variation in the developmental level of children's behavior by comparing performance on isomorphic tasks in a play or a nonplay situation. Manuilenko (1948), for example, asked young children to stand still without moving for as long as possible. When this task was made part of a game in which they were to imagine themselves to be soldiers standing guard at Lenin's tomb, they were able to control themselves and stand still for a significantly longer period than when simply instructed to do so. For older children, the play setting had no effect on their behavior. Many years later, Ivanova (2000) replicated this result, although she found that play/nonplay differences in level of behavior occurred at a younger age than had been true half a century earlier.

Not surprisingly, a number of experiments that focus on synchronic variation in children's manifest levels of conceptual development also introduce a play element. Thus, for example, Nielsen and Dissanayake (2000) studied children's understanding that others can hold and act upon a false belief in both a standard false belief task and in their peer play at preschool. The children clearly displayed such understanding when at play but not in the standard experimental situation.

Finally, the effect of the experience accumulated in the course of an experiment itself was long ago demonstrated by Alexander Zaporozhets and his colleagues (Zaporozhets and Lukov 1941). In one such demonstration, preschoolers were asked if different objects would float or sink. They were then given, for example, a tin toy shovel, asked whether it would float (they said, "yes"), and then allowed to test their prediction. Because the toy shovel was placed carefully on the water, it floated. Subsequently they were given a series of metal objects, none of which floated. When again given the tin shovel, they declared that it would sink. When it floated, they denied it was floating! Eventually, given many contrasting examples, they began to generalize correctly about which objects would float and which would not. The interpretation of these results may be disputable. But the influence of the child's experience in the course of the experiment, the "context," is not.

Synchronic Variation Reconsidered

Vygotsky's proposal that play constitutes a unique form of activity that is a special source of motives for children's thinking and acting in early childhood was part of a larger proposal to reconceive the idea of stages of children's development in relation to the "leading activity" that corresponded to children's age rather than to entirely "inside the head" stage theories of the sort offered by Piaget. This proposal provides a potential bridge between Russian cultural-historical developmental theory and approaches placing heavy emphasis on synchronic variability that derive from non-Russian developmentalists sympathetic to Vygotsky's ideas. However, as currently formulated, the Russian proposal, in the same spirit as the notion of "social situation of development," tends to assume that there is an invariant sequence of leading activities and that only a single kind of activity can play a leading role in organizing cognitive performance at a given time. Here we offer two examples, one empirical from American research and one from comments that Vygotsky made about the heterogeneity of manifest conceptual abilities, to suggest the possibility that multiple forms of activity (and modes of conception) can coexist in the same persons in the course of time spans too brief to be considered as candidates for general changes in stages of development. We then complete our discussion with some remarks on ways to promote more inclusive conceptual agreement and to pinpoint areas in need of closer scrutiny.

Heterogeneity of "Leading" Activity in the Course of a Single Game Episode

The following example is a description by an undergraduate in a child development field course playing a computer game, "Mystery House," with two girls, Jamie (age 8) and Lisa (age 6) (see Cole and Subbotsky 1993 for more extended treatment). This game was one of many choices of activities for the children as a part of a special after school program called the "Fifth Dimension" (see Cole and the Distributed Literacy Consortium 2006). The computer on which the game was implemented is now quite outdated. Its graphics were primitive, and all commands were entered by typing simple two-word instructions. Players entered a house where mysterious things happened, including lights going out and people dying at the hands of a murderer. The object of the game was to discover who the murderer was.

The conventions for writing the fieldnotes included the requirement to write about the writer's moods and thoughts at the start of the session and as detailed an account as possible. Several "leading" activities were potentially present, each associated with different age periods: affiliation, the need to be loved and accepted; play; learning; peer interaction; and work (at least on the part of the undergraduate). The fieldnotes (written by Jill Silverstein) begin as this undergraduate meets up with a child:

Right away I was anxious to get started since I knew that Jamie had been looking forward to working with me again after last Thursday. But this day was special . . . it started out different and ended up being one of the greatest experiences of my life. Never before have I exerted so much energy in the fifth dimension. . . . Leaving the library I was wiped out but really felt like I made a difference in two beautiful children's lives. Actually I went home to sleep for hours. WOW was it worth the extra energy!

And the reason for this sudden burst of energy came from the fact that Jamie requested me as her partner. I don't know why this meant so much to me but I guess it was because I wasn't quite sure the kids were liking me. [Appearance of affiliation as central motive]. First thing Jamie tells me that Lisa her sister was going to play with us "a little" since she really was not in the mood to play full out. Jamie acted very motherly and quite protective of Lisa. She made sure that I understood that Lisa would not be a big part of our team. This was a great opportunity to give Lisa, only 6, freedom to do or not to do.

As we get started with Mystery House, Lisa sits back and observes, but the minute I explained to them the purpose of the game, the objectives and strategies, she piped up her ears and got into it. After the first five minutes or so, Lisa was full-fledged into the game and we couldn't have progressed through the different rooms of the house without her help. [Play becomes the leading activity for children.]

All three of us were stunned when we realized that the reason we couldn't go and look in the refrigerator because the computer would not eat our command to "look Refrigerator"—UNTIL we wrote "GO TO REFRIGERATOR." This made all three of us stop and think, HMMM, why can't we look there?? AHAAAA! We must GOOOOOOO there first, then we can look. [Adult enters into play with children, learning enters as a motive.]

Here are some of the goals we had, when we started the game. . . . We should try to get through as many rooms of the first floor of the house and collect as many objects on our way as possible, while at the same time, staying away from the "masked killer" who was somewhere roaming the house. But we were also looking for the killer at the same time, so this in turn affected our decisions about what to gather as we ventured through the house. For example, when a knife was lying in the kitchen sink, we grabbed it! For protection of course.

The children really rely on the pictures on the screen. *[Adult engaging in analytic work in the course of playing.]* I say this because two times, the picture affected our next step. For example, Lisa saw the stove in the kitchen as one that was "never looking" and thus, didn't need to be lit by matches. Rather she informed me that it was "not an old fashioned stove and that her mom doesn't have the kind that needs matches any more." So, when I suggested that we light the stove for some light, the first reaction Jamie had was that it was a bad idea because the house could catch on fire if we lit the stove and then left the kitchen to search other rooms. Lisa also thought my idea wasn't a good one because of the fact that the stove looked like an electric range (as opposed to gas). *[Logical reasoning and inference by six-year-old in context of play.]*

So we went with Lisa's idea and kept our eyes open for a candle. When that candle finally turned up, you wouldn't believe how excited they got!!!! It was as if they accomplished so much. *[Children are now deeply involved in play.]*

The game doesn't count matches, and we couldn't actually go through the whole day lighting matches time after time that the lights shut off, but they both realized that there was a more efficient way of doing things, and they could save a lot of time with a permanent time source. Plus, I think Lisa was getting really scared. She said, "Jill, I hope that lights don't go out again, I hate the dark. And what if the killer sneaks up behind us when the lights go off?" *[Border between fantasy play and real life becomes obscured.]*

I could really go on and on about the amazing interaction that took place between all three of us. But I want to illuminate one more incident that took place which really stood out in my head. We are outside in the back porch of the "Mystery House" and we adventurously risked going through the gate. It was as if we were actually tiptoeing through this scary place always in the lookout for the killer. Lisa was so scared but having fun at the same time. Anyways we find ourselves in the graveyard and instead of there being a dead body lying there, as we had found in most of the other rooms, there was a live person digging graves!!!!!!!!!

But as we are thinking about what to do with the gravedigger—should we kill him with the knife we got or should we talk to him or should we sneak away without him seeing us and go get the dagger and come back later and kill him???—I ask them why they think he is the killer and not just an innocent bystander.

Jamie: Well, why is he alive if he's not the killer?

Lisa: Plus why won't he talk to us?

Jamie: He looks pretty suspicious to me.

Me: You can't always tell things that easily. He may be innocent.

Lisa: Well why is he digging six graves then? He obviously knows that six people will die and he's preparing to bury them.

Jamie: That has to be him. UNLESSSS, the killer asked him to dig the graves as a favour!!!!!

Lisa: That would mean that Joe (gravedigger) knows who the killer is!

Jamie: Maybe Joe's friends with the killer.

Lisa: We should kill him.

Jamie: Yeah either way he's bad.

[Logical reasoning by two young children and adult in the midst of the fantasy.]

So they both looked to me for final approval and I made sure they understood that they were risking getting killed since all they had to kill him was a butter knife. So we decided to get another weapon and come back.

As this example makes clear, not only are the girls able to be a "head taller" but a "head shorter" in the course of a single stretch of a joint game play mediated by the computer game and each other.

Heterogeneity in Level of Adult Conceptual Thought: Toward Convergence

We hope we have made the case in the foregoing discussion that, in principle, context (despite the ambiguities in its various usages) plays a role both in Russian, Vygotskian conceptions of human thought and in the formulations of their American admirers. While emphases differ

(American researchers appear to place more emphasis on demonstrations of synchronic variability associated with variations in context/situation/ activity while Russian researchers place a greater emphasis on diachronic, developmental change), both groups are wrestling with the issue of how to achieve a more systematic approach to an understanding of thought and its development, both historically and ontogenetically. We close by citing two clear statements from the Russian tradition that signal this point of essential agreement.

First, note the words of L. S. Vygotsky concerning synchronic variability from his monograph *Thought and Language*—in this case with respect to the level of conceptual development manifested by adults:

> However, these processes of transition [towards thinking in concepts] are not mechanical processes, where each new phase begins only with the completion of the previous one. The developmental process is much more complex. *The various genetic forms co-exist,* just as strata representing different geological epochs coexist in the earth's crust. This is more the rule than the exception for the development of behavior generally. Human behavior is not consistently characterized by a single higher level of development. Forms of behavior that emerge very recently in human history dwell alongside the most ancient. The same can be said about of the development of the child's thinking. A child who mastered higher forms of thinking, a child who mastered concepts, does not part with the more elementary forms of thinking. In quantitative terms, these more elementary forms continue to predominate in many domains of experience for a long time. As we noted earlier, even adults often fail to think in concepts. The adult's thinking is often carried out at the level of complexes, and sometimes sinks to even more primitive levels. When applied in the domain of life experience, even the concepts of adults and adolescents frequently fail to rise higher than the level of pseudoconcept. They may possess all the features of the concepts from the perspective of formal logic, but from the perspective of dialectical logic they are nothing more than general representations, nothing more than complexes.   (1987:160)

We relate, second, the words of Peeter Tulviste, an Estonian student of Alexander Luria's, concerning synchronic variability associated with cultural history, as based upon his cross-cultural research on syllogistic reasoning:

There is an obvious connection between various forms of activity and the heterogeneity of thinking. This is true between and within cultures. The reason for the heterogeneity of verbal thinking must not be sought in the accidental preservation in society or in the individual of "old," "lower," or "previous" sociohistorical or ontogenetic stages of thinking. Instead, it must be sought in the multiplicity of activities that are distributed in society and carried out by the individual. Heterogeneity developed through social history such that with the development of material and mental production new forms of activity appeared. These new forms of activity required new types of thinking and gave rise to them. At the same time, to the degree that earlier forms of activity, which fulfill some role in the society, are preserved, the "old" types of thinking that correspond to them are preserved and continue to function.   (1986:24–25)

The current challenge facing those concerned with understanding the relation of thought and its development to its context is to resolve the residual uncertainties of the past by formulating in clear and consistent terms the specific references of their use of the term "context," how the use of this term relates to their notion of activity, situation, and environment, and how investigations focusing on cultural-historical and ontogenetic change can most fruitfully be brought into alignment with each other.

Note

1.   It should be noted that Dash and Das (1987) report no differences between schooled and nonschooled Indian children in response to everyday and non-everyday syllogistic reasoning problems, but stated that both schooled and nonschooled subjects "seemed to do poorly when empirical and contingent truths interfered with logical inferences."

References

Barkhudarov, S. G., et al. 1958. *Dictionary of the Russian Language* [in Russian]. Moscow: State Publishing House of Foreign and National Dictionaries.

Borke, H. 1975. Piaget's mountains revisited: Changes in the egocentric landscape. *Developmental Psychology* 11:240–243.

Bronfenbrenner, U. 1979. *The Ecology of Human Development*. Cambridge, MA: Harvard University Press.

Cole, M. 1988. Cross-cultural research in the sociohistorical tradition. *Human Development* 31:137–151.

———. 1996. *Cultural Psychology: A Once and Future Discipline*. Cambridge, MA: Harvard University Press.

Cole, M., S. R. Cole, and C. Lightfoot. 2004. *The Development of Children*. 5th ed. New York: Worth.

Cole, M., and the Distributed Literacy Consortium. 2006. *The Fifth Dimension: An After-School Program Built on Diversity*. New York: Russell Sage.

Cole, M., and N. Gajdamaschko. 2007. Vygotsky and culture. In H. J. Daniels, M. Cole, and J. Wertsch, eds., *The Cambridge Companion to Vygotsky*, 193–211. New York: Cambridge University Press.

Cole, M., J. Gay, J. A. Glick, and D. W. Sharp. 1971. *The Cultural Context of Learning and Thinking*. New York: Basic Books.

Cole, M., and E. Subbotsky. 1993. The fate of stages past: Reflections on the heterogeneity of thinking from the perspective of cultural-historical psychology. *Revue suisse de psychologie* 52:103–113.

D'Andrade, R. G. 1989. Culturally based reasoning. In A. Gellatly, D. Rogers, and J. A. Sloboda, eds., *Cognition and Social Worlds*, 132–143. New York: Oxford University Press.

Dash, U. N., and J. P. Das. 1987. Development of syllogistic reasoning in schooled and unschooled children. *Indian Psychologist* 5:15–20.

Das, J. P., and U. N. Dash. 1990. Schooling, literacy, and cognitive development. In C. K. Leong and B. S. Randhawa, eds., *Understanding Literacy and Cognition: Theory, Research, and Application*, 217–244. New York: Plenum.

de Loache, J., and A. Brown. 1979. Looking for Big Bird. *Quarterly Newsletter of the Laboratory of Comparative Human Cognition* 1:53–57.

Dias, M. G., and P. L. Harris. 1988. The effect of make-believe play on deductive reasoning. *British Journal of Developmental Psychology* 6:207–221.

———. 1990. The influence of the imagination on reasoning by young children. *British Journal of Developmental Psychology* 8:305–318.

Dias, M., A. Roazzi, and P. L. Harris. 2005. Reasoning from unfamiliar premises: A study with unschooled adults. *Psychological Science* 16:550–554.

Greenfield, P. M. 1966. On culture and conservation. In J. S. Bruner, R. P. Olver, and P. M. Greenfield, eds., *Studies in Cognitive Growth*, 225–256. New York: Wiley.

Irvine, J. 1978. Wolof magical thinking: Culture and conservation revisited. *Journal of Cross-Cultural Psychology* 9:300–310.

Ivanova, F. F. 2000. The development of voluntary behavior in preschoolers: Repetition of Z. V. Manuilenko's experiments. *Journal of Russian and East European Psychology* 38:6–21.

Karpov, Y. V. 2005. *The Neo-Vygotskian Approach to Child Development*. New York: Cambridge University Press.

Kozulin, A., B. Gindis, V. S. Ageyev, and S. M. Miller, eds. 2003. *Vygotsky's Educational Theory in Cultural Context*. Cambridge: Cambridge University Press.

Luria, A. R. 1976. *Cognitive Development: Its Cultural and Social Foundations*. Cambridge, MA: Harvard University Press.

Manuilenko, Z. V. 1948. Razvitie proizvol'nogo povedeniya u detei doshkol'nogo vozrasta [The development of voluntary behavior in preschoolers]. *Izvestiya APN RSFSR* 14: 43–51. Cited in *Journal of Russian and East European Psychology* 43 (2005): 11–21.

McDermott, R. P. 1983. The acquisition of a child by a learning disability. In S. Chaiklin and J. Lave, eds., *Understanding Practice: Perspectives on Activity and Context*, 269–305. New York: Cambridge University Press.

Mescheryakov, B. G., and V. Zinchenko. 2000. Выготский и современная культурно-историческая психология Критический анализ книги М. Коула/Вопр. психол. 2. С. 102.

Nielsen, M., and C. Dissanayake. 2000. An investigation of pretend play, mental state terms, and false belief understanding: In search of a metarepresentational link. *British Journal of Developmental Psychology* 18:609–624.

Scribner, S. 1977. Modes of thinking and ways of speaking: Culture and logic reconsidered. In P. N. Johnson-Laird and P. C. Wason, eds., *Thinking: Readings in Cognitive Science*, 483–500. Cambridge: Cambridge University Press.

Scribner, S., and M. Cole. 1981. *The Psychology of Literacy.* Cambridge, MA: Harvard University Press.

Siegal, M. 1991. *Knowing Children: Experiments in Conversation and Cognition.* Hillsdale, NJ: Erlbaum.

Tulviste, P. 1986. Ob istoricheskoi getergennosti verbal'nogo myshleniya [The historical heterogeneity of verbal thinking]. In Y. A. Ponomarev, ed., *Myshlenie, obshchenie, praktiki: Sbornik nauchnykh trudov* [Thinking, communication, practice: A collection of scientific works]. Yaroslavl: Yaroslavl Pedagogical Institute.

——. 1991. *The Cultural-Historical Development of Verbal Thinking.* New York: Nova Science.

van der Veer, R., and J. Valsiner. 1991. *Understanding Vygotsky: A Quest for Synthesis.* Oxford: Blackwell.

——. 1994. *The Vygotsky Reader.* Oxford; Blackwell.

Vygotsky, L. S. 1929. The problem of the cultural development of the child, II. *Journal of Genetic Psychology* 36:414–434.

——. 1934. Fascism in neuropsychology. In van der Veer and Valsiner 1994:327–337.

——. 1978. *Mind in Society: The Development of the Higher Psychological Processes.* Cambridge, MA: Harvard University Press.

——. 1981. The genesis of higher mental functions. In J. V. Wertsch, ed., *The Concept of Activity in Soviet Psychology*, 144–188. Armonk, NY: Sharpe.

——. 1987. *The Collected Works of L. S. Vygotsky* 1: *General Psychology.* Ed. R. W. Rieber, A. S. Carton, and N. Milnick. New York: Plenum.

——. 1997. *The Collected Works of L. S. Vygotsky* 3: *The Problem of the Theory and History of Psychology.* Ed. R. W. Rieber and J. Wollock. New York: Plenum.

——. 1998. *The Collected Works of L. S. Vygotsky* 5: *Child Psychology.* Ed. R. W. Rieber, M. J. Hall, and J. Glick. New York: Plenum.

Vygotsky, L. S., and A. R. Luria. 1930. Tool and symbol in child development. In van der Veer and Valsiner 1994:99–174.

———. 1993 [1930]. *Studies on the History of Behavior: Ape, Primitive, and Child*. Hillsdale, NJ: Erlbaum.

Wason, P. L. 1968. Reasoning about a rule. *Quarterly Journal of Experimental Psychology* 20:273–281.

Wertsch, J. V. 1985. *Vygotsky and the Social Formation of Mind*. Cambridge, MA: Harvard University Press.

———. 1991. *Voices of the Mind*. Cambridge, MA: Harvard University Press.

———. 2000. Communication: An arena of development. In N. Budwig, I. C. Uzgiris, and J. V. Wertsch, eds., *Advances in Applied Developmental Psychology*, 109–129. Westport, CT: Ablex.

Winegar, L. T., and J. Valsiner, eds. 1992. *Children's Development Within Social Context*. Hillsdale, NJ: Erlbaum.

Wozniak, R. H 1992. Co-constructive, intersubjective realism: Metatheory in developmental psychology. In W. Kurtines, M. Azmitia, and J. Gewirtz, eds., *The Role of Values in Psychology and Human Development*, 89–104. Oxford: Wiley.

Zaporozhets, A. V., and U. D. Lukov. 1941. The development of reasoning in young children. *Soviet Psychology* 18:47–66.

Contributors

Igor M. Arievitch is professor in the Department of Education at the College of Staten Island of the City University of New York. He is a developmental and educational psychologist working within the framework of cultural-historical activity theory. His studies focus on the role of learning in students' cognitive development and on methods of developmental teaching. Among other topics, his recent publications address the concepts of cognitive tools, internalization, and non-automaticity and the function of technology in education.

Sunil Bhatia is an associate professor of human development at Connecticut College. His research examines how globalization and migration have forced us to redefine the meaning of culture, identity, community, acculturation, difference and development in the field of cultural psychology. His book *American Karma: Race, Culture, and Identity in the Indian Diaspora* (New York University Press) was published in July 2007. His articles have appeared in *Human Development, Theory & Psychology, History of Psychology, Culture & Psychology,* and *Mind, Culture, and Activity.*

Michael Cole is distinguished professor of communication, psychology, and human development at the University of San Diego and director of the Laboratory of Comparative Human Cognition. He was a postdoctoral fellow at Moscow State University in 1962–1963 under the directorship of A. R. Luria. He has conducted research in Africa and Mexico and has written extensively on questions of culture and development, the organization of classroom instruction, and the design of after-school activities for children.

Blaine J. Fowers is professor of counseling psychology at the University of Miami and a fellow of the American Psychological Association. His theoretical work reinterprets and enriches our understanding of psychological research and practice with the resources of virtue ethics. In the Constitutive Goals Project, he is studying higher-order goals and investigating the empirical links between these goals and human flourishing. His books include *Virtue and Psychology: Pursuing Excellence in Ordinary Practices* (American Psychological Association), *Beyond the Myth of Marital Happiness* (Jossey-Bass), and *Re-envisioning Psychology: Moral Dimensions of Theory and Practice* (Jossey-Bass).

Mark Freeman, professor of psychology at the College of the Holy Cross in Worcester, MA, is the author of *Rewriting the Self: History, Memory, Narrative* (Routledge), *Finding the Muse: A Sociopsychological Inquiry Into the Conditions of Artistic Creativity* (Cambridge University Press); and numerous articles on memory, self, and autobiographical narrative. He is currently finalizing two additional book projects: the first addresses the phenomenon of hindsight and the second explores the centrality of the Other, both human and nonhuman, in psychological life.

Natalia Gajdamaschko, vice president of the International L. S. Vygotsky Society, teaches in the Faculty of Education, Simon Fraser University, Canada. Trained in Moscow, she has served as a visiting research fellow at the Vinson Institute of Government and at the Torrance Center for Creative Studies at the University of Georgia (US), and was the 1993 recipient of an advanced scholars award by the International Research and Exchange Board (IREX). She has presented papers at numerous international congresses in the fields of educational theory, gifted education, and educational psychology.

Kenneth J. Gergen is a senior research professor at Swarthmore College and director of the Taos Institute. His contributions to dialogues on social construction, the self, and cultural change are internationally acclaimed. Among his major works are *Realities and Relationships: Soundings in Social Construction* (Harvard University Press), *The Saturated Self: Dilemmas of Identity in Contemporary Life* (Basic Books), and *An Invitation to Social Construction* (Sage). His forthcoming *Relational Being: Beyond the Individual and Community* (Oxford University Press) will elaborate on his contribution to the present volume.

Rom Harré was for many years the university lecturer in philosophy of science at Oxford University and fellow of Linacre College. Currently he is distinguished professor in the Psychology Department of Georgetown University in Washington DC, and director of the Centre for Philosophy of the Natural and Social Sciences at the London School of Economics. His publications include, among others, *Causal Powers: Theory of Natural Necessity* (with E. H. Madden; Blackwell), *Varieties of Realism: A Rationale for the Natural Sciences* (Blackwell), *Modeling: Gateway to the Unknown* (Elsevier), and *The Explanation of Social Behaviour* (with P. F. Secord; Blackwell).

Hubert J. M. Hermans is emeritus professor of psychology at the University of Nijmegen, Netherlands. In his early work he devised a self-confrontation method for the assessment of one's personal meaning system. Later he developed, together with colleagues, dialogical self theory. He is initiator of a series of international conferences on the dialogical self and is president of the International Society for Dialogical Science (ISDS; www.dialogicalscience.org).

Suzanne R. Kirschner is associate professor of psychology at the College of the Holy Cross in Worcester, MA. She received her doctorate from Harvard University, where she also taught. She is the author of *The Religious and Romantic Origins of Psychoanalysis: Individuation and Integration in Post-Freudian Theory* (Cambridge University Press), as well as numerous articles on the interconnections between psychological theories and socio-cultural forces. She is a fellow of the American Psychological Association and a past president of the American Psychological Association's Division 24 (Theoretical and Philosophical Psychology).

Eva Magnusson is professor of psychology and gender studies at the Umeå University, Sweden. She was recently director of the Center for Gender

Studies at the Umeå University, and earlier head of research at NIKK, the Nordic Center for Gender Research in Oslo, Norway. Her recent research focuses on identities, power, and negotiations of activities and responsibilities in heterosexual couples with children.

Jeanne Marecek (Ph.D., Yale University) is Kenan Professor of Psychology at Swarthmore College. She is co-editor of the book series Qualitative Psychology (New York University Press) and associate editor of *Feminism & Psychology*. Her research concerns the sociocultural context of suicide and self-harm in Sri Lanka. Her work has been supported by the National Science Foundation (NSF), the National Institute of Mental Health (NIMH), and the National Institute of Child Health and Development (NICHD), and she has been a Fulbright scholar and a fellow of the Swedish Collegium for Advanced Studies in the Social Sciences (SCASSS).

Jack Martin is Burnaby Mountain Endowed Professor of Psychology at Simon Fraser University. His research interests are philosophy and history of psychology, social-developmental psychology, and educational psychology, with particular emphasis on the psychology of selfhood and personhood. His most recent books include *Psychology and the Question of Agency* (with Jeff Sugarman and Janice Thompson; SUNY Press) and *The Psychology of Human Possibility and Constraint* (with Jeff Sugarman; SUNY Press).

Frank C. Richardson is professor of educational psychology at the University of Texas, Austin. He has authored, co-authored, or edited several books, including *Stress, Sanity, and Survival* (New American Library), *Re-envisioning Psychology: Moral Dimensions of Theory and Practice* (with Blaine J. Fowers and Charles Guignon; Jossey-Bass), and *Critical Thinking About Psychology: Hidden Assumptions and Plausible Alternatives* (with Brent Slife and Jeffrey Reber; American Psychological Association), and numerous articles and chapters on topics in psychotherapy theory, the philosophy of social science, and psychology and religion. He is a recent past president of Division 24 (Theoretical and Philosophical Psychology) of the American Psychological Association.

João Salgado, Ph.D., is director and professor of the master's program in clinical and health psychology at the Instituto Superior da Maia (ISMAI), Portugal. He is also a psychotherapist and the director of the counseling service of his university. His main research interests involve the theoretical and methodological developments of a dialogical perspective within psychology, and the applications of this framework to the fields of psychotherapy and clinical psychology.

John Shotter is emeritus professor of communication at the University of New Hampshire and also works for the KCC Foundation in London. His long-term interest is in the social conditions conducive to people having a voice in creating the conditions of their own lives. He is the author of several books, including *Social Accountability and Selfhood* (Blackwell), *Conversational Realities: Constructing of Life Through Language* (Sage), and *"Getting It": Withness-Thinking and the Dialogical . . . in Practice* (Hampton Press, in press).

Anna Stetsenko is a professor in the Ph.D. programs in developmental psychology and urban education at the Graduate Center, the City University of New York. Her focus is on developing cultural-historical activity theory, especially in applications for teaching and learning. She has published widely on this topic, drawing on her firsthand involvement with Vygotsky's school at Moscow University (1970s through 1980s) and her later international research and teaching experiences around the globe.

Jeff Sugarman is professor of education at Simon Fraser University. He is co-author (with Jack Martin) of *The Psychology of Human Possibility and Constraint* (SUNY Press) and (with Jack Martin and Janice Thompson) *Psychology and the Question of Agency* (SUNY Press). He is a fellow of the American Psychological Association and the American Educational Research Association. His work is concerned with the psychology of personhood and the application of historical ontology and hermeneutics to psychological study.

Index

variation, 260, 270–72; variations in meaning of, 254–61; Vygotskian notion of, 16, 237, 253, 255–60. See also development; Vygotsky

context-stripping, 95

conversation: agentive hermeneutic view of, 167; cognition as, 35–36; production of masculinities and, 96, 97–101; thinking as, 100

Cooley, Charles, 3

cooperative activity, 11

Côté, J., 199

Counselling Psychology Quarterly, 195

counterpositions, 192

creativity, 83

critical realism, 42–43

critique, forms of, 70–71

Crossley, Michelle, 95

cultural anthropology, 4

cultural borrowing, 16

cultural competence, 129

cultural differences, inquiry into, 129

cultural-historical activity theory (CHAT), 11, 14, 19, 21, 231–32; background, 232–34; development as collaborative process of transforming the world, 240–42; foundational worldview and premises of, 235–46; object-related activity and mind, 242–45; sociopolitical context, 246–49; transactional worldview, 235–40

cultural-historical psychology, 1, 4

cultural inconsistencies, 128–29

cultural psychology, 4, 84; identity in, 206–9; toward transnational, 219–24. See also Indian diaspora

culture, 17; identity and, 8–9, 152–57, 206–9; likened to text, 18–19; nation, conflation with, 221–22; politics of acculturation, 213–19; as positions in the self, 199–200

Culture & Psychology, 195

D'Andrade, Roy, 117, 268–69

Darwin, Charles, 235

Darwinism, 235–36

Davidov, B. J., 129

deep history, 147–52, 155

de Loache, J., 270

Derrida, Jacques, 3

Descartes, Rene, 2, 41, 52

description, 40–41, 63

descriptivisms, 117–18

determinism, 12–13, 21–22, 176; co-determinism, 238; feminist views of, 88; social constructionism and, 119–20; supplements and, 78–79; underdetermination, 159, 162–64, 166–68

development: of children within a single culture, 269–71; co-existing forms of, 276; as collaborative process of transforming the world, 240–42; social referencing, 59–60; synchronic variation, 260, 270–72; zone of proximal, 38, 270, 275. See also context

developmental continuity, 53

developmental emergence, 160, 166–68

developmental theory, 4, 19, 31–38; general law, Vygotsky's, 257–58; laws, replacement of by social and semantic conventions, 34–35; play, studies of, 270–71; social construction of minds, 32–33; Vygotsky's, 38–43

Dewey, John, 3, 236, 240, 241

dialectical materialism, 240–42, 249

dialogical approaches, 5, 9, 13, 18–19

dialogical realm, 51–54

dialogical self: body in the mind, 192–93; collective voices, 190–91; dominance and social power, 184, 189–91; as minisociety, 189; multiplicity-in-unity, 184, 187–89, 200; power and relative dominance, 184; spatial and embodied, 184, 191–94; the-other-in-the-self, 184–87;